THE GODS
THAT FAILED

THE GODS THAT FAILED

—

*How Blind Faith in Markets
Has Cost Us Our Future*

LARRY ELLIOTT
and
DAN ATKINSON

NATION
BOOKS

New York

Published by Nation Books, A Member of the Perseus Books Group
116 East 16th Street, 8th Floor
New York, NY 10003

Nation Books is a co-publishing venture of the Nation Institute and the
Perseus Books Group

Books published by Nation Books are available at special discounts for bulk
purchases in the United States by corporations, institutions, and other
organizations. For more information, please contact the Special Markets
Department at the Perseus Books Group, 2300 Chestnut Street, Suite 200,
Philadelphia, PA 19103, or call (800) 810-4145, ext. 5000, or e-mail
special.markets@perseusbooks.com.

Designed by Brent Wilcox

Library of Congress Cataloging-in-Publication Data
Elliott, Larry.
    The gods that failed : how blind faith in markets has cost us our future /
Larry Elliott and Dan Atkinson.
        p.   cm.
    Includes index.
    ISBN 978-1-56858-602-1 (alk. paper)
    1. Financial crises.   2. Capitalism.   3. Economic history—1945–
4. Economic security.   I. Atkinson, Dan.   II. Title.
    HB3722.E45 2008
    330.973—dc22

                                                                2008045884

10 9 8 7 6 5 4 3 2 1

This book is dedicated to our families.

Larry would like to thank his wife, Carol, and his daughters, Ursula and Eowyn.

Dan would like to thank his wife, Sarah, and his sons, Aloysius, Aidan, and Fergus.

CONTENTS

CHAPTER 1

Under the Volcano

1929–1973–20??

*Behind us was a dark and dreadful cloud, which, as it was broken
with rapid zigzag flashes, revealed behind it variously shaped masses
of flame: these last were like sheet lightning, though on a larger scale.*

— PLINY THE YOUNGER,
account of the eruption of Mount Vesuvius

*Gatsby believed in the green light, the orgiastic future that year
by year recedes before us. It eluded us then, but that's no matter—
tomorrow we will run faster, stretch out our arms farther.*

— F. SCOTT FITZGERALD,
The Great Gatsby

*I came to the conclusion that we're perhaps living on the edge of a vol-
cano. Oil supplies, copper or wheat or nitrate supplies—inflation—
any one of a number of things could push us over into the lava flow.*

— LEE MACKENZIE,
The Brothers: A Clean Break

Between September 7 and October 7, 2008, the great global chain
letter that had been the turbocharged free market economy ran
out of subscribers. On September 6, it was possible to believe—just—
that the credit crunch and accompanying financial crisis might simmer

1

down and that, with extensive adjustment and much trimming of the sails on Wall Street and the City of London, life would return to normal in money markets and in the financial services industry.

By October 8, hollow laughter would have greeted such a suggestion.

On September 6, optimists could still—just—make the case that we had been here before, and that the turbulence of 2007–2008 was merely a more painful rerun of the events of 1997–1998, when the meltdown of Far Eastern economies was followed by Russia's defaulting on its external debt in August 1998, leading to the insolvency and rescue of the Long Term Capital Management (LTCM) hedge fund in the autumn of that year.

By October 8, such a Panglossian view would have put its proposer in serious danger of committal to a care institution.

On September 6, even doomsayers thought twice before making comparisons with the other great postwar economic crisis, the one that erupted in the autumn of 1973.

By October 8, such comparisons seemed inadequate as even sober commentators leapfrogged the energy shock and hyperinflation and went straight to the granddaddy of all crises, the 1929 Wall Street crash and its aftermath. Before long, parallels with the Great Depression were rolling off newspaper presses like Model A Fords off a prewar Detroit assembly line.

September 7 to October 7—one month, the standard payment period for commercial invoices. This was the month in which the bill for fifteen years of excess was presented in full, a bill that Wall Street, the City, and other financial centers were incapable of paying. As a consequence, governments in Washington, London, and Continental Europe stepped in with direct and indirect financial support totaling trillions of dollars. Three mortgage companies (two British, one American), one insurer, one European bank, and $700 billion of toxic subprime "assets" were nationalized during this time. One investment bank (Lehman Brothers) was allowed to fail, and one sovereign state, Iceland, teetered on the brink of insolvency. The hero class in the investment banks and brokerages, the "masters of the universe" made famous by Tom Wolfe in his 1988 novel *The Bonfire of the Vanities*, had been bailed out by the national governments they had long affected to despise and tolerate only so long as these authorities provided "competitive" conditions in which they could operate—low taxes and light regulation.

This month formed a great divide, separating the past from the future. On one side, it was still possible to believe that the system could be fixed in a sort of grand-scale version of the LTCM bailout. On the other, it was stunningly obvious that turbocharged global finance as a whole was every bit as insolvent as all those unfortunate business ventures that start with the dread words: You're a super cook, darling—let's open a restaurant!

As a failed utopia, the financially driven free market system was now up there in the same gallery as the Tanzanian road to socialism, Juan and Eva Peron's *Justicialismo* movement, and Major C. H. Douglas's social credit campaign. No number of lavishly produced booklets by pro-market think tanks could change this. The card sharps had been found out, the masters of the universe had rattled the begging bowl, the racket had unraveled, and the scam was over.

The Accidental Socialist:
Henry Paulson and the Nationalization of Wall Street

It was fitting, somehow, that the paroxysms of September–October 2008 should have started with the nationalization on Sunday, September 7, of the two giant U.S. mortgage institutions, the Federal National Mortgage Association (Fannie Mae) and the Federal Home Loan Mortgage Corporation (Freddie Mac), at a potential cost to the U.S. taxpayer of more than $5 trillion. Both institutions had their roots in the era of President Roosevelt's New Deal (although Freddie Mac was a more recent creation), both epitomized the curious blend of state intervention and boisterous free market rhetoric that characterizes so much of American economic life, both played a major role in extending home ownership to millions of Americans over the generations, both were supposedly private sector entities with shareholders, both were assumed to operate under some sort of guarantee from the federal government, and both were taking a hammering from the crisis over subprime mortgage loans and their potential to blow up bank balance sheets.

Finally, in a twist that summed up so much of the market madness of the time, Fannie and Freddie were quite innocent in terms of subprime mortgages. They had never been involved in this market. But as mortgage default rates rose, Fannie and Freddie's losses on previous business started to mount—and the shares fell, losing more than 85 percent on the year.

This was bad news for the U.S. banking system, given that shares in Fannie and Freddie had long since been a pillar of banks' capital structures, rock-solid securities that had been as good as cash. No longer. Fannie and Freddie, which guaranteed three-quarters of all new mortgages, were running out of capital, threatening to deepen the pall of depression hovering over the property market. Furthermore, the two institutions faced a witching hour in September 2008, needing to refinance more than $200 billion in bonds. Investor resistance was a real danger; as *The Economist* noted on August 30, 2008, "The collapse of just one bond auction could send shock waves around the world."

For Treasury secretary Henry Paulson, the options were narrowing. For weeks, he and his colleagues had pointed out to anyone who would listen that the Treasury had made colossal sums available to Fannie and Freddie should they be needed. This is the classic central banker's maneuver to restore confidence in a troubled institution. In times gone by, bars of gold would be loaded into a stagecoach and carried into the bank, the hope being that the panic would subside and the same bars would then be quietly shipped out the back door onto a second stagecoach and taken away again.

Often it worked. This time it did not. By early September, Paulson faced two choices, neither very palatable. One was to refinance Fannie and Freddie for tens of billions of dollars. In normal times, this would have been preferable to nationalization, especially for a Treasury secretary in a Republican administration. But these were not normal times, and the prospect of responsibility without power, in terms of effectively bailing out the management and shareholders with taxpayers' money, did not appeal, certainly not in an election year.

Nationalization, by contrast, would at least align those paying the piper (U.S. taxpayers) with management of the entities concerned (via Treasury control).

"Fannie Mae and Freddie Mac are so large and so interwoven in our financial system that a failure of either of them would cause great turmoil in our financial markets here at home and around the globe," Paulson declared. He added that he hoped the intervention would "accelerate stabilisation in the housing market" by bringing down the cost of home loans. (*Financial Times*, September 8, 2008.)

To an outsider, coming from the relatively straightforward home loan arrangements of Britain or Ireland, the activities of Fannie and Freddie, even in normal times, were unusual and complex, using, as they did, implicit government backing to stimulate the supply of mortgages below a certain size. But by the time Paulson and his colleagues had taken full control, Fannie and Freddie's method of operation was looking positively Byzantine. These nationalised entities would each pick up a $100 billion cash injection from the government, to allow them to meet their debts.

In addition, it [the government] would buy mortgage bonds backed by these companies starting with an initial $5bn purchase, and provide an unlimited liquidity facility to them until the end of next year . . . Fannie and Freddie will be allowed to grow in the short term to $850bn each, but from 2010 onwards they will have to shrink their portfolios by 10 percent a year until they reach $250bn. Officials hope this will reduce the future risk to taxpayers. (*Financial Times*, September 8, 2008.)

But then Fannie and Freddie (along with their solvent sisters Sally Mae, the student loan company, and Ginnie Mae, supplier of mortgages to low-income people) were peculiarly American institutions, so it was unsurprising that both their fate (nationalization) and the form in which this fate manifested itself, in terms of the labyrinthine proposals mentioned above under which the entities would first grow and then contract, rather like a man playing the accordion, would also be peculiarly American.

Could it be there were no real lessons to be learned as to the health of the rest of the American and global financial system?

Commenting on the eve of nationalization, *The Economist* seemed to think so:

> Nationalisation should not be the end of the story. The giants' assets should be liquidated over time, or the entities broken up and privatised. The companies' size and strange structures carry a big cost for American finance. Backed by cheap government funding, their bosses have speculated with the gusto of hedge-fund managers—and lost. ("Fire the Bazooka," *The Economist*, August 30, 2008.)

Indeed, as the dust settled on the Fannie and Freddie affair, the next crisis to break over Wall Street seemed to bring out some of the old free market steel in Paulson and his colleagues.

Lehman Brothers, founded in 1850, was Wall Street's fourth largest investment bank. But in September 2008, it was nursing $14 billion of losses from high-risk property loans that had gone bad. Over the weekend of September 13 and 14, talks were under way to find either a buyer or a rescuer. But as Saturday turned into Sunday, sounds from or near to the U.S. Treasury were suggesting there would be no help this time from the federal government. Not to worry, suggested some commentators, as the British bank Barclays was keen to buy. The only problem was that Barclays had been playing down this idea for at least forty-eight hours by the time it pulled out of talks on the Sunday.

Come Monday, and Lehman was forced into bankruptcy, jeopardizing 27,000 jobs worldwide. At the same time, fellow investment bank Merrill Lynch agreed to an emergency takeover for $50 billion by Bank of America. One of the grandest names on Wall Street had been rescued by an institution founded barely one hundred years earlier to serve Italian immigrants in California. Indeed, Bank of America's original name was Bank of Italy.

Paulson's tough new line did not last long. As Lehman was carted off to the breaker's yard, a potentially far more serious crisis blew up. American International Group (AIG), the world's biggest insurer, was in deep trouble. Within a day of the death of Lehman, it was clear there would be no rueful shake of the head from Paulson and his colleagues when AIG rattled the begging bowl. For those, and there were many on both sides of the Atlantic, who wondered how an insurance company could get caught up in what was essentially a crisis of banking, investment, and securities trading, the answer was simple. AIG had used complex derivatives to insure vast quantities of corporate debt and personal mortgages. Battered by claims on defaulting mortgages, the group's liquidity was running low.

On September 16, the federal government took charge of AIG in return for $85 billion in credit. The following day, the spotlight swung across the Atlantic to Britain, where the ghastly prospect had reared its head of a collapse in the country's best-known mortgage lender, the HBoS group, an acronym formed of the two original constituents, the Halifax—a home loan giant with a long history—and Bank of Scotland, a grand Edinburgh institution that enjoys the ancient privilege of being able to print its own banknotes.

Despite repeated reassurances, HBoS was seen by investors as uniquely vulnerable to the slide in both house prices and housing market activity in 2008. On September 17, it emerged the government had used its good offices to arrange for Lloyds TSB, a sound bank, which had been criticized in pre–credit crunch days by investors for its stodgy approach, to pay £12 billion for HBoS. There was no government subsidy involved—at least, not the sort denominated in money. But ministers made it clear they would use special powers to exempt the takeover from competition laws, which would normally have stood in the way of the creation of a bank with a 30 percent market share. This was deeply ironic, coming from a government that had taken great pride in allegedly removing all competition decisions from political interference and placing them instead in the hands of disinterested experts.

Thursday, September 18, was an unusual day in that no major financial institution went bust and there was no large-scale call on public funds to rescue Wall Street and the City from the consequences of their folly. But the day that followed was to make good this deficiency, in generous measure.

Paulson, his appetite for socialist solutions to capitalism's woes now fully whetted, unveiled an extraordinary $700 billion plan to nationalize Wall Street's toxic waste, the worst of the bad loans sitting on banks' books, thus (it was hoped) giving banks the confidence to return to the fray and start making loans again, to each other and to both corporate and individual customers.

He told a press conference in Washington, "America's economy is facing unprecedented challenges and we are responding with unprecedented action."

"There will be ample opportunities to debate the origins of this problem. Now is the time to solve it. This bold approach will cost American families far less than the alternative—a continuing series of financial institution failures and frozen credit markets unable to fund economic expansion."

Referring to the week's events as a crisis after many others had done so, he said it was no longer viable to treat each financial body blow on a case-by-case basis: "We must now take further, decisive action to fundamentally and comprehensively address the root cause of our financial system's stresses."

Markets rocketed on both sides of the Atlantic as investors and traders joyfully forgot their supposed hatred of this sort of blatant state interference. London's FTSE 100 index saw its biggest ever one-day rise, up 8.8 percent, while on Wall Street shares extended Thursday's late rally, the biggest in six years.

Sometime over the weekend, these same investors must have thumbed through their junior high guides to the U.S. Constitution and been reminded that the only organ of the federal government entitled to borrow money was not the Treasury Department but the Congress. Given the state of the public finances, this money would most certainly have to be borrowed—and this was an election year.

A week of jittery market activity followed, and then on September 29 the Paulson plan was sunk by a 225–208 defeat in the House of Representatives. Members of Congress were struck by their constituents' unwillingness to see their money used to bail out Wall Street bankers.

The package was tweaked to secure its passage through Congress a few days later, on Friday October 3, 2008. But by then the euphoria had worn off, and shares on Wall Street closed down.

During all this excitement, the British government was not idle, although it had a rather smaller stage on which to play. Bradford &

Bingley, a onetime building society (the British equivalent of a savings and loan institution), had carved itself a seemingly profitable niche in providing mortgages to people who wished to acquire rental properties. Essentially these were home loans for amateur landlords. So-called buy-to-let mortgages had flourished during the cheap money era of the early and mid-2000s as average rents had far outstripped the cost of borrowing.

Now, with the buy-to-let boom unraveling, B&B was fighting for survival. On September 29, it emerged the bank's £21 billion deposit base and 197-strong branch network would be sold to Spanish bank Santander, with the £52 billion loan book being nationalized. But, perhaps sensitive to criticisms of having exposed taxpayers to danger in the Northern Rock nationalization, the government structured this nationalization in such a way that the first £15 billion of liabilities would fall on other banks, not the government. Once this became clear, bank shares duly tumbled.

The Last Illusion: Fortress Europe

As we shall see, the early shudders of the financial earthquake of 2007–2008 were felt almost as strongly in Continental Europe as elsewhere, but by the late summer of 2008, the crisis could plausibly be presented as one of Anglo-Saxon supercharged capitalism run riot.

After years of being lectured by free market commentators about their "rigid" economic structures in contrast to the dynamic and flexible British and American models, it would have been surprising had the Continent's leaders not taken the odd pop back now that the Anglo-Saxons were in trouble.

And they did.

On Thursday, September 25, 2008, French President Nicolas Sarkozy, speaking in Toulon, said, "The market economy is a regulated market, a market that is at the service of development, at the service of society, at the service of all. It is not the law of the jungle," predicting the end of laissez-faire capitalism.

The same day saw German finance minister Peer Steinbruck being more outspoken. "When we look back ten years from now," he told journalists on Thursday, "we will see 2008 as a fundamental rupture." The United States, he said, would lose its role as a finance superpower and added, "We must civilise financial markets, and not just through moral appeals against excess and speculation."

But this picture of solid European finance standing firm while the cream puffs of the Anglo-Saxon world crumbled started to darken in the week ending Saturday, October 4, 2008. In a few short days, the begging bowl had been rattled by Continental institutions as it became clear that banks in the euro zone faced similar potential dangers to those in the supposedly more freebooting financial centers of Wall Street and the City of London.

During that week, two of Belgium's five biggest banks—Fortis and Dexia—were bailed out by the Belgian government in alliance with the Dutch, French, and Luxembourg authorities. Fortis, a Belgian-Dutch institution, won a $15 billion capital injection while Dexia, a Franco-Belgian municipal lender, got $8.64 billion.

In the same week, Hypo Real Estate mortgage bank, Germany's second biggest commercial property lender, was bailed out to the tune of €35 billion.

At the end of the week in question, on Saturday October 4, President Sarkozy hosted a meeting in Paris of the four European Union members that are also members of the Group of Seven rich nations: France, Italy, Germany, and Britain, with the guests represented by German chancellor Angela Merkel, Italian prime minister Silvio Berlusconi, and British prime minister Gordon Brown. Large-scale Paulson-style rescue plans were not agreed on; instead, a more general pledge was made that no major European institution should be allowed to fail.

Earlier in the week, the Irish and Greek governments had announced 100 percent guarantees for all personal bank depositors, a move understood to have occasioned much tut-tutting among the Big Four in Paris over "unilateral action." Twenty-four hours after the Paris meeting, the British Treasury was seeking urgent clarification of news that Germany was planning to follow the Irish and Greek leads, something Merkel had apparently omitted to mention the day before. It emerged on the Monday that the Germans did not plan to pass new legislation to guarantee deposits and that the pledge had been rather vaguer than it first appeared.

Meanwhile, the Hypo rescue agreed to the previous week had collapsed on Saturday, and a more costly €50 billion rescue had been arranged on Sunday night.

Europeans may have been less prone to take out subprime mortgages and other toxic debt, not least because cautious Continental lenders would not make them available. But their banks seemed almost as likely to have dived into the market to buy up other countries' subprime lending, as were banks in the countries concerned. The crisis was not "out there," whether in the trailer parks of Middle America or even in the bank headquarters of London or New York. It had moved from the periphery to the center, to the heartland of European economic respectability.

Most bizarre of all was the case of Iceland, which, in the early days of October 2008, appeared close to national bankruptcy. A country of 304,000 people previously best-known for its fishing industry and spectacular scenery had sprouted an enormous financial sector that had snapped up foreign assets and given the island nation the appearance of a sort of giant private equity fund. As its currency slid, a cloud settled over some of the country's banks. This was of more than passing interest in Britain, for example, where Iceland-owned assets included the House of Fraser department store group and West Ham soccer club.

But perhaps the most telling piece of news during this period had little to do with high finance and everything to do with the way the balance of power was shifting in the world.

On Monday it was reported that the film studio DreamWorks, cofounded by Steven Spielberg, had agreed to a joint venture with one of India's biggest entertainment conglomerates, the Reliance ADA Group, a big player in Bollywood, India's film business.

The BBC reported, "Now the new studio will make movies in the US, putting large amounts of Indian money into America's film industry. It is a story of Hollywood meets Bollywood in a $1.5 billion deal."

It seemed that Reliance was buying DreamWorks out of an unhappy marriage with Paramount Pictures in 2006. As an illustration of what the future may hold, the union of one of the totemic figures of the American film industry and the vigorous new wealth of the developing world was hard to beat. This seismic shift in power and wealth from the west to the east may prove to be the most enduring legacy of the month that shook the world. If so, the West will have lost its preeminence not because of the machinations of the Indians, the Chinese, or any other external factor but through allowing itself to be ruled by a set of ideas, the governing concepts of the turbocharged market economy, the gods that have failed. It is to these that we now turn.

The Mountain Dwellers: Meeting the Modern Market's Governing Spirits

The ancient Greeks believed their twelve most important gods and goddesses lived on Mount Olympus. Each had a special significance. Zeus, the lord of the gods, ruled the sky; he was responsible for thunder and lightning. Poseidon, his brother, was the king of the sea; he could ensure that a traveller returned safely home to port. Aphrodite was the goddess of love, Ares the god of war, Apollo the god of the sun and music. This book highlights the activities of a new class of superfinancier and helpers—the New Olympians—in national and international organizations such as central banks. We believe they are merely a subsidiary "hero" class that represents the Big Ideas that rule on Mount Olympus, the "gods," if you like, or the governing spirits.

We identify twelve such gods and goddesses hovering above and directing modern Western economies. These guiding principles are far from new; indeed the world of the New Olympians, both the gods and their hero-servants, would, barring the personal computer, the mobile phone, and blanket smoking bans, have been familiar enough to the characters in an F. Scott Fitzgerald book set in the late 1920s.

Until mid-2007 the governing rules of life in the early twenty-first century went largely unchallenged. Partly this was because those in charge believed that all was for the best in the best of all possible worlds. Partly it was because there was deemed to be no alternative to the dominant model, however flawed. And partly, perhaps most importantly, it was because nobody was really sure what was happening up there on Mount Olympus. Or at least they found it convenient to pretend that they didn't know what was happening. Once Pandora's box flew open, however, that excuse sounded increasingly hollow.

Greek mythology provides plenty of raw material for a book about the failings of modern financial markets. There is the story of King Midas, who found the ability to turn all he touched into gold a curse. The tendency of markets to veer between the wild optimism of booms and the manic depression of busts is akin to the life led by poor Persephone, condemned to live six months of every year in Hades. But Pandora—a gift from the gods whose beauty belied her baleful influence on the lives of mortals—makes the best metaphor.

Pandora was fascinated, obsessed even, by the box that had been handed to her husband Epimetheus by his brother Prometheus, the titan who according to legend was chained to a rock and had his liver pecked out daily by a vulture for having the temerity to steal fire from the gods. Prometheus had told Epimetheus that on no account was the box to be opened, but Pandora, believing that it might contain precious jewels that would enhance her beauty, was not to be deterred.

Eventually she could contain herself no longer and decided to peek into the box. She lifted the lid a fraction, but to her horror found that the box did not contain diamonds and gold but a host of nasty creatures that swarmed over the world bringing all the curses of mankind—plague and old age, disease and dishonesty.

August 9, 2007, was the moment the lid came off the modern version of Pandora's box. Few realized it at the time, although there had been a sprinkling of soothsayers warning that the sky was darkening with bad omens. To be sure, the financial markets wobbled, with the Dow Jones industrial average losing almost 400 points in the worst day for Wall Street for four months and the index of London's blue chip shares down by more than 100 points. But reports that the European Central Bank in Frankfurt and the Federal Reserve in Washington had made cheap funds available to banks was confined to the business pages. This was, so editors believed, simply another market wobble. After all, the Dow had closed at an all-time high of above 14,000 only three weeks earlier after the Fed had given reassurance that there would be no contagion effects to the rest of the U.S economy from the problems in the U.S. subprime mortgage market. On the front page of *The Guardian* the top story concerned global warming; the back pages were looking forward to the start of the soccer season that coming weekend. In the United States, the baseball season was in full swing.

The role of Pandora in August 2007 fell to the giant French bank, BNP Paribas. It announced that it had blocked withdrawals from three investment funds because of what it called the "complete evaporation" of liquidity. A BNP spokesman said it was a technical issue, which was only partly true. While the link between falling house prices in California and the bottom line of one of France's biggest commercial banks was certainly convoluted, the reason for BNP's action was simple: despite employing some of the country's best mathematical brains, it could not put a price, with any great confidence, on the investments it had made in U.S. asset-backed bonds. Like Pandora, the ECB and the Fed tried desperately to slam the lid back down again. Like Pandora, they failed.

Our list of the twelve gods of the modern Mount Olympus, the ruling ideas served by the overpaid heroes of the City and Wall Street, begins with *globalization*. The ancient Greeks worshiped Zeus; today's cosmopolitan elite pays homage to a world without borders. Everything stems from the acceptance that economic power has shifted from the nation-state to the global market. The sinews of the modern economy are the trade routes that take goods from Shanghai to Los Angeles and capital back in the other direction. Governments that seek to meddle with the global market do so at their peril; the experience of François Mitterrand in the early 1980s tends to be cited as the last gasp for Keynesian state intervention. In the modern world, governments are not supposed to tame globalization but to ready their citizens to compete in a world of cutthroat competition.

There is a wrong way and a right way to do this. The wrong way is to adopt a protectionist approach, putting tariffs on foreign steel or banning a foreign company from buying your ports (as the U.S. has done) or seeking to prevent cheap food from undercutting your farmers (as the French have done). The right way is to invest in education, skills, and science in the belief that this will "brain-up" your population and create a knowledge economy that will find an upmarket niche in a world awash with cut-price goods. This is Gordon Brown's approach.

The twin brother of globalization is *communication*. While the arrival of the telegraph in the first half of the nineteenth century marked a revolution in the way information can be transmitted, the development of powerful digital technology has transformed the way the world works. Had a French bank run into difficulties as a result of financing Napoleon's wars in 1807, for example, it would have taken days for the news to arrive in London, and weeks for it to get to New York. Yet when BNP announced that it was having problems with its hedge funds, every dealer in Wall Street and Canary Wharf knew what had happened within seconds. Some argue that the change between the globalization at the end of the nineteenth century and what exists today is that the gold standard has been replaced by an information standard. Walter Wriston, the former chairman of Citibank, once noted, "What it means, very simply, is that bad monetary and fiscal policies anywhere in the world are reflected within minutes on the Reuters screens in the trading rooms of the world. Money only goes where it is wanted and, once you tie the world together with telecommunications and information, the ball game is over. It's a new world, and the fact is, the information standard is more draconian than any gold standard" (quoted in Philip Bobbitt, *The Shield of Achilles*, Allen Lane, 2002).

Nation-states, despite the impact of globalization and communication, retain considerable power. They control the flow of imports into their markets; they have controls on the movement of capital; they run industries that are considered to be strategic; they believe that some sectors of the economy—health and education—should be shielded from the full blast of competition. These are, however, impediments to the smoother running of the global market and thus need to be removed. The World Trade Organization—a supranational body with punitive powers over governments that transgress its rules—started a new round of talks in November 2001 designed to open up markets in agriculture, manufacturing, and services. The International Monetary Fund and the World Bank insist that poor countries receiving financial assistance should abandon state control of their mines, banks, and energy companies. In Brussels, the European Commission is dedicated to the removal of the restrictive practices and state subsidies that throw sand under the wheels of the single market. The next three gods are, therefore, *liberalization, privatization,* and *competition.*

Finance is the sector of the economy that has benefited most from these developments. International banks have always tended to have global reach, and they benefit more than any other sector from rapid communication. It was in their interest to have barriers on capital removed. They picked up hefty fees for organizing privatization, and competition allowed them to wipe out weaker competition.

During the summer of 2007 it became apparent just how powerful the sixth god—*financialization*—has become. In countries like Britain, the expansion of the City of London had been the engine of the economy's growth—the fastest-growing parts of the finance sector expanded at around 7 percent a year between 1996 and 2006. The increasing size of the financial sector was accompanied by greater power. At one level, this meant that Merrill Lynch, Goldman Sachs, and PriceWaterhouseCoopers were able to attract the best brains from the best universities in the annual trawl for promising graduates, with the summer internship between the second and third year replacing what had once been the InterRail tour round Europe. There was an opportunity cost to other sectors of the economy from a state of affairs where the City was able to secure a disproportionate amount of young talent. At a wider level, this mirrored the transfer of income from the "real" to the financial economy. Furthermore, the opportunity cost of one sector receiving a disproportionate amount of young talent was mirrored by a transfer of income from the "real" sector of the economy to the financial sector. Manufacturing output stagnated, while the income for those not working in the City—or in those industries such as financial PR or law firms arranging takeover bids—tended to grow at best only modestly.

Financialization, argued its proponents, is good for a country like Britain. It made London the hub of global finance, encouraged innovation, and—by allowing the market to decide where capital should go—made the economy more stable. Whether this proves to be true in the long term remains to be seen. In the short term, economic growth did not accelerate, productivity did not surge, there was no miracle cure to the balance of payments and only rare glimpses of trickle down. One commentator summed up the triumph of financialization as follows: "Economic growth has been tepid, median wages have stagnated, and income inequality and economic insecurity have both risen. Moreover, there are concerns that the business cycle generated by financialisation may be unstable and end in prolonged stagnation" (Thomas Palley, "Financialization: What It Is and Why It Matters," Levy Economics Institute, November 2007).

As events unfolded in late 2007 and early 2008, this started to look like an accurate assessment. Up until that point, it was easy to argue that the first six gods out of Pandora's box were beneficial to the global economy and at worst neutral. Privatization in developing countries, for example, was heralded as a way of preventing corrupt ruling cliques from siphoning off profits into Swiss bank accounts. Globalization was specialization on a grand scale, the logical conclusion to the sort of division of labor that Adam Smith and David Ricardo had envisaged two hundred years ago. The modern world not only means that we can keep in touch by email with our cousins in Cape Town and buy an agreeable Malbec from an Argentinian vineyard in the foothills of the Andes, but also allows our pension fund to buy shares in an Indian software company. On paper, this world of greater choice, freedom, and opportunity sounds splendid. It is certainly preferable that modern communications technology allows Mozart's clarinet concerto to be heard on a CD player in any living room rather than being the exclusive preserve of the court of the Austro-Hungarian emperor in Vienna. In reality, however, the world does not work this way and that's because the remaining six gods in Pandora's box have such potentially dangerous properties. These are *speculation, recklessness, greed, arrogance, oligarchy,* and *excess.*

Speculation is not always harmful. Britain's fifteen years of uninterrupted economic growth from 1992 onward was the direct consequence of the Conservative government being forced to leave the European exchange rate mechanism following an attack on the pound orchestrated by George Soros. Absent the need to use excessively high interest rates to defend sterling, growth picked up and unemployment came down. Yet the activities of the big banks and the hedge funds in the first half of 2007 had no noble purpose. Far from rectifying a glaring public policy error, they exploited a problem in the private sector—granting mortgages to Americans who couldn't afford them. Financialization had created an inverted pyramid. Instead of having a broad-based productive economy supporting a financial sector, which had speculation as one of its lucrative but less important activities, a diminished productive sector supported an ever bigger financial sector that saw speculation as the reason for its existence.

The risks of speculation are magnified when the speculator behaves recklessly. A millionaire placing a $1,000 bet on red in a well-run casino is speculating, but at (just about) even money could hardly be said to acting imprudently. Not so the jobless gambler who mortgages his house to back a hunch that the 50 to 1 outsider will win the Derby. The history of the past five years is marked by reckless behavior, not just from the banks and other financial institutions that loaded up on investments backed by American subprime mortgages but from the central banks that were playing with fire when they provided cheap money to maintain the speculative frenzy, the ratings agencies that give securities AAA ratings because it was a way of securing business from investment houses, and the real estate brokers who kept on selling subprime loans even when the U.S. housing boom was clearly over.

As with Pandora, there were plenty of warnings. As with Pandora, the actors in our modern Greek tragedy could not help themselves. As in all tragedies, the central figure has a fatal character flaw. For Macbeth it is ambition, for Othello jealousy, for Hamlet indecision. The tragedians of 2007 and 2008 displayed not one but two central flaws that help explain their recklessness: greed and arrogance.

Greed will never be expunged from financial markets; the pursuit of riches is, and always has been, a factor motivating those who buy and sell shares, bonds, currencies, and commodities. Nor is it uncommon to find that brokers and dealers do better out of asset price bubbles than their customers; Fred Schwed wrote a book published in 1940 perceptively titled *Where Are the Customers' Yachts?* (Wiley Investment Classics).

Every so often, however, the money lust becomes so pronounced that it crosses the dividing line between cupidity and criminality. In the late 1980s there was an outcry in Britain when mortgage salespeople exploited the opportunities provided by financial deregulation to persuade homeowners to take out endowment mortgages rather than repayment loans, and convinced those with inflation-proof public sector pensions to switch into much less attractive portable personal pensions.

In both cases, the motivation was the fat commission the salesperson could make by closing a deal and the upfront fees charged by the firms selling the products. Since 2002, a similar wave of selling has been evident in the U.S. real estate market, with senior citizens who have only a tiny amount outstanding on their loans tricked into remortgaging their homes at ruinous rates of interest by unscrupulous mortgage brokers.

The financial equation—from top to bottom in the industry—was skewed toward generating the maximum amount of business, and, because it was more lucrative that way, the riskier the better. Real estate brokers assumed they could not lose; if subprime borrowers failed to keep up their payments the home would be repossessed and sold at a profit in an ever rising market; those dabbling in mortgage-backed securities believed what their "rocket scientist" mathematicians and ratings agencies told them: that they were all gain and no pain. Five months into the crisis, the mood was more contrite. Panelists at a session at the World Economic Forum in Davos on risk management were asked how the big banks of North America and Europe had failed to spot the potential losses from subprime. The one-word answer from a group that included the chairman of Lloyd's of London and the chief risk officer of the insurance company Swiss Re was "greed."

As one participant put it, "Those running the big banks didn't have the first idea what their dealers were up to but didn't care because the profits were so high."

It goes without saying that those responsible for the speculative bubble of early 2007 could not conceive that Bear Stearns would announce problems with its hedge funds in late July or that BNP's problems would give credit markets the equivalent of a stroke a couple of weeks later. That was where the arrogance kicked in. The superheroes of the New Olympian order are the brightest and the best of their generation. Their activities were making massive profits, a good chunk of which were being paid out in seven-figure bonuses that kept property markets humming in the Cotswolds and the Hamptons. Could it be remotely possible that Citigroup, Merrill Lynch, and UBS were guilty of crass stupidity and that their glittering palaces were little more than Potemkin villages?

It was unthinkable, and even when cracks did start to appear in the edifice, the New Olympian class managed to blame everyone but themselves. This arrogance stemmed from the not unreasonable belief that big finance was now too big to fail and there was a loud and insistent demand that the monetary authorities step in with unlimited quantities of financial assistance.

The response to the market meltdown helps illustrate the final two principles that govern the modern world. One is that, despite the lip service paid to democracy, Western societies are effectively run by moneyed oligarchies, who have as little time for their wage slaves as did the ruling elite of ancient Athens.

It is tempting to say that the final scourge to escape from the modern Pandora's box was weakness, because it was certainly apparent in late 2007 and early 2008 that the apparent strength of the financial markets was illusory. The happy-go-lucky mood evaporated instantly, with the write-down of losses accompanied by some token sackings of executives and followed by more stringent lending for the real victims of the credit crunch—individuals and businesses forced to pay more when they borrowed. In the UK, loans worth 125 percent of the value of a home disappeared and lenders rediscovered the virtues of thrift when they started to demand that first-time buyers save up for a sizable deposit to be eligible for a loan. Weakness, though, cannot really be included as a principle of the New Olympians, since nobody willingly seeks to be weak. Rather, our twelfth and last principle is excess. It is an axiom of the global order that there is never too much of anything: never too much growth, never too much speculation, never too high a salary, never too many flights, never too many cars, never too much trade. It was for that reason, perhaps, that the financial crisis was accompanied by rising inflation (as demand for oil and food pushed up prices globally) and by almost daily evidence of the impact of global warming: losses in the financial markets, hardship for seniors facing more expensive heating and food, climate change. There were no prizes for guessing which the New Olympians considered the most pressing issue for policymakers.

We opened this chapter with the month that changed the world. But this came after more than a year of global financial turbulence. We are reminded of Humpty Dumpty, an egg-shaped character in a British nursery rhyme who "has a great fall" and who, despite the best efforts of "all the king's horses and all the king's men," cannot be put back together again.

If September and early October 2008 marked the point at which Humpty was proved to be irreparable, seven days in January showed just how great his fall had been.

Winter Lightning: Ninety-Six Hours That Shook Mount Olympus

In the week ending Saturday, January 26, 2008, the New Olympians were in deep trouble. On Monday, January 21, Chancellor Alistair Darling said he had given up on hopes of persuading a private sector buyer to assume the £24 billion that stricken bank Northern Rock owed to the Bank of England, which had pumped in the money to keep the Rock in business. The Rock had been brought to its knees by drinking deep of the cup of commercial liberalization and financial engineering. Darling proposed that taxpayers should gulp down a big draught of the same medicine. He announced plans to turn the £24 billion into bonds that would be sold on the open market, with a government guarantee. Whoever ended up owning the Rock would have to put aside a portion of the future income from customers' mortgage payments to pay the dividends on the bonds. Put in layperson's terms, this is how the bond scheme worked. Someone owes you money and cannot pay you back; you take that person's IOU and sell it to a third party, thus getting your money back. But the only reason the third party will touch this IOU with a barge pole is that you have guaranteed it—in effect, you have underwritten someone else's debt to you.

Thus did the sort of financial engineering in which the Olympians specialize come full circle. Having put one of the UK's largest mortgage lenders deeply in debt to the public purse, it was now being employed by ministers, it was hoped, to package up that debt and sell it to someone else. But any hopes that this would expedite a sale of Northern Rock to the private sector were cruelly disappointed on February 17, 2008, when Darling announced that the bank was to be nationalized.

On the day after Darling's bond scheme was announced, Tuesday, January 22, the Federal Reserve Board stunned financial markets with the sudden announcement that the U.S. official rate of interest was to be cut by 0.75 percentage points to 3.5 percent. This was the biggest single cut in twenty-three years. It was also the first time the Fed had cut the rate other than on its scheduled meeting date since a between-meeting cut in September 2001 after the terrorist attacks on New York and Washington. The move by Fed chairman Ben Bernanke and his colleagues reeked of panic and was reminiscent of nothing so much as a drug pusher desperately hoping that one more fix will get his groggy customers back on their feet. The Fed statement seemed anything but reassuring:

> [We] took this action in view of a weakening of the economic outlook and increasing downside risks to growth. While strains in short-term funding markets have eased somewhat, broader financial market conditions have continued to deteriorate and credit has tightened further for some businesses and households. Moreover, incoming information in-

dicates a deepening of the housing contraction as well as some softening in labor markets. . . . Appreciable downside risks to growth remain.
The Committee will continue to assess the effects of financial and other
developments on economic prospects and will act in a timely manner as
needed to address those risks.

It did that all right, with another cut, this one of 0.5 percentage
points to 3 percent, on January 30. The communiqué read: "Financial
markets remain under considerable stress, and credit has tightened
further for some businesses and households. Moreover, recent information indicates a deepening of the housing contraction as well as
some softening in labor markets."

But guess what? "[Downside] risks to growth remain . . . [We] will
continue to assess the effects of financial and other developments on
economic prospects and will act in a timely manner as needed to address those risks."

This all sounded very much like bureaucrat-speak for "Help!"

Since the share price falls of October 1987, the Fed had responded to any threat to asset prices by pumping the system full of
cheap money through cuts in interest rates. There seemed not a
glimmer of understanding at the Fed that the crisis of 2007–2008
was the working out of twenty years of this policy, not the result of
insufficient application of it. After a day's respite, the week's third
bombshell went off on January 24. French bank Société Générale,
one of the country's most respected financial institutions, announced it faced a $6.6 billion hole in its accounts and needed an
emergency cash injection from shareholders of $7.4 billion. Blame
was immediately ascribed to a "rogue trader" of the type familiar
from the 1990s (Nick Leeson, the British trader who broke Barings
Bank in 1995, was probably the best known). The name in the frame
was that of Jerome Kerviel, a thirty-one-year-old Paris-based trader
working on the bank's European equities derivatives desk. According to the January 25, 2008, edition of the *Financial Times*, "He was
already being portrayed by the governor of the Banque de France
yesterday as a 'genius of fraud.'"

Kerviel had made large, unauthorized bets on European stock markets and had managed to keep them from the attention of those above him at SocGen, but SocGen has said that direct financial gain did not seem to be his motive. Furthermore, the very expression "rogue trading" in contexts such as these suggests some deeply deviant activity far removed from the usually straight-laced world of financial services. In fact, taking bets (speculation, in other words) is what traders are paid to do by the investment banks and commodities houses that employ them.

For Société Générale, there was one crumb of comfort. Elsewhere in the above-mentioned *Financial Times* report it was noted that the fraud also overshadowed SocGen's announcement the previous day of a $2.7 billion hit from the U.S. mortgage crisis, in addition to the $506 million of write-downs taken in the third quarter.

Every cloud, it seems, still has a silver lining.

The Pride and the Fall: Hubris Explained

The Greeks gave us the word hubris, which means insolent pride toward the gods. Many might argue that Alan Greenspan was guilty of just such presumption in his self-serving memoir: "I would tell audiences that we were facing not a bubble but a froth—lots of small local bubbles that never grew to a scale that could threaten the health of the overall economy" (*The Age of Turbulence*, Allen Lane, 2007).

Traditionally, hubris was followed by nemesis—retribution and downfall—and through most of 2008, there was plenty of evidence to suggest that the age-old pattern was repeating itself. House prices were falling, consumer confidence was collapsing, borrowing conditions were being toughened, and inflation was rising. Banks in the West were increasingly looking to sovereign wealth funds—state-owned companies from oil-rich or export-heavy countries—for injections of capital to compensate for the write-downs on their bad loans. Cassandras tend to be lonely figures, but by the spring it was as if the battlements of Troy were heaving with prophets of doom jostling to make themselves heard.

Big financial crises tend to go through a number of distinct phases. The first phase is the *wild boom:* the period when there is plenty of easy money to be made and the mood is euphoric. This was the world in early 2007, as private equity firms went on the prowl for takeover victims and the financial markets boomed. The second phase is marked by *denial:* a refusal to accept that the manic behavior is having malign consequences and needs to end. After a brief period of denial in the spring and early summer of 2007, the crisis entered its third phase: *panic.* At this point, the walls of the temple start to buckle and there is a rush for the exit. In most cases, panic is followed by recovery. Not every period of financial turmoil is followed by recession, and precious few recessions lead to slumps. Some do, however, with 1929 the most obvious example.

On these rare occasions, the fourth phase of the crisis is capitulation as it becomes clear that the crisis is far, far worse than previously appreciated and that the conventional policy response is not adequate to deal with it. This book explains why this, indeed, is shaping up to be the "Big One." We trace the origins of the crisis, how it unfolded, and what its implications may be. The final chapter looks at what could be done to cut the New Olympians down to size and make the world a saner, safer place.

These, then, are the inhabitants of our twenty-first-century Mount Olympus, the "gods" (each of which embodies one of the big ideas of modern-day economics and finance) and their pampered servants, the "heroes," the investment bankers and central bankers, the hedge fund managers and private equity buccaneers. As with the characters of ancient mythology, both the gods and the heroes share their privileged existence with titans and exotic monsters: incorporated companies, offshore investment vehicles, exotic financial instruments, and the like. From time to time, the gods, heroes, titans, and monsters have lived together on tropical tax haven islands, as well as in legal fictions such as the Eurodollar market.

The heroes are, as in the ancient world, mortals who have achieved near divine status through their allegiance to the gods and through their sporadic (and hard to verify) claims to have tamed the various titans and monsters. But the gods, the heroes, and the titans/monsters, fascinating or frightening as they may be, can be banished, if we have the courage. It is to be hoped that we have. Ending on a hopeful note is, we believe, fitting, since hope was the last thing to emerge from Pandora's box.

CHAPTER 2

The Rock and the Bear

A Tale of Two Banks

Q: How many fingers do you have?
A: Ten.
Q: Count them.
A: One, two, three, four, five . . .
Q: And the other hand makes ten, nine, eight, seven, six?
A: Yes.
Q: Five and six make?
A: Eleven.

— English children's playground riddle

As a cashier I was particularly inept because I could never get the tills to balance.

—ADAM APPLEGARTH,
chief executive of Northern Rock, quoted in
The Independent on Sunday, September 16, 2007

Celebrating 20 years as a public company has give us the opportunity to reflect on our past success and focus on the drivers of a profitable future.

—Bear Stearns annual report, 2006

They both had tough, no-nonsense names. They were both institutions that reveled in the idea that they were outsiders, run by people born on the wrong side of the tracks. They both flourished during the heady days of the mid-2000s, pushing to the very limit the freedom to trade afforded by deregulated global capital markets. Both had dabbled extensively and—as it proved—disastrously in the exotic new financial instruments available in global markets. And both—one in New York, one in Newcastle—were the first big casualties in the United States and Britain of the crash of 2007–2008, and became symbols of how a heady brew of arrogance, greed, and recklessness could have dire results. Bear Stearns and Northern Rock were not the only banks to collapse; they were certainly not alone in making decisions that looked stupid to their customers in hindsight (and to us in foresight). But their demise provided the first hard evidence that the palace of Olympus was crumbling and that the gods had failed.

Bear Stearns was one of America's oldest investment banks when it fell like a collapsed soufflé in March 2008. Founded in 1923, the Bear had survived the Wall Street crash of 1929 and had $18 billion in cash reserves nestling in its coffers when rumors started to swirl around Wall Street that the bank was in trouble. At first the executives running the company shrugged off the rumors, issuing statements from the company's offices in Midtown Manhattan that there was no cause for concern. The power of the electronic herd meant that after a week of frantic selling Bear Stearns was swallowed up by J.P. Morgan Chase in a rescue brokered by the Federal Reserve and the U.S. Treasury.

On March 11, 2008, Bear Stearns shares were trading at more $63; less than a week later they were worth just $2 each. With one last growl of its shareholders, Bear Stearns was gone.

If there was a tiny crumb of comfort for what was then America's fifth biggest investment bank (a sector of the economy that six months later had gone the way of the dodo), it was that it avoided the long, lingering death of Britain's banking basket case—Northern Rock. The Rock, as it was known, had been on life support for five months when the British government finally realized that the lack of a private sector bidder for the bank meant there was no alternative but nationalization.

Northern Rock's problems were hidden from its customers (although not from Britain's asleep-at-the-wheel financial regulators), until the revelations from Bear Stearns in the summer of 2007 that it was having difficulties with two of its hedge funds brought an abrupt end to the mood of sunny optimism in the world's booming financial markets. The Bear's problem was that it had made big bets on securities whose value depended on the U.S. housing market, and by the summer of 2007 real estate prices were in free fall. In June, the bank pledged $3.2 billion in loans to cover subprime losses and investor redemptions; a month later it wrote to clients of the hedge funds admitting that they contained "very little" or "effectively no value" for investors. Within a fortnight, "closed for business" signs were put up in the global money markets as concern that Bear Stearns was not alone in having problems with mortgage-backed securities left banks unwilling to trade with each other.

Yet many banks, Northern Rock among them, depended on the wholesale money markets for the day-to-day cash that allowed them to go about their normal business of granting home mortgages. Without access to what were known as the securitization markets, Northern Rock was like a car without fuel. The strains were quickly felt. And when behind-the-scenes attempts by UK authorities to broker a rescue became public knowledge, Northern Rock was the subject of the first run on a major bank in Britain in almost 150 years. Customers queued outside its branches for three days in mid-September 2007 demanding their money. Only when the government promised to guarantee all savings did the panic stop.

"A Deep Desire to Get Rich": The Rise and Fall of Bear Stearns

The swallowing up of Bear Stearns by J.P. Morgan and the nationalization of Northern Rock were among many attempts by the authorities in New York, Washington, London, Frankfurt, and Brussels to draw a line under the crisis. At root, there was a failure to comprehend that the gods of deregulation and liberalization had so comprehensively failed. Wedded to the old belief system, the high priests of the new Olympus tried to recreate the world as it had been—or as they thought it had been—before August 2007. There was a sense that with perhaps just one more injection of cash from the Federal

Reserve, the Bank of England, and the European Central Bank, or one more private sector bailout lubricated with a sweetener from the taxpayer, it would be possible to restore confidence to the markets and reopen them for business on lines pretty much unchanged from before. For a time, the high priests seemed to be right. The bailout of the Bear was followed by a three-month spring rally in stock markets and a slight easing of the tension in money markets. The relief, though, was short-lived. The U.S. Treasury was forced to announce in July that it was prepared to provide financial support for Fannie Mae and Freddie Mac, which between them underwrite half of the mortgages in America, and this time the rally on stock markets lasted just two weeks. When Hank Paulson announced that he was taking Fannie and Freddie into conservatorship—nationalization by any other name—the rally lasted twenty-four hours. By the end of September 2008 the ideological retreat was complete. The U.S. government had nationalized the biggest U.S. insurer, AIG, and it had agreed to use public money to buy up $700 billion of so-called toxic waste from banks—the worthless securities that had looked like good bets in the years when the markets were booming. In March 2008 it had taken a week to see the demise of Bear Stearns; in September 2008 it took a week to get rid of the rest of the American investment banking industry. Lehman Brothers? Allowed to go bust after the U.S. Treasury decided there would be no Bear Stearns–style bailout. Merrill Lynch? Taken under the wing of Bank of America. Morgan Stanley? Goldman Sachs? Faced with market mayhem, the last men standing converted themselves into commercial banks in order to get easier access to credit from the Fed's money tap.

Bear Stearns had always been a company that did things its own way. It was founded by three men—Joseph Bear, Robert Stearns, and Harold Mayer—in the Roaring Twenties, and one of the company's proudest boasts was that it survived the Great Crash without laying off a single employee. In Wall Street's pecking order, Bear Stearns was the fifth biggest investment bank but lacked the patrician hauteur of Morgan Stanley or Goldman Sachs. Many of its staff lived in the less fashionable boroughs of New York rather than in the exclusive town houses of the Upper East Side. "Bear was bridge and tunnel and proud of it," said one writer (Bryan Burrough, "Bringing Down Bear Stearns," *Vanity Fair*, August 2008). "Since the days when the Goldmans and Morgans cared mostly about hiring young men from the best families and schools, the Bear cared about one thing and one thing only: making money. Brooklyn, Queens, or Poughkeepsie; City College, Hofstra, or Ohio State; Jew or gentile—it didn't matter where you came from; if you could make money on the trading floor, Bear Stearns was the place for you. Its longtime chairman Alan 'Ace' Greenberg even coined a name for his motley hires: PSDs, for poor, smart, and a deep desire to get rich."

Some of Greenberg's PSDs were, it is fair to say, hard-nosed about the way they got rich. There was some irony in the fact that on two occasions in the 1990s Bear Stearns showed no mercy to companies that had found themselves in financial difficulty when their trade in exotic instruments went sour. A dry run for the crisis of 2007 occurred in 1994, when a surprise decision by the Fed to raise interest rates caused turmoil in the market for collateralized mortgage obligations, an early form of the mortgage-backed securities of the 2000s. David Askin ran a hedge fund with a $2 billion CMO exposure and leverage of 3 to 1, modest by the standards of the recent past. Higher borrowing costs played havoc with the complicated math on which the CMO model was based because it reduced the value of the fund's fixed income assets. Creditors had the right to demand additional collateral to secure their loans, and when Askin tried to sell some of his CMO paper he found that its value was virtually zero. Bear Stearns proved the most aggressive of Askin's creditors and moved to seize the company's assets.

This was not the only early warning of the trouble that lay ahead in the crisis of 2007–2008. Long Term Capital Management was a hedge fund founded in 1993 by John Meriwether, a former trader at Salomon Brothers. Among the partners were Myron Scholes and Robert Merton, who had come up with a "sophisticated" mathematical model for pricing investments. (Experience has shown that the actual definition of "sophisticated" is "incomprehensible and wrong.") Predictably enough, the whiz kinds at LTCM came unstuck in the summer of 1998 when their model failed to take account of the possibility that the Russians would show the same ruthlessness to invading bond dealers as they had to Napoleon and Hitler. When the Kremlin defaulted on its debts, LTCM was left in a parlous position. Its creditors, with Bear Stearns again leading the pack, demanded extra collateral. Fearing the unwinding of LTCM's heavily leveraged positions (100 to 1 by the time it folded), the Fed chairman, Alan Greenspan, passed the hat round to Wall Street for contributions. Bear Stearns alone was prepared to tell the Fed chairman to get lost, and took some delight in doing so. Many of those running the company when the Fed and the Treasury took charge of the bailout believe that the severity of the terms imposed reflected the relish the Fed and the Treasury took in taking revenge on the arrivistes of 46th Street.

Ralph Cioffi was the archetypal Bear Stearns employee. He commuted to Manhattan each day from his home in New Jersey and loved cracking jokes almost as much as he liked making money. He had one of the best track records in fund management and was a longtime devotee of mortgage-backed securities. During the boom years for the real estate markets, Cioffi and his clients did well, recording average monthly gains of at least 1 percent. But as the housing market headed south from 2006 onward, the two hedge funds he managed started to rack up losses. Cioffi's main fund was called the High-Grade Structured Credit Strategies Fund (notably, not one of the five words proved to be true). Investors always find it hard to accept that their losses are deserved rather than the result of sheer bad luck, and Cioffi was not the sort of man to cut his losses. Instead, just like Bassanio in *The Merchant of Venice*, he took the classic option of the gambler who has just lost a small fortune and doubles his bets in the hope of coming out whole. Bassanio's gamble almost cost his friend Antonio a pound of flesh; Cioffi's ship never came in. Instead, he set in motion a series of events that led to the collapse of the bank.

Cioffi's High-Grade Structured Credit Strategies Fund was leveraged not twice but thirty-five times; his new fund was leveraged one hundred times on the grounds that the U.S. housing market could not conceivably continue to weaken. Sadly for Cioffi it did, and the

deterioration in the housing market in late 2006 and 2007 left the
funds with even bigger exposure. He tried to reassure investors that
all would eventually be well, but by the spring of 2007 even Cioffi's
incurable optimism had started to wane. Rather than come clean, he
decided to create a new company called Everquest Financial that
would sell shares to the public. The only assets of the company, it
transpired, were the worthless mortgage-backed securities, which
Cioffi could not trade in the markets. Presumably Cioffi imagined
that none of his investors would be any the wiser. Predictably, however, the scam came to the attention of *Business Week* and the *Wall
Street Journal*, and the flotation of Everquest Financial was subsequently pulled. Cioffi asked for more time and begged his creditors
not to seize his limited and depleted capital. Given Bear's own record
and the crash in the summer of 2007, the plea was not heeded. Merrill Lynch, by this stage aware that High-Grade Structured Credit
Strategies Fund was another term for Ponzi scheme, proved happy
enough to accept the Rottweiler role that Bear Stearns had played in
previous crises, seizing collateral and forcing Bear Stearns to pledge
up to $3.2 billion to bail out the two funds. It made little difference;
the funds filed for bankruptcy anyway.

The news did not get any better during the fall. A few days after
the collapse of Northern Rock in the UK, Bear Stearns announced
that third quarter profits were down 61 percent to $171 million. At
this stage, though, there was still hope that the financial storm
would—like that of LTCM in 1998—quickly blow over. Jimmy
Cayne, Bear's chief executive, said, "Most of our businesses are beginning to rebound." They weren't. The bank's president, Alan
Schwartz, insisted, "The market is in the very early stages of recovery." It wasn't.

Cayne and Schwartz were right about one thing, however: banks
needed to be very careful about touting around for partners willing to
inject the fresh capital needed to make up for the losses on subprime.
In the febrile environment of late 2007 and 2008, any short-term gain
from the new investment was offset by the clear signal that the institution was like a limping wildebeest struggling to keep up with the
herd. As such, Bear made only halfhearted attempts to bolster its

capital base. It forged one link with CITIC, a state-owned Chinese lender, under which both institutions agreed to invest $1 billion in each other. Cayne and Schwartz ignored the constant background noise on Wall Street that Bear was ailing, but the New York rumor mill had plenty to feed on. In November, the bank said it was cutting its workforce by 4 percent of the worldwide total, and in December announced that it had lost $854 million in the fourth quarter and had been forced to write down $1.9 billion as a result of the continuing problems in the mortgage market. Far from rebounding, Bear had posted the first quarterly loss in its eighty-five-year history; to make matters worse, it was sued by Barclays for misleading the British bank about the performance of Cioffi's two collapsed hedge funds. Cayne, who had been attacked in the financial press for his laid-back (some might say virtually horizontal) management style, appeared to recognize the writing on the wall for him personally: he cashed in $15.4 million of Bear Stearns stock in the quiet trading days between Christmas and New Year. In the light of what was to happen to shares in Bear Stearns less than three months later, it was one of Cayne's better decisions. It was certainly one of his last as CEO; he resigned on January 8, 2008, but maintained the role of chairman.

It was the curse of Bear Stearns that its CEO always seemed to be a long way from the front when the shooting started. The only thing Cayne had been shooting in the summer of 2007 was pars and birdies at the country club. In March 2008, when the bank's New York headquarters was turned into a bunker, Cayne's successor, Alan Schwartz, was hosting the Bear Stearns media conference at the Breakers hotel in Palm Beach, Florida. Schwartz left New York on Thursday, March 6, with a degree of concern about the Bear's exposure to three hedge funds—Thornburg Mortgage, Carlyle Capital, and Peloton Partners—all of which had been reported the previous day to be about to buckle under their losses from the financial crisis. Bear Stearns had lent to all three hedge funds and there was talk (as there had been almost every day since August) that all was not well at the bank.

Schwartz was right to be worried because his bank was about to be hit by the sort of irresistible pressure that had toppled Northern Rock the previous September. There was a difference, however. The wounds at the Rock were highly visible; anybody with access to a TV could see the customers patiently waiting to withdraw their savings. Bear Stearns died of internal bleeding, a massive hemorrhage that wiped out $18 billion of capital in a week's trading and left the company facing the choice of bankruptcy or an ignominious takeover.

The bank's decision to accept the $2 a share bid (later raised to $10) inevitably prompted speculation as to who killed Bear Stearns. In truth, there were as many potential murderers as in an Agatha Christie detective story. Was it the ruthless hedge fund dealer sensing easy pickings? Was it one of the rival banks—Goldman Sachs or Credit Suisse—that turned off the financial life-support machine when they realized the Bear was losing strength fast? Was it CNBC, the TV channel chirping away in every Wall Street dealing room, with its decision to run stories about the Bear's ill health on little more than market tittle tattle? Or was it the lawman—Henry Paulson of the U.S. Treasury—who struck the fatal blow by insisting that a line of credit negotiated by Bear Stearns for twenty-eight days would, in fact, be good for only forty-eight hours.

This whodunit has a messy, unsatisfactory outcome. Nobody will ever know for sure who killed Bear Stearns. The events of the week starting on Monday, March 10, 2008, suggest that many of the suspects—perhaps all of them—fired the gun. A rumor on the previous Friday turned into a sharp sell-off in the Bear Stearns share price on the following Monday, which was then picked up by CNBC. The report led to a further frenzy of selling, with seven times more Bear Stearns shares than normal changing hands on that day.

On Tuesday, the Federal Reserve unveiled a new lending scheme designed to make it easier for Wall Street firms to tackle the credit crunch. The move did not help, since in the highly charged atmosphere of that week it was assumed that the move was designed to help a specific bank with a cash flow problem—Bear Stearns. By Wednesday, the crisis had entered a fresh phase, with hedge funds withdrawing their cash and firms like Goldman Sachs and Credit Suisse instructing their staff to be wary about doing business with Bear Stearns. On Thursday, the Bear found that it was unable to roll over its $30 billion of loans in the overnight New York money markets, leaving it with only two options—file for a Chapter 11 bankruptcy petition or find an emergency transfusion of cash.

Thursday night saw a deal pieced together designed to get Bear Stearns through the one remaining trading day to the weekend so that a more comprehensive plan for its future could be worked out. Bear Stearns, as an investment bank, was not eligible to borrow funds from the Fed's discount window, but J.P. Morgan was. The Fed lent $30 billion to J.P. Morgan, which in turn lent it to Bear Stearns. It made a difference on Friday, but only for an hour, after which the selling recommenced. By the time Wall Street traders left for the weekend, the $18 billion capital cushion that Bear Stearns enjoyed at the start of the week had all but disappeared.

The final wound came from Paulson. He telephoned Schwartz to say that Bear Stearns had until the start of the new working week to find a buyer. J.P. Morgan spent the weekend working out what the troubled investment bank was worth and came to the conclusion that it was worth a lot less than the $32 a share at which it had closed on Friday night. The due diligence experts fretted about the large inventory of untradeable mortgage-backed securities, and it was suggested that the offer be in the region of $8 to $12 per share.

Had Bear Stearns shareholders been hoping to raise the price closer to $32 a share, they were not helped by a sharply critical article in the *New York Times* by Gretchen Morgenson (March 16, 2008), which said the bank had often operated in the "gray areas of Wall Street," that it had provided "munificent lines of credit to public-spirited subprime lenders" and had a delinquency rate on subprime mortgages that was double the industry average. The author said it was difficult to know how much the $46 billion in mortgages on the Bear Stearns books was actually worth. "According to Bear Stearns's annual report, $29 billion of them were valued using computer models 'derived from' or 'supported by' some kind of observable market data. The value of the remaining $17 billion is an estimate based on 'internally developed models or methodologies utilizing inputs that are generally less readily observable.' In other words, your guess is as good as mine."

Before the market turmoil began in 2007, the Bear Stearns share price had traded as high as $170 a share. On Sunday, March 16,

Cayne and the other Bear Stearns shareholders were told by J.P. Morgan that they would be offered $4 a share for their stock. At that point Paulson intervened once more—to say that the offer was too generous. He insisted that $2 a share was quite enough. Cayne growled furiously, but the Bear was dead.

Northern Rock: Just Like a Rolling Stone

If Bear Stearns was an elite bank that wanted to be a loner, Northern Rock was a loner bank that wanted desperately to be part of the elite. Unlike the Bear, the Rock was physically rather than emotionally detached from the rest of the UK financial system, based as it was in Newcastle, some three hundred miles north of London in the northeast of England.

Northern Rock was the perfect totem for the British economy under Labour, with its rise and fall neatly book-ended by Tony Blair's premiership. Created as a building society (the British equivalent of a savings and loan institution) in 1965 from two Victorian lenders, it converted to a bank in October 1997, five months after Labour came to power. By the time Blair announced in May 2007 that he was resigning as prime minister, it was for a short period offering more new mortgages than any other lender.

The Rock began as a medium-size regional building society, but by 2007 it had become a flashy, stop-at-nothing bank. Its rapid growth saw it become the biggest private sector employer in its hometown and was seen as the triumph of the service sector driven renaissance of a economy that for two centuries had been synonymous with the rise and fall of British manufacturing. It came from a region that had a history of producing business chiefs who, like Icarus, were tempted to fly a little too close to the sun. It was seen as an example of Britain's transformation into a knowledge economy right up to the point when it was clear the people running it were not quite so smart after all. It took high risks. It was greedy and arrogant.

In short, the financial crisis that engulfed Gordon Brown's fledgling government in the autumn of 1997 had its origins in a region synonymous with Labour machine politics and in the sector of the economy—housing—that was emblematic of the borrow-and-spend country Britain had become over the previous decade. Just as there had been fears that the economy was growing too dependent on speculation to keep it moving, so there were concerns that Northern Rock was too dependent on one form of financing—borrowing from the City's money markets. In both cases, the warnings were ignored.

The aggressive marketing of Britain as an offshore financial sector with a light-touch regulatory regime meant those managing Northern Rock were allowed to run the bank not just with a highly risky Plan A but without the backup of a Plan B. In that sense, there was an obvious parallel with Bear Stearns, but there were differences too. The collapse of Northern Rock exposed the weakness of the government's vaunted system for overseeing the financial sector. Dividing responsibility among the Treasury, the Bank of England, and the Financial Services Authority looked good on paper, but failed in its first real test. As one of the main participants put it, "The system worked well in peacetime. This turned out to be a different kind of war."

Moreover, the crisis exposed both the superficial nature of the alleged transformation of the economy in the decade after 1997 and the intellectual bankruptcy of New Labour as it floundered around for months looking for a third-way solution to the future of the bank. America has remained an industrial power of the first rank despite the migration of jobs south to Mexico and west across the Pacific to China in recent decades. The U.S. leads the world in aerospace, computer hardware, and the audiovisual industry. Britain, by contrast, has been kept going in the past decade by three engines of growth: the housing market, the City of London, and the public sector. By 2008, all three had stalled and the money-go-round was fast slowing down.

Finally, for all the justifiable criticism in the U.S. that Paulson and Bernanke were too soft on Wall Street, they at least tended to act speedily and decisively. The same could not be said of Labour's handling of Northern Rock. There were only two real options: to let the bank go into administration or to nationalize it. The first meant job losses, 6,000 of them in a part of the world where the political map was dominated by Labour red; the second ran the risks that the government would be accused of turning the clock back to the bad old days of the 1970s, when Britain was seen as the sick man of Europe and a string of loss-making companies were bailed out by the state.

So instead of the clean free market solution or a state ownership solution, the Treasury called in the New Olympians to help sort out a problem caused by . . . the New Olympians. Goldman Sachs presented a number of options. One was that a private company should take over Northern Rock, with the Treasury standing behind the new owners with a £55 billion government guarantee. The government strained every sinew to make the public-private partnership work—anything to avoid the stigma of nationalization.

Put another way, for six months Labour flunked making the only realistic decision, to nationalize, while trying to come up with an Olympian escape plan. In the end, even New Labour shied away from handing a fat taxpayer-funded check to Sir Richard Branson, founder the Virgin commercial empire, so that he could have the profit while the state took the risk. Less than a year after the chief executive of Northern Rock, Adam Applegarth, had harbored hopes of elevating his bank into the big league, it was belatedly taken under the wing of the state. Goldman, interestingly, had told Darling from the moment it was consulted that nationalization was the best bet.

Applegarth was a no-nonsense Geordie, the nickname given to people from the northeast of England, and he had never sought to disguise what he was up to at Northern Rock. The bank lacked the branch network of its rivals, a handicap that before the financial deregulation of the 1980s and 1990s would have hindered its expansion plans. Up until the late 1960s, British banks held 25 percent of their assets in liquid form so that they could be sold easily in the event of trouble, but the gradual easing of controls meant there was a steady decline in the size of the cushion provided by rock-solid investments such as bonds and an increase in holdings dominated by residential mortgages.

Two other trends also disturbed what had once been the placid waters of the home loan business. Mortgage lenders had traditionally relied heavily (and in the case of many of the smaller building societies, exclusively) on their retail savings to finance their lending business, but by the time Applegarth took over at Northern Rock it was commonplace for lenders to borrow in the world's money markets. In addition, from the turn of the millennium, lenders also developed a taste for securitization, which involved bundling up parcels of mortgages and selling them for a lump sum.

Year after year of 20 percent growth saw Northern Rock expand its share of the UK mortgage market rapidly; it more than tripled under Applegarth from 6 percent to 19 percent, but at a cost. Mortgage lenders make their profits from the spread between the rate at which they borrow and the rate at which they lend, and Northern Rock saw its spreads compressed to levels that were lower than those of its rivals.

This did not affect its profits, because the business was expanding so fast; nor, despite the fact that in 2002 it started to offer mortgages worth 120 percent of a home's market value, did it have the "trailer trash" problem of U.S. subprime lenders.

Just like Cioffi at Bear Stearns, Applegarth convinced himself that what he was doing was prudent and safe. Yet Northern Rock lacked adequate alternative sources of funding if, for any reason, there was no appetite in the markets for its securitization issues. This was a threat not unlike that to Achilles after his mother made all of his body immortal barring the ankle by which she held him as she dipped him in the River Styx—small but potentially deadly. In both cases the danger was ignored until it was too late.

Mervyn King, the governor of the Bank of England, noted after the crisis broke that Northern Rock had neglected to take the same sort of precautions as Countrywide, the biggest U.S. mortgage lender and an institution that was heavily exposed to subprime loans. Countrywide had taken out insurance so that it could call on extensive lines of credit should it get into trouble; Northern Rock could call on only £1.5 billion at a time when its loan book was worth more than £100 billion. When the global financial markets froze up in August 2007, the Rock was left fatally exposed.

Both the Bank of England and the FSA knew that there was a risk of a problem. In December 2006, the tripartite authorities—the

Bank, the Treasury, and the FSA—had conducted a "war game" to simulate a crisis at one of Britain's high street banks. The mock-up came up with one striking conclusion: the UK's compensation scheme for depositors was far less generous than that in the U.S. and clearly inadequate. In the event that a bank failed, depositors would get only the first £2,000 of their savings back in full, and then 90 percent of the next £31,500. This, it was agreed, created an incentive for customers to get their money out of a troubled bank as quickly as possible. The Treasury, which has responsibility for the scheme, started work on an improved scheme but saw no reason to make it a priority.

In the days before financial liberalization, it was said that financiers in London sailing too close to the wind would have an audience at the Bank of England at which the governor would raise an eyebrow, this being sufficient to bring an immediate halt to the risky behavior. Between the war game in December 2006 and August 2007 both the Bank and the FSA metaphorically raised an eyebrow but to little effect.

At a meeting in July 2007 to announce his appointment, the new chief executive of the FSA, Hector Sants, said "sudden and abrupt" changes in normally liquid capital markets were being ignored by some banks. When it came to action against specific banks, the FSA was less aggressive. Under the terms of the new system of financial regulation brought in by Gordon Brown in 1997 there was no doubt that Sants was the man directly responsible for Northern Rock, but the FSA had picked up the mood music from the government: the City is our friend. Ministers sought to contrast the easygoing atmosphere of London with the stifling regulations that burdened the financial sector in New York, particularly after Congress passed the Sarbanes-Oxley Act to clean up corporate governance in the U.S. following the Enron and Worldcom frauds.

The Bank had misgivings about the cavalier attitude to risk being displayed by banks—not just in the UK but in the U.S. and Europe as well—and may have had an inkling that Northern Rock, with its dependence on the City for the bulk of its funding, was one of those sailing close to the wind, it did not become formally involved until the crisis had broken. Sir John Gieve, the deputy governor of the Bank of England, said on September 20, 2007, "I was concerned in a general way about the growth of wholesale lending. Did I know the details of Northern Rock's position before this blew up? No I did not."

The FSA, on the other hand, knew what was happening at Northern Rock. But far from telling Applegarth to act more prudently, the City watchdog appeared to endorse his strategy. In May, Northern Rock succeeded in securitizing a package of mortgages worth £5.75 billion. By then more than two-thirds of its £110 billion mortgage lending had been financed by short-term loans or securitizations—bond issues—mostly through Granite, which owned 70 percent of its mortgage book by the time the bank hit trouble.

The FSA said it had warned Northern Rock that a review of its borrowings was needed but was brushed aside. The watchdog has admitted it was toothless and with hindsight should have insisted. "Northern Rock didn't foresee anything going wrong with its model," said one FSA source (interview by authors). "It wasn't in their mind-set." Nor, apparently, was it in the FSA's mind-set, and in the circumstances of, at best, benign neglect it was hardly surprising that the Rock carried on regardless until August 9, 2007, when the announcement by BNP Paribas that it had made losses in the U.S. subprime market brought paralysis to the world's money markets. Only at this stage did he realize the perilous position his bank was now in, and he cut back on lending. It was, of course, far too late.

King, who just before the BNP Paribas announcement confessed that he did not know how serious the July tremors in the global markets would prove to be, now had his answer. On August 14, the Bank of England was told just what had been happening at Northern Rock. To its horror, the Bank found that Northern Rock was less a bank than one of the fancy new vehicles that had been created to trade in mortgage-backed securities. "By August 9, 2007, it was basically a 'gigantic SIV.' It had gigantic maturity mismatch. It had assets it couldn't sell and it couldn't borrow against them because other banks were hoarding liquidity" (Mervyn King, interview by authors, November 2007).

At both the FSA and the Bank, there was now the unmistakable clang of stable doors being slammed. Northern Rock was subjected to an intensive monitoring of its means of financing itself and plans began to be drawn up for Bank of England support. Every aspect of this proposal—its merits, the mechanics, and its legality—was explored. Every aspect bar one: what might happen if depositors made a run on Northern Rock.

In the early days of the crisis, King took a tough line. He was reluctant to bail out banks like Northern Rock that had behaved foolishly for fear that it would encourage a repeat of the folly in the future. There was much talk of "moral hazard," and despite lobbying from the FSA, the Bank of England refused to lend money to Northern Rock. Attention then switched to the possibility of finding a "white knight" for Northern Rock: a rival bank that would buy the stricken institution. One potential buyer was found in Lloyds TSB, another UK banking chain, but talks foundered after King refused to countenance the idea of providing £30 billion in loans to Northern Rock for the next two years.

Facing down the FSA, which backed the idea of a takeover by Lloyds TSB, King argued that it was not the Bank of England's job to support takeovers. If the government wanted to use money in this way, it would need to make the facility open to all comers, and that might involve sums of £300 billion, enough to prompt fears that the entire British banking system was at risk. The Treasury again backed the governor and by September 10 the idea of a takeover for Northern Rock was dead in the water.

Northern Rock now had no choice but to turn to the Bank of England for help. Under the government's tripartite system of regulating the financial markets, both the Bank of England and the FSA were required to make separate assessments of how serious the situation was before seeking the approval of Darling for emergency help. Both decided that the Northern Rock's enfeebled state and the risk of contagion to the rest of the system warranted emergency assistance from the Bank of England. The FSA also judged that Northern Rock was solvent, exceeded its minimum regulatory capital requirements, and had a good quality loan book. Darling had a reputation for being the

Cabinet's safe pair of hands but had been grappling with an intensifying financial crisis from his first few weeks at the Treasury. He rubber-stamped the request.

The Bank of England court, made up of the great and the good of the City, convened on the evening of Thursday 13 to hear the shocking truth that a bank was going bust and needed rescue. On September 14 a profits warning from the Northern Rock coincided with a statement by the tripartite authorities that the Bank of England stood ready with its lender of last resort facilities to help not just the Newcastle-based bank but any other institution that might run into trouble during the global market turbulence. It was all too late, though, because by then the lines had formed outside every Northern Rock branch in the country.

Despite the TV images, the authorities waited to see if the panic would subside once Northern Rock customers knew that the bank now had a cast-iron guarantee that would keep it trading. Saturday, however, saw even longer lines. On Sunday morning—which by unhappy coincidence was the fifteenth anniversary of Black Wednesday in 1992, when sterling was ejected from Europe's exchange rate mechanism—the chancellor, Alistair Darling, met Callum McCarthy, chairman of the FSA, and King at the Treasury. It was agreed the next step would have to be a blanket commitment to safeguard all deposits in Northern Rock. Again, however, the decision was taken to delay an announcement. Treasury insiders say this was for two reasons. First, it was felt that if Darling said something on Sunday night or on the radio on Monday morning it might make matters worse. Second, and somewhat implausibly given the abortive discussions of the previous few weeks, there was still hope that a bid from Lloyds TSB could be arranged. Unsurprisingly, that hope proved forlorn. The lines formed once more outside branches and by Monday afternoon, with shares falling in Alliance & Leicester and Bradford & Bingley, two other vulnerable UK banks, it was clear that there could be no further delay.

Darling used a press conference with Paulson to announce that deposits in Northern Rock, and any other bank that might experience similar difficulties, would be guaranteed. The run was over.

But if September 17 proved to be the high-water mark of the affair, it quickly became apparent that there were far-reaching implications for the government, for financial regulation, and for the mortgage market.

In the months between September 2007 and the moment in February 2008 when Darling finally announced that Northern Rock was to be taken into public ownership, the Labour government saw its political hegemony and economic competence challenged for the first time in more than a decade. It was forced to take a dispassionate look at its core philosophy: that the best solution to any problem was a market solution. The search for a private sector solution to Northern Rock was a long and tortuous one, involving virtually every cadre of the New Olympian order: investment banks, private equity firms, the European Union, whole armies of lawyers. The crisis for the bank, and for the tripartite system of regulation—the Bank of England, the FSA, and the Treasury—was far from over.

Gradually it became apparent to Darling that potential bidders for Northern Rock wanted to privatize the profits from running the lender while nationalizing the risk. They wanted the taxpayer to pick up the tab if things went wrong, and in those circumstances Darling at last concluded that it was time for the almost superstitious terror of nationalization to be abandoned. There was a belated realization that a "private sector solution" in the world of the New Olympians actually meant featherbedding the private sector with large dollops of public money. This, as Paulson found seven months later when he unveiled his $700 billion plan to buy up Wall Street's "toxic waste," was not especially popular.

Aside from the fate of the bank itself, the fallout from Northern Rock produced no end of suggestions for tightening the supervision of banks and generally ensuring that such a collapse can never happen again. There was, rightly, a focus on the role of the Financial Services Authority, and the rightness or otherwise of Gordon Brown's decision in 1997 to take banking supervision away from the Bank of England and hand it to the FSA.

The FSA has always seen itself as a sort of service company and was launched in the late 1990s as a world-class regulator, which suggested that from the start it saw those whom it regulates as customers to be satisfied rather than as the sources of potential instability or even fraud. It was not alone in facing criticism for its failure to do its job properly.

Aftermath: Regulators in the Stocks

In September 2008, U.S. government auditors published a severe indictment of the Securities and Exchange Commission's decision to ignore "numerous potential red flags" in the run-up to the collapse of Bear Stearns and its failure more generally to exercise adequate supervision over the investment banking industry.

David Kotz, the inspector who oversees the SEC, found "serious deficiencies" in the way it supervised Bear Stearns, applying little or no pressure on the bank to comply with voluntary accounting rules. He concluded that SEC investigators "became aware of numerous potential red flags prior to [the] Bear Stearns" collapse, concerning its mortgage-related assets, high leverage, and failure to comply with the spirit of regulatory standards, but they "did not take action to limit these risk factors."

In the wake of Northern Rock, it was clear that the difficulties with financial regulation were more systemic than they were in the U.S. The problem was the FSA itself, a lumbering monster created by the cross-fertilization of New Labour's twin loves for large, bureaucratic "strategic" units on the one hand and for the financial services industry on the other. There was much merit in the idea of putting "prudential" institutions—banks, fund managers, and big insurers—back under the supervision of an expanded new wing of the Bank of England, but the government preferred more modest reforms that left day-to-day supervision of individual banks to the FSA while beefing up the Bank of England's role in monitoring the health of the financial system as a whole. Nor was there any hint that the government intended to restrict the proportion of funding that mortgage lenders could raise on the wholesale money markets. Such funding ought to smooth the gaps that occur between an institution's deposits and loans but must never become the mainstay of funding. At the time of writing, Darling was awaiting a report on how to reopen the dormant securitization market.

As for Northern Rock, it was still in business, albeit in a slimmed down form. Labour instructed the new management team at the bank to prepare for a return to the private sector as soon as possible; mortgage holders were persuaded to find other lenders. As was the case across the industry, there was no question of new borrowers being offered loans well in excess of the value of their property. On the contrary, first-time buyers were asked to put up deposits of up to 25 percent as security against rapidly falling house prices. The bank was also told explicitly by the Treasury in September 2008 not to poach depositors from other banks. The irony was that a year after depositors had been desperate to get their cash out of Northern Rock they were clamoring to put it back in. The loss of faith in banks was so widespread that the state guarantee for Northern Rock made it one of the safest banks in Britain.

The U.S. and the UK were not the only countries to experience housing bubbles in the easy credit environment tolerated by central banks in the aftermath of the terrorist attacks of 2001; Ireland and Spain were among those where real estate bust followed real estate boom. What was different about the world's two biggest Anglo-Saxon economies, however, was that the shock waves from the property crash had a much more profound impact on the U.S. and British banking systems than on the more tightly regulated and more risk-averse banking systems of Continental Europe. Spain's system of banking regulation, for example, differed in two important ways from those of Britain and the United States. First, banks had to set aside provisions against assets in off-balance sheet assets as they did to on-balance sheet assets. Second, they were subject to "dynamic provisioning," a process whereby provisions rise when lending is rising quickly.

What marked Britain and the U.S. out from the pack was the messianic belief in the system that failed so comprehensively in the case of Northern Rock and Bear Stearns. The collapse of each bank was not a one-off, not a tragic mistake, but emblematic of economies built on the freedom of banks and other financial institutions to transform themselves from solid institutions into risky peddlers of debt. We need to retrace the road to the Bear and the Rock back to its starting point. Perhaps surprisingly, the intellectual journey to credit-crunched Manhattan and Tyneside began sixty years earlier on a mountain in Switzerland.

CHAPTER 3

Let's Go Round Again

The Free Marketeers' Sixty Years War

For the first 80 years of this century, the left has been in the ascendant. Those who argued for rationalism and planning in human affairs put their faith in the power of the state. Socialism enjoyed the support of most intellectuals. Now, under the patronage of Margaret Thatcher and Ronald Reagan, the liberal revival is enjoying some success.
— DAVID GRAHAM AND PETER CLARKE,
The New Enlightenment

The Empire may have disintegrated and the UK may now be a third-rate power, but the City of London has staged a comeback which would be the envy of any child movie star reaching maturity.
— IRA SCOTT, quoted by Margaret Reid in
The Secondary Banking Crisis, 1973–5

"I'm a 19th Century liberal," says Miss Callendar. "You can't be," says Howard, "this is the 20th Century, near the end of it. There are no resources." "I know," says Miss Callendar, "that's why I am one."
— MALCOLM BRADBURY, *The History Man*

This particular journey began on All Fool's Day 1947, when the conspirators gathered in a Swiss hotel overlooking Lake Geneva. These were not conspirators with murder in their hearts, let alone blood on their hands, but with ideas in their heads. This awesome collection of brain power included Friedrich von Hayek, Ludwig von Mises, Karl Popper, and a youthful Milton Friedman among the thirty-eight participants meeting at the Hotel du Parc on Mont Pelerin to chart the fight-back for classical liberalism against what was seen as the tyranny of the collective.

It ended, as we saw in Chapter 1, in the autumn of 2007, with Bob Diamond, the chief executive of Barclays Bank, orchestrating a campaign in the City of London to demand that Mervyn King, governor of the Bank of England, capitulate to demands from London's financial elite for cheap money to rescue them from the consequences of their own stupidity. Whether Hayek and his colleagues would have sided with Diamond and his cronies is doubtful. The Mont Pelerin society was formed to roll back the power of the state, and was hostile to any notion of featherbedding. Logically (Hayek and Popper were thinkers who prided themselves on their capacity for logic), they would have opposed handouts to investment banks just as they would have opposed the Common Agricultural Policy or giving blank checks to ailing manufacturing firms. King himself contrasted the dependency culture among investment banks with the hard-nosed view of the modern world taken by British manufacturers. Industry, the governor noted in the aftermath of the run on Northern Rock, knew that it was pointless and even self-defeating to plead for cuts in interest rates to bring down the value of the pound. The result would simply be higher inflation, which would negate the beneficial impact of cheaper exports. Industry, perhaps, through bitter experience, knew that life was tough; manufacturers expected to work hard to make a profit and they knew that some among their number would go to the wall. Investment banks, by contrast, saw no reason why any of their charmed circle should suffer a fall in profitability, let alone go out of business.

Such is the law of unintended consequences. The free market fight-back against the postwar consensus culminated in the rich and powerful sucking deep and long on the teat of the state. It swept away a form of subsidy that sought to defend the jobs and living standards of ordinary people with another form of subsidy that put money in the hands of those with seven-figure bonuses. The evolution of the global economy in the six decades from a series of spring seminars in a Swiss canton to the fallout from mortgage defaults in Las Vegas trailer parks was not smooth or linear. It took years, many years in fact, for the Mont Pelerin conspirators to see their plans come to fruition. So how did it happen? How did the world of 1947—when financial interest was caged so that ordinary folk could be guaranteed work and income security—turn into a world where the only freedom that mattered was that of Goldman Sachs and J.P. Morgan to continue making money?

What do we mean by "ordinary folk"? Pretty much everybody apart from the very rich. Paul Krugman in his recent book, *The Conscience of a Liberal*, argues that the New Deal helped create a middle-class America. We would claim that the same applies to Britain with regard to the welfare state policies pursued after 1945. Between the 1929 crash and the late 1950s, the purchasing power of the median family in the United States doubled, while the real incomes of those in the top 0.1 percent of earners had halved. At least four factors lay behind what Krugman calls the great compression: stronger trade unions, sharply progressive taxation, controls on the free movement of capital, and managed trade. A fifth factor, immigration controls, also contributed to rising real incomes of blue-collar workers.

From Riot to Market Renaissance: The Legacy of the Year of Living Dangerously

At first free market ideas were confined to some well-funded think tanks and the fringes of academic economics. The attempt to revive eighteenth-century liberalism had limited appeal at a time when the New Deal, the welfare state, and other versions of the mixed economy were delivering unprecedented prosperity. That began to change in the year that became a hinge between the social democratic settlement and the bastardized form of the free market that we now find ourselves with.

Although it may appear curious to some, that year was 1968, the year students took to the streets of Paris, demonstrators protested against the war in Vietnam, and riots engulfed the Watts ghetto of Los Angeles. It was the year theater censorship was abolished in London. It was the year Lindsay Anderson made the film *If* about a group of schoolboys mounting an insurrection at their public school. It was the year the first abortion clinic opened in Britain; it was the year rock's aristocracy—the Beatles, the Rolling Stones, Bob Dylan—ditched psychedelia and made plain, unadorned albums that returned them to their roots. But for all that and more, it was the moment, a bit like El Alamein in 1942, when the tide turned.

It was a pivotal year, but not in the sense that is sometimes suggested today. Some of those supposedly in the vanguard of the revolution sensed that the impact of the counterculture would be transitory and superficial. Interviewed by Robin Blackburn and Tariq Ali for the underground magazine *Red Mole* in January 1971, John Lennon summed things up like this: "Of course, there are a lot of people walking around with long hair now and some trendy middle-class kids in pretty clothes. But nothing changed except that we all dressed up a bit, leaving the same bastards running everything."

To which we would merely add that the trendy middle-class kids in pretty clothes have cut their hair, wear sober suits, and make speeches in praise of free markets and welfare reform (for the poor and middle classes, if not the rich).

At one level, of course, 1968 was a logical conclusion to the anti-colonial spirit of the postwar era; the difference only that the protests were directed at the new hegemony in the Western Hemisphere, the United States, for its war in Vietnam, rather against the empire on which the sun now only very intermittently rose. There are those in their fifties in Britain who look back fondly on the days when they swarmed outside the American embassy in Grosvenor Square, something that the fight against global terrorism has long since made impossible.

Yet at another level, the 1968 protesters were the solvent that started the process of dissolving the postwar settlement. This was not so much that the violence in Detroit, Paris, and London engendered a conservative backlash (although it did) but that the protesters willingly allied themselves, in a rather bizarre echo of the 1939 Ribbentrop-

Molotov Pact, with the sleepers of the new right in an attack on the postwar order. While one wing of the protest movement took to the streets in pursuit of the traditional working-class demands for higher wages and a shorter week, the other wing, the middle-class student wing, was inimical to the bourgeois Keynesian state, with its top-down control and emphasis on material well-being. This sense of distaste at the trappings of Western democracy was fully manifested in the 1970s with the flowering of violent revolutionary groups such as the Baader-Meinhof gang in Germany and the Red Brigades in Italy. Once captured by the "Nazi pig state," however, they would wax lyrical about habeas corpus and police brutality, suddenly demonstrating an ability to tell the difference between a justice system run by the Federal Republic of Germany or the Italian state and one run by the Gestapo. Nor was the cultural underpinning of 1968 built on sturdy foundations. By the early 1970s, when they were all safely tax exiles in the south of France, the idea of the Rolling Stones singing "Street Fighting Man" seemed rather absurd, although "Street Fighting Accountant" doesn't have quite the same ring about it.

As Peter Doggett notes in a recent book, on the same day in December 1969 that police arrested members of the Charles Manson family in California, Mick Jagger was in London with the Stones' business adviser, Prince Rupert Lowenstein, discussing ways of minimizing certain tax liabilities (*There's a Riot Going On: Revolutionaries, Rock Stars, and the Rise and Fall of 1960s Counter-Culture*, Canongate, 2007).

The year 1968 saw severe and growing strains on the postwar settlement of both Lord Keynes and Lord Beveridge (and their transatlantic equivalents), mixing economic management and social welfare, not least because a second generation was coming into adult life that had known nothing but the state-guaranteed prosperity of the time and was not minded to be grateful for it. This predisposition to take abundance for granted was epitomized by the behavior of the Lyndon Johnson administration, which tried simultaneously to fight a war in Southeast Asia, increase welfare spending at home, and keep a lid on taxes. In some ways, President Johnson and his lieutenants were grand-scale versions of the self-centered Benjamin Braddock character played by Dustin Hoffman in the film of the previous year, *The Graduate*. Both Braddock and Johnson seemed to take for granted America's nearly limitless capacity to generate wealth.

In the inevitable international financial dislocation that followed Johnson's unsustainable economic, military, and social policies, the renascent freebooting financial speculators sniffed their first openings. Hitherto thought of as disreputable figures confined to entrepôts such as Tangier or Macao, outside the Bretton Woods system, they were coming to the center stage as important players in the Eurodollar and other financial markets. The suspension of U.S. gold payments in 1968 to all overseas dollar holders other than national governments was a harbinger of what was to come, with the Tet offensive by the North Vietnamese leading to the first concerted pressure on the American currency in the postwar era.

Sterling had been devalued the previous autumn and the 1968 weakening of the dollar's link to gold presaged the devaluation of the U.S. currency in August 1971. The Bretton Woods system was coming apart.

Few periods in recent history have aroused as much passion and dispute as 1968. Almost before it ended, its legacy was being fought over by radicals, liberals, conservatives, and people from just about every viewpoint. Through the eyes of Malcolm Bradbury's fictional left-wing lecturer Howard Kirk it was "the radical year . . . Everything seemed wide open; individual expectations coincided with historical drive" (*The History Man*, Secker &Warburg, 1975). Kirk's hopes went unfulfilled, however, as did those of many real-life '68ers: "By the end of 1968 that dream was in a ragged state. The cries of rage had all been in vain; the new age was conclusively stillborn. Nixon was in the White House and the [Vietnam] war went on" (David Downing, *Future Rock*, Panther, 1976). What is more, after being in power for only eight of the past thirty-six years (and even then with the nonideological Dwight Eisenhower as president) the Republicans had, in Richard Nixon, a perhaps unlikely harbinger of a period of Republican domination of the White House that has seen only three Democrats—Jimmy Carter, Bill Clinton, and Barack Obama—as chief executive and commander in chief. And two of these Democrats had a noticeable conservative bent, hailing as they did from southern states. The old Democrat alliance of the industrial North and the patrician East went down to defeat under candidates Walter Mondale (1984), Michael Dukakis (1988), and John Kerry (2004).

It was a far cry from the days when most Republicans had felt tied in to the postwar settlement. Writing to his brother Edgar in 1954, Eisenhower said, "Should any political party attempt to abolish social security, unemployment insurance and eliminate labor laws and farm programs you would not hear of that party again in our political history. There is a tiny splinter group, of course, that believes you can do those things. Among them are H. L. Hunt (you possibly know his background), a few other Texas oil millionaires, and an occasional politician or business man from other areas. Their number is negligible and they are stupid."

In the half decade from 1968 to 1973, the postwar system lost its moorings. The economic squalls associated with rising public spending in the United States became the hurricane inflation winds of a fivefold increase in oil prices. After years of rapid economic growth, the Keynesian model listed in the doldrums of unemployment. And below decks, there was talk of mutiny. From the late 1950s there had been creeping attempts to circumvent the strict controls on the movement of capital, with the U.S. authorities choosing not to control the rise of the Eurodollar market, which found its home in the City of London. Despite its name, the market had nothing much to do with Europe and simply described any pool of American dollars held outside the United States and available for loans and investments unregulated by the U.S. authorities.

Through the Eurodollar market, despite increased domestic capital controls, U.S. banks were largely enabled to continue their foreign lending from their overseas bases, and U.S. multinational corporations enabled to meet their borrowing and investment needs throughout the period (Robert Brenner, "The Economics of Global Turbulence," *New Left Review*, May–June 1998, 117).

As such, there were reasons, perhaps almost hidden at the time, for the new right to be quietly cheerful as the students prised the cobblestones from the boulevards of the Latin Quarter to hurl at the police and as the Russian tanks rumbled into Prague later in the summer to crush Alexander Dubček's attempt at liberal communism. They may even have quoted Winston Churchill, who, on the occasion of the 8th Army's victory over the Afrika Korps, explained the battle's significance thus: "Now, this is not the end," said the then prime minister. "It is not even the beginning of the end. But it is, perhaps, the end of the beginning." As we shall now see, the "beginning of the end" for the postwar order was not to be long delayed.

The Better Tomorrow: From Welfare State to Market State

As an opening to a new premiership, it was not auspicious. The Opposition had just won, against almost all the predictions of the opinion polls.

> There was a large crowd in Smith Square, outside Conservative Central Office, through which Mr [Edward] Heath had to thrust his way without police protection. One disappointed citizen stubbed out a lighted cigarette on his neck, burning him painfully. (Douglas Hurd, *An End to Promises*, Collins, 1979.)

To this day, Mr. Heath (he was knighted long after leaving office) is seen as someone who was burned again and again by the pressure of outside events. The surprise winner of the June 1970 general election, he has gone into the history books as having entered office on a near-Thatcherite radical program of creating "a new economic order, deliberately based on the disciplines of a market economy" (Harold Wilson, *Final Term*, Weidenfeld & Nicolson, 1979). Heath had promised a "quiet revolution" (Hurd, *End to Promises*), and his 1970 manifesto had been entitled A Better Tomorrow. In the conventional reading of the unhappy and crisis-torn government of 1970–1974, early attempts by the Heath government at forcing British industry into the cold shower of market "discipline" ran into two insuperable, linked obstacles: the strength of organized labor (relatively short-lived) and the amalgam of crises that were to kill off what the French called the *trente glorieuses*— the thirty golden years from the mid-1940s to the mid-1970s.

And there seemed to be something in this. Between taking office and the end of 1971, the Tories, backed by their own laws to control trade union activity, had attempted to break the back of pay inflation with a pay policy, applied only to the public sector, called N Minus One, under which each settlement had to be lower than the last one. Defeats at the hands of local authority workers in 1970 were balanced by better results against power station workers at the turn of the year and the Union of Post Office Workers in 1971. Meanwhile, the government insisted loss-making companies would be allowed to fail, that there would be no state rescues for "lame ducks."

This second pillar of the policy was to collapse more quickly than the confrontation with the unions. In February 1971, the government faced not so much a lame duck as a lame pterodactyl, the now bankrupt engineering group Rolls-Royce. Best known for its luxury cars, the company's strategic value related to aircraft engines, and its collapse threatened to leave a number of airlines and air forces in the lurch. Heath's immediate decision to nationalize the company contrasted sharply with Gordon Brown's dithering over Northern Rock and was subsequently vindicated, as Rolls-Royce is today one of Britain's few manufacturers of international stature.

The subsequent Rolls-Royce bailout killed off the lame duck policy, and one year after the company's insolvency the government agreed to a rescue package for Upper Clyde Shipbuilders (UCS), scene of a world-famous "work-in" to beat off the threat of closure. But by this time, the Tories' reasonably hot streak in terms of industrial action had gone cold, courtesy of the 1971–1972 miners' strike.

The shipbuilders' less probable allies included John Lennon and Yoko Ono, who delivered flowers to the work-in with a card attached declaring: "Oppression is bad for you." But they were merely at the far edge of a long platform of middle-class support for the strikers of the Heath era.

In the early 1970s, playwright Arnold Wesker spent time as a guest of the *Sunday Times*. In one editorial meeting, the paper discusses its attitude toward pay disputes. Wesker mused, "It has always seemed manifest lunacy to me that workers are expected to be happy, civilised, fulfilled and unfearful of the future, doing the work they do for the wages they receive" (*Journey into Journalism*, Writers and Readers Publishing Cooperative, 1977).

Bernard Levin, not usually counted a friend of union activists, wrote thus on a pay dispute on the railways: "Has he [Edward Heath] any idea what a man earning £20 a week feels when he sees speculators about to make untold millions by befouling Piccadilly Circus and Covent Garden and indeed any other bits of any other city that they can get their hands on?" (*The Times*, May 30, 1972).

Christopher Booker, another writer not always in sympathy with the unions, concentrated on Heath's personality in the crisis that engulfed his government: "Amid the greatest collapse in share prices and property values since 1929, the 'second' miners' strike, the 'Three Day Week' and all the rest, the Heath government in March 1974 finally fell (Heath himself being simply not psychologically equipped, with his wooden, unvisionary stubbornness, to do anything other than make the situation worse)" (*The Seventies*, Allen Lane, 1980).

Referring to a time when the fall of Edward Heath was still in the future, Paul Foot—in some ways the epitome of upper-middle-class radicalism—put it this way: "So it was that the miners' strike of 1972 transformed British industrial relations. . . . All this led to an unparalleled blossoming of democracy. Political discussion and debate, for so long confined to parliamentary chambers, suddenly became part of the daily lives of many thousands of workers. Anyone even remotely involved in those nine dramatic weeks can testify to that" (*The Vote*, Viking, 2005).

But what Foot called "the industrial and democratic volcano of 1972" was a peak, never to be scaled again, in the alliance between organized labor and liberal-minded middle-class intellectuals. As noted above by Booker, a second miners' strike, two years later, helped tip Heath's Conservatives out of office, but only just. The Tories won more votes than had the incoming, minority Labour government.

Heath's attempts to bring greater control and order to trade union affairs and hence to industrial relations had not emerged from a clear blue sky in the summer of 1970. Organized labor had not featured as an election issue in 1966, and, as we shall see later, it was routine at this time for schoolchildren to be taught that the growth of the unions was a type of social progress. But by the late 1960s, under the twin pressures of higher inflation and the rise of a new, more militant breed of shop steward, the number of days lost to strikes started to rise, and the Labour government decided to act. A Royal Commission under Lord Donovan had been set up as early as 1965 to look at the modernization of the unions, and when it reported in June 1968 it recommended a number of largely voluntary reforms to industrial relations.

Barbara Castle, then secretary of state for employment and productivity, decided to go much further; in January 1969 her draft white paper, In Place of Strife, proposed compulsory registration of trade unions, with strike ballots and cooling-off periods in certain circumstances.

The proposals were defeated by internal Labour Party opposition, as Heath's legal framework was destroyed by the turmoil of the mid-1970s. But for organized labor, the clock was ticking, despite a general feeling that, having seen off Castle and Heath, the unions were invincible.

Away from political and industrial battles, cultural changes augured poorly for the future of the twenty-year intellectual fascination with the authenticity of British working-class life, expressed in innumerable "kitchen sink" plays and television dramas, in popular music and art photography.

On television, the quintessential gritty northern series, *Z Cars* (BBC TV, 1962–1978) was well past its creative peak, most of its senior actors having been despatched south to solve crime in the more middle-class pastures of *Softly, Softly* (1966–1976), a successful spin-off. The two main characters in *The Likely Lads* (BBC TV, 1964–1966) returned in *Whatever Happened to the Likely Lads?* (1973–1974), a rhetorical question as what had "happened" was that one had joined the middle class and the other remained resolutely upwardly immobile.

Popular music, along with professional sport, had been a traditional escape route from the back streets, and, indeed, a number of major rock acts spent the early 1970s ruminating on the humble backgrounds of the modern British star, some more convincingly than others. In many cases, these ruminations had an elegiac quality. Alan Price, formerly of the Newcastle band the Animals, went further than most, reprising one of the legendary moments of Labour history, the Jarrow March of unemployed workers to London in October 1936 ("Jarrow Song," 1974). David Bowie's alter ego Ziggy Stardust confined himself to recalling that an old mate had joined the army to escape poverty and to name-checking postwar Labour health minister Aneurin Bevan. Elton John's rock star narrator in "Goodbye Yellow Brick Road" hinted, improbably, at a farming background ("I'm going back to my plough"). Interestingly, the era's indisputably working-class band, Slade, produced a string of best-selling records containing almost no references to blue-collar British life, the narratives, such as they were, being set in a sketchy Middle America in which raunchy women drink whisky and obey the injunction: "Girls grab the boys."

On screen, the disengagement between the intellectuals and the working class was illustrated by the gulf between two depictions of two youths at tough comprehensive schools. *Kes*, released in 1969, was based on a novel of the previous year by Barry Hines entitled *A Kestrel for a Knave* (Michael Joseph). In an evocative and moving film, the main character, Billy, nurses an injured kestrel back to health.

Eight years later, in April 1977, BBC's *Play for Today* broadcast "Gotcha!" written by Barrie Keefe and featuring a sixteen-year-old school dropout who, on the spur of the moment at the end of his last term, takes two teachers hostage. The youth is never named, underlining the fact that none of his "teachers" can remember who he is. The play ends with the youth being overpowered by one of the male teachers, who then beats him up.

Keefe presumably hoped the audience would sympathize with a youth facing the resurgent specter of unemployment and deplore the violence to which he was subjected. In the atmosphere of 1977, he may well, had there been a reliable method of measurement, have been disappointed.

In fact Heath had not failed but succeeded: both the "market economy" and the need to "discipline" the trade unions were firmly on the agenda, although neither had been an issue during his first general election as leader in 1966. True, he had failed to remain as prime minister. But that was of no great interest to anyone other than himself. And this failure was far from preordained; he fell probably because of confusion as to his choice of weapons, rather than choice of battlefield:

> [Heath] was . . . trying to go in contradictory directions. On the one hand he was trying to take the unions on board into a tripartite management of the domestic economy; on the other he was attacking them with his industrial relations legislation; on the one hand seeking an investment boom in Britain via cheap credit; on the other unwittingly allowing the introduction of a system which explicitly promised increases in interest rates [a forerunner of the current system of Bank of England independence] to "control" the supply of credit. (Robin Ramsay, *Prawn Cocktail Party*, Vision, 1998.)

Heath may well have been confused as to the compatibility of European social market democracy on German lines and the unfettered capital markets the City demanded. But his most enduring domestic legacies (this is not the place to consider the effects of his successful attempt to take Britain into what was then the European Community) were, first, the beginning of the process whereby the City would be freed from the postwar controls that it found so irksome and, second, the embedding of the trade unions as a problem in much of the public mind.

The "freeing" of the City centered on a package of changes mendaciously entitled Competition and Credit Control (CCC), under which banks would be allowed to wriggle free of much of the regime under which they had been supervised. The official interest rate (bank rate) would cease to be what it had been since the 1940s—effectively an instruction issued by the Bank of England—and became instead the "market-driven" minimum lending rate. City bankers, through the package proposed by the Bank of England, were being given back control of borrowing costs.

Furthermore, interbank borrowing would no longer use as security certain assets (chiefly government securities) held by the borrowing bank. Instead, these banks would simply pledge their own paper as security, a change that was to have profound implications more than three decades later in the Northern Rock debacle. Lending limits were lifted. "Here is the authentic voice of the British banker struggling to throw off the restrictions of government and begin seriously milking the British economy" (Ramsay, *Prawn Cocktail Party*).

Adopted as government policy in September 1971, CCC had nothing much to do with either control or competition, but a lot to do with credit. Even Tory grandee Edward du Cann, himself a merchant banker, was alarmed when attending a meeting of backbench MPs at which the package was discussed: "I looked round the room and wondered how many of the MPs present fully comprehended . . . [the package] I doubt whether more than half a dozen had the least idea" (Edward du Cann, *Two Lives*, Images, 1995).

He added, "It was generally supposed that all that was occurring was the replacement of one system of control by another: it was certainly not appreciated, perhaps not even by the banking sector generally, that the competition part of the package meant virtually unbridled liberalism, leading to new and unforeseen risk."

Put another way, "it was simply the old order being re-imposed on the British economy. This was the climax of all those attempts since the post-war era to get rid of government controls. Under the new system the banks could lend what they liked and, when it was decided that there was too much credit in the system, they would put the interest rates up. What a truly wonderful racket!" (Ramsay, *Prawn Cocktail Party*).

One might have thought the financial market cataclysm of 1973–1974, much of it directly resulting from the inflationary and destabilizing effects of the "reforms," would have buried CCC. Far from it. A theme of this book is that all setbacks for financial interests are treated as temporary and all advances are treated as permanent, an approach summed up admirably by this wonderful, fictional conversation:

Sir Desmond Glazebrook: "Surely a decision's a decision?"
Sir Humphrey Appleby: "Only if it's the decision you want. If not it's just a temporary setback." (From *Yes, Minister*, BBC TV, March 30, 1981.)

Thus the head of the Labour government that took office in March 1974 wrote later: "It is only fair to say that . . . some of the main features of CCC still operate in the City, and are working." (Wilson, *Final Term*.)

Indeed, the 1974–1979 Labour government gave a (probably unintended) forward shove to the unshackling of the City in 1976, when the Restrictive Practices Act was extended to cover the supply of services as well as goods. Shortly afterward, Labour referred the rulebook of the London Stock Exchange to the Office of Fair Trading. Two aspects of the exchange's operations were likely to be of particular concern: the system of "minimum commission," under which small shareholders were effectively subsidized on their share deals by large ones, and firms were prevented from full-blooded competition, and "single capacity," under which brokers, market makers, and merchant bankers had to be separate from each other.

This reference led directly to the Big Bang reforms of 1986; at that time, it seemed ironic that a Labour government had been responsible for the huge enrichment of City partners now free to sell up their stakes to the new breed of investment banks. It seems less ironic now, after ten years of Labour's obeisance to the financial sector.

Heath's financial legacy rolled on after his departure: through the abolition of exchange controls in 1979, privatization (which he started in a small way in the early 1970s, selling the Thomas Cook travel agent and a clutch of bizarrely government-owned pubs in the Carlisle area), and perhaps above all from the phenomenon of the 2000s described in sepulchral tones by younger financial journalists as "private equity," a grand-sounding phrase for the sort of asset stripping that flourished during the Heath years.

As for the second strand of the Heath legacy—mounting hostility to organized labor—it is worth recalling that, until the early 1970s, the rise of the trade unions had been regarded as an indicator of social progress: "The Trades Union Congress, an organisation which has been called the 'Parliament of the Workers', has met almost every year and has now come to be recognised as the spokesman for workers of this country. Today it is a much-respected organisation and is

consulted by governments on all matters concerning working people"
(*Hamlyn Children's Encyclopedia*, 1971).

By the end of the 1970s, it was very different. Many, perhaps most,
of the million-plus workers involved in the so-called winter of discontent in 1978–1979 were much worse off than the miners and others
who had enjoyed such a large measure of public sympathy in the earlier
part of the decade. But you would not have known it from the broadcast coverage, which has traditionally (because of the legal obligation to
supply balance) been fairer to the unions than the press has been:

> [In an interview with the regional secretary of the health service union
> CoHSE] What if somebody did die, would we be able to sue CoHSE?
> (BBC Radio Birmingham, February 5, 1979.)

> Well-cherished the weekend that lies ahead because on Monday we're
> due for more industrial action. One and a half million public service
> workers will be staging a day of action, a euphemism for a one-day
> strike. (*Today*, BBC Radio 4, January 19, 1979.)

> [In an interview with a union representative, these three questions were
> asked] How do you justify putting lives at risk? If somebody dies will it
> be on your conscience? Is . . . more money worth a life? (BBC2 News,
> January 19, 1979.)

> [Questioning a union official] One understands the basis of your claim,
> but isn't the strike by ambulancemen potentially one of the most disas-
> trous things that could happen to society? (BBC1 Nationwide, January
> 16 1979; quotes taken from *A Cause for Concern*, 1979.)

Press comment, by and large, was more hostile still. Heath had succeeded; the trade unions were now an issue, perhaps one of the top
three or four issues in the public mind. And his own reputation, in relation to his struggle with the trade unions, tended to rise as the decade
progressed. His former political secretary Douglas Hurd was in no
doubt Heath had been a man ahead of his time. In 1977, he compared
the work of the Heath administration with that of a fictional govern-

ment in 1931, insisting on rearmament. Even had it lost office, turfed out by an appeasement-minded electorate, and its new warplanes been scrapped by a pacifistic Labour government, said Hurd, "By 1939 the British people might have looked back with regret."

By apparently comparing 1970s trade unionism with 1930s fascism, Douglas Hurd (later to hold a number of senior Cabinet positions) showed the extent of even moderate Conservative opposition to organized labor. It marked also the distance traveled by center-right politicians since the postwar decades in which their support for the social and economic settlement could be taken for granted. It is to the ferocity of the attack on this settlement that we now turn.

Target for Tonight: The Mixed Economy

Whether or not the inaugural meeting of the Mont Pelerin society had been a deliberate attempt to ape the meeting in a New Hampshire hotel three years earlier that had pieced together the architecture for the postwar international order and given it its name, Bretton Woods, the collection of economists and political theorists who met for nine days in Switzerland in the spring of 1947 had an entirely different vision of the postwar world. What's more, they knew they were in it for the long haul.

The West, less than two years after the Red Army had unfurled the hammer and sickle over Berlin's Brandenburg Gate, could hardly have been less promising for those who believed in the power of market forces to provide the best possible combination of prosperity and freedom. The retreat from liberalism prompted by the economic slump of the 1930s had been hastened by the need to harness the power of the state to defeat Hitler. Seeking a theme for the 1945 general election, Winston Churchill had borrowed from Friedrich Hayek's seminal 1944 work, *The Road to Serfdom*, to claim that a vote for Clement Attlee's Labour Party would result in bringing the Gestapo to Britain, if not immediately, then at some point in the future once the initial good intentions of those dedicated to planning the economy hardened into a form of totalitarianism. Churchill's attack flopped. Attlee, a cricket-loving First World War major and former social worker, was not the sort of person the average British voter could imagine armed with a rubber truncheon in a torture chamber. Furthermore, he cleverly exploited paranoia about all things German by using an election broadcast to emphasize the "von" between the "Friedrich" and the "Hayek." More to the point, perhaps, the tide of collectivism was at its height. Not only was there enormous respect for the part communist Russia had played in the defeat of Hitler, but there was a sense that it had only been by pulling together that Britain had survived in the dark days from the summer of 1940 to the arrival of the United States in the war in December 1941. There was a demand that the same meticulous planning that had characterized the war economy should be used to confront the problems of peacetime, and in particular the five giants identified in the 1942 Beveridge report—want, ignorance, squalor, disease, and idleness.

The luminaries of the Mont Pelerin society knew what they were up against. Hayek drew comparisons with the undercover struggle waged by resistance fighters in the war, urging his friends to "raise and train an army of freedom fighters" (from Hayek's paper "The Prospect of Freedom," quoted in Richard Cockett, *Thinking the Unthinkable*, Fontana, 1995, p. 104). He added, "If we do not flinch at this task, if we do not throw up our hands in the face of overwhelming public opinion but work to shape and guide that opinion, our cause is by no means hopeless. But it is late in the day and we have not too much time to spare."

Hayek was right about that. Faith in Wall Street and big finance generally had been shattered by the Great Depression, so much so that President Roosevelt was able to launch the sort of populist attack in his inauguration speech that today would be found only in the pages of *Socialist Worker*. Yet with unemployment at 25 percent and industrial production down by 50 percent in three years, FDR had the public on his side when he said of those who had enjoyed the fruits of the Gilded Age: "True they have tried, but their efforts have been cast in the pattern of an outworn tradition. . . . They have no vision, and when there is no vision the people perish. The money changers have fled from their high seats in the temple of our civilization. We may now restore that temple to the ancient truths. The measure of the restoration lies in the extent to which we apply social values more noble than mere monetary profit."

As Howard Wachtel wrote in his book *Street of Dreams* (Pluto, 2003, p. 182):

> These were words Wall Street had never before heard from Pennsylvania Avenue, but their defences were down, having been shattered by a financial and economic reality and decades-long public debate. Now the representatives of a popular politics on Main Street had the upper hand, and the Street found itself in an unfamiliarly defensive position.

Roosevelt kept up the pressure. Speaking to Adolph Berle, a professor at Columbia University and a former member of FDR's original brains trust, after Berle accepted an offer to join the New York Stock Exchange's advisory board, the president said, "The fundamental trouble with this whole stock exchange crowd is their complete lack of elementary education. I do not mean lack of college diplomas, etc., but just inability to understand the country or public or their obligations to their fellow men. Perhaps you can help them acquire a kindergarten knowledge of these subjects. More power to you" (quoted in Steve Fraser, *Wall Street*, Faber & Faber, 2005, p. 391).

It was Roosevelt who referred to the new era's stock market seers and fantasists as object lessons in how the country had departed from the basics of Ben Franklin republicanism. It was Roosevelt who decried Samuel Insull's pyramid of watered stock, its arbitrary write-up of assets, its milking of subsidies and vast overcharging of customers. It was the president who confirmed a long held populist suspicion that fewer than three dozen private banking houses and stock-selling adjuncts in the commercial banks "have directed the flow of capital within the country and outside it, pledging that the government would become the effective counterweight to this financial oligarchy."

Roosevelt backed his words with action. The Glass-Steagall Act of 1933 protected ordinary depositors by banning commercial banks from acting like investment banks and by establishing an insurance fund, the Federal Deposit Insurance Corporation. In 1934, the Securities and Exchange Act legislated for transparency in the financial markets, creating the Securities and Exchange Commission to police Wall Street. Wachtel says the essence of the new legislation was that caveat vendor replaced caveat emptor.

The third pillar of the new postcrash system involved the installation of a populist banker from Utah, Marriner Eccles, as chairman of the Federal Reserve Board. He reformed the central bank by putting control of interest rates under an open market committee, thus removing it from the hands of Wall Street's so-called money center banks, those with a large market presence and a major role in providing funds for corporations and governments.

> The regulatory regime established during the 1930s prevailed until its undoing in the deregulatory movement of the 1980s. In that half century the American economy grew faster than in any other comparable period in its history. It was also the only such half-century without a single or even minor financial crisis on Wall Street, which had become used to one every ten years or so from its origins in 1792 to the 1930s. (Wachtel, *Street of Dreams*, p. 187.)

Roosevelt's scathing remarks had an echo in Britain, where John Maynard Keynes said, "Speculators may do no harm as bubbles on a steady stream of enterprise. But the position is serious when enterprise becomes the bubble on a whirlpool of speculation" (*The General Theory of Employment, Interest, and Money*, 1936). A decade earlier, when Winston Churchill had been persuaded against his better judgment to return Britain to the Gold Standard, the future prime minister wrote in a February 1925 memo to Treasury Permanent Secretary Otto Niemeyer that he "would rather see finance less proud and industry more content."

Yet, despite all this, Hayek's faith was rewarded. Unlike the left after the setbacks of the 1970s, the believers in classical free market liberalism did not throw in the towel. Even though the Great Depression was a far more serious economic crisis than that triggered in autumn 1973 by the energy cartel, the Organization of Petroleum Exporting Countries (OPEC), Hayek and his friends never doubted that they would eventually be proved right. As such, they ignored the nationalization of the coal mines in Britain that took place three months before Mont Pelerin; they were undeterred when the National Health Service introduced socialized medicine little more than a year later; they saw the "we're all in it together" spirit of the classic Ealing comedy film *Passport to Pimlico* as a challenge, something to be shaped and guided as Hayek put it, rather than something that implied surrender. As far as the Mont Pelerin conspirators were concerned, the postwar settlement was the equivalent of the *Titanic*, seemingly unsinkable but inevitably heading for disaster. As we shall see later in this chapter, the postwar consensus hit the iceberg in 1968. Although the band played on for a few more years, it slipped beneath the waves five years later.

So what was it about the postwar settlement that the classical liberals loathed so much? As we have seen, it was a somewhat bloodless and technical construct whose shorthand name—the mixed economy—captured admirably its blend of welfare, state economic management, and private enterprise. It was a very far cry indeed from the totalitarian state feared by Hayek and colleagues, which was hardly surprising since the two men who did more to bury classical liberalism (John Maynard Keynes and Franklin Delano Roosevelt) were both from the patrician class in their respective countries. Neither Lord Keynes nor President Roosevelt was remotely interested in creating a workers state to mirror that in the Soviet Union; they saw themselves as practical men seeking to cope with the world as it was rather than as how it should be if the economic textbooks were right. Keynes did not want to abandon private enterprise in favor of state socialism anymore than Hayek did, but neither economist thought that a wholly market economy was possible. Responding to *The Road to Serfdom*, Keynes said, "You agree that the line has to be drawn somewhere, and that the logical extreme is not possible. But you give us no guidance whatever as to where to draw it . . . but as soon as you admit that the extreme is not possible, and that a line has to be drawn, you are, on your own argument, done for since you are trying to persuade us that as soon as one moves an inch in the planned direction you are necessarily launched on the slippery path which will lead you in due course over the precipice."

Sequel: The Market Comeback:
From Arthur Halley to the Abbey National

Credit where it is due: the financiers, the offshore capitalists, the investment bankers, and the speculators fought back from an extraordinarily unfavorable position immediately after the war to perhaps the key position in the world economy. It is hard to recall now just how despised were the financial traders and traffickers of the early postwar period, both in political discourse (Harold Wilson's famous "gnomes of Zurich") and in fiction (at least two Ian Fleming villains, Hugo Drax and Auric Goldfinger, are metals speculators). They were the shadowy, wealthier, and often expatriate counterparts of the coupon clippers and the dividend drawers, the faded rentier class living in Eastbourne or Cheltenham and doomed to extinction in the new Britain of the postwar world. Even the relatively respectable merchant banks were treated with suspicion and widely thought to have a limited future. Until the late 1960s, the activities of financial interests were severely curtailed by instruments such as exchange control, high and selective levels of taxation, strict banking regulation, and official surveillance. Emerging from the intellectual and economic chaos of forty years ago, those representing that interest are now perhaps the most important figures on the economic stage. Their opinions are sought on financial and political issues, and their "confidence" must be maintained at all costs by those (such as central bankers) charged with economic management. Their "contribution" to the public good is routinely praised by politicians, even when it amounts to little more than asset stripping. National laws and international treaties entrench their position. They argue that their dominance is the "natural" order of things, and that political or social action can only "distort" this natural order.

Until the 1970s, they confronted a system that combined strict official control over finance and industry, tight supervision of banking, and active management of the economy in the interests of the many, coupled with a hands-off approach to people's personal lifestyles and attitudes, whether of the traditional variety or, as the 1950s and 1960s progressed, the freewheeling sort. This formula has since been turned on its head—a remarkable achievement. But then the financial interests and their intellectual companions were not just determined but were as wise as serpents. They treated every reverse as temporary and every advance as permanent. In the first category, not including the sweeping measures of the 1945 Labour government, were the defeat in the highest levels of government of the Operation Robot proposals to float the pound in 1952, the import surcharge of the post-1964 Labour government, the nationalization of aerospace and shipbuilding in the 1970s, and, at the same time, the imposition of "corset" arrangements on British banks. The second category included the above-mentioned Heath liberalization of the City, the 1979 abolition of exchange control, the granting of operational independence to the Bank of England's Monetary Policy Committee, and the entire post-1979 privatization program.

Despite the energy crisis and rampant inflation in the 1970s, victory for the free marketeers was far from assured. Well into the early 1970s, fashionable Western political leaders (such as they were) remained on the center-left: Olaf Palme, Willy Brandt, Shirley Williams. Center-right leaders (Richard Nixon, Edward Heath) were forced into center-leftist economic management once initial attempts to restore old-fashioned "market discipline" had failed. Indeed, the first two or three years of Margaret Thatcher's first government had all the hallmarks of a period of high inflation, high unemployment, and confrontation with trade unions that had marked the first two years of Heath in office. As the crisis of the mid-1970s deepened, the smart money would probably have been staked on a further shift to the left in the Western democracies as the cheap energy and cheap money that had, from a leftist perspective, papered over the cracks in the postwar system started to evaporate.

In 1976, the French commentator Jean-François Revel (a committed socialist with a skeptical view of his fellow leftists) wrote scathingly, "Yes, you [other socialists] loftily claim to possess the only remedy, to offer the only possible choice. Every day we read titles of this sort: 'Socialism: The Only Solution to the World Crisis.' You talk as if you had in your hands a completely constructed society, a fully proven solution with an obviously favourable balance sheet" (*The Totalitarian Temptation*, Secker & Warburg, 1977).

Thus the battle for untrammelled financial markets was long and bitter. It was engaged on every front, from the populist (such as privatization and the liberalization of credit markets) to the diplomatic (getting governments to sign away in treaty agreements their rights to aspects of economic management) to the social (deriding opponents as hopelessly old-fashioned and harboring disreputable prejudices) to the engagement of state forces in head-on confrontations with organized labor (such as the 1981 strike by air traffic controllers in America and the 1984–1985 miners' strike in Britain).

Gusting behind these developments, helping them move along, were the warm zephyrs from the fallout from 1968. If Hayek, Friedman, and company would have been a little long in the tooth convincingly to pose as 1960s "faces," this was less of a problem for someone who was a major influence on the man who was to become perhaps the single most important figure in the fantastical bubble economy of the early twenty-first century—Federal Reserve Board chairman Alan Greenspan.

Ayn Rand was a Russian-born and Soviet-educated thinker who took advantage of a visa to visit American relatives in 1925 to leave the Soviet Union for good. Fiercely intelligent, strikingly attractive, and utterly outspoken, she founded the movement that she called objectivism and which would probably now be recognizable as right-wing or free market libertarianism. While not exactly a first division 1960s celebrity, she was well-known and had a large number of followers, particularly in North America, the 1970s hard rock band Rush among them.

She called capitalism the "unknown ideal." She dismissed as slavery the taxing of one person in order to make welfare payments to another (i.e., the routine operation of Western systems of social benefits), and believed the unfortunate ought to rely entirely on charity. Flatly opposed to any kind of regulation of monopolies, Rand described big business as "America's persecuted minority," wrote scathingly about the student rebellion of the 1960s, and employed the word "altruist" as a term of abuse.

An unlikely hipster? Not so fast. She opposed conscription as another form of slavery, fiercely opposed the war in Vietnam, despised the politics of consensus, and—perhaps inevitably—loathed with a vengeance the Democratic Party leader, U.S. President Lyndon Johnson, someone whose policies encompassed pretty much all that she saw wrong with the world (*Capitalism: The Unknown Ideal*, Signet, 1967).

With views such as these that chimed exactly with those of the student rebels and the "underground," Rand was a whole lot funkier than Hayek; she even teased dark-suited Greenspan by calling him "the Undertaker" (Alan Greenspan, *The Age of Turbulence*, Penguin, 2007).

This sort of thinking took a little while to drift across the Atlantic, but drift it did. In 1975, British author Terry Arthur produced an extremely funny book billed as "a plain man's guide to British politics" with the cheeky but not entirely inaccurate title (then or now) *95 Percent Is Crap*. Trawling through the political statements of the recent past (which included two general elections in the course of 1974), Arthur skewered again and again the dishonest formulations and double-speak of British politicians, ably assisted by excellent cartoons from Michael Cummings. Only on a careful second reading would one realize the skewering comes from one direction only—that of the free market perspective—with Tory politicians being attacked on the same grounds as Labour and Liberal ones. It may take a careful third reading to spot that the publisher is Libertarian Books of Bedford.

Linked to this sort of hip and unstuffy free market thinking was a new type of populism that sought to make the cause of financial deregulation the cause of the ordinary people. It is hard to pinpoint the start of this movement or its originators. Suffice to say that, by the end of the 1970s, deregulation was seen as a vote winner on both sides of the Atlantic. Intriguingly, it was to be sold with a leftist slant in both Britain and the United States.

In America, the airline deregulation bill that passed in 1978 was sponsored by Senator Edward Kennedy. President Jimmy Carter was to oversee the deregulation of a number of other industries, including rail and truck transport, communications and finance. Regulation had traditionally been seen as a way to protect the public. Increasingly, it was being portrayed as a conspiracy against the public.

The hero of Arthur Hailey's 1975 novel *The Moneychangers* is a liberal banker called Alex Vandervoort, whose long-standing girlfriend is a feminist lawyer. Hailey has Vandervoort interviewed by the *New York Times*, where Vandervoort blends social liberalism with a call for bank deregulation: "[Vandervoort] What ought to happen is that laws should stop protecting banks and protect people instead." "By protecting people you mean letting those with savings enjoy the maximum interest rate and other services which any bank will give?" "[Vandervoort] Yes, I do." There is more in the same vein.

A real-life Vandervoort was a British businessman called Clive Thornton. As chief general manager of the Abbey National Building Society, he broke away in 1983 from the system whereby the Building Societies Association met monthly to fix mortgage rates. From now on, the Abbey would do its own thing. Within a few years, the old system had fallen apart and mortgage rates had become completely deregulated.

But in contrast to Sir Freddie Laker, who had battled the big airlines in the late 1970s to bring fares down on transatlantic routes, Thornton never came across as the typical hard-boiled Tory entrepreneur. Indeed, in the years immediately following Abbey's 1983 move, he became associated with leftish projects such as reviving the fortunes of the Labour-supporting paper, the *Daily Mirror*, and with launching a radical new title, *News on Sunday*.

In the euphoria that followed the collapse of the old fixed system of interest rates, and with it the "queue" under which would-be mortgage borrowers had first to build up a track record of savings, few seemed to notice that the net effect of deregulation, over time, would be to raise the cost of home loans. Indeed, six years after Abbey went its own way on interest rates, it became the first building society to turn itself into a bank, with members becoming holders of shares that could be sold for a windfall profit.

This in turn was part of a wider populist movement to "widen" share ownership, usually through the sale at below-market prices to the public of shares in former nationalized industries. It seemed everybody was on board the people's privatization express other than out-of-touch characters such as the Earl of Stockton (formerly Harold Macmillan), who warned against "selling the family silver," or the Law Lords, who effectively asked in 1986 how the government could sell something (the Trustee Savings Bank) that it did not actually own.

Of course, the various elements of the market revival—populist, diplomatic, social, and so on—did not operate in isolation. For example, the Single European Act, which became operative in 1992 and severely restricted the ability of European governments to carry out effective economic intervention, was advertised through the British authorities' populist campaign Europe Is Open for Business. In turn, the post-1992 European Commission required nationalized industries to be run on commercial lines, adding to the impetus for privatizations, some of which involved attempts at mass share ownership. Social contempt for old-fashioned unionized "male" jobs and workforce "inflexibility" could be fostered by (rarely repeated) bonus payments from companies in return for employees adapting to new technology and by staff share schemes.

By the late 1980s, novelist David Lodge could envisage a trendy English lecturer writing to his similarly employed girlfriend informing her of a career switch to merchant banking. Part of his rationale speaks volumes about the change in attitudes:

> You and I, Robyn, grew up in a period when the state was smart: state schools, state universities, state-subsidised arts, state welfare, state medicine—these were things progressive, energetic people believed in. It isn't like that any more. (*Nice Work*, Secker & Warburg, 1988.)

The Not So Great Defender (Or, Where Was the Left?)

As noted earlier, if 1968 was the year in which financial interests began to test the notion of shrugging off the superstructure of the postwar settlement, it was also the year in which the middle-class leftist intelligentsia began, tentatively, to do the same thing. The onetime home of the likes of George Orwell started to give up on the Western working class as ever likely to abandon material advancement and turn instead to cultural improvement (the goal of the inside left) or start a revolution (the goal of the outside left). In no apparent need of their self-appointed saviors, the "workers" ceased to be the great ally and became instead the enemy—as, by happy coincidence, they were becoming to the new, aggressive breed of financiers and superrich.

Some middle-class leftists drifted away from political engagement of any kind and into well-heeled employment; their allegiance became a sort of fashion accessory, something the sharp-eyed spotted fairly quickly. In his column of television criticism in the *Observer* on October 8, 1978, Clive James had great fun:

> The Italian Marxist composer Luigi Nono (BBC 2) proclaims the necessity for contemporary music to intervene in something called the sonic reality of our time. Apparently it should do this by being as tuneless as possible. There were shots of Nono's apartments to indicate that he is even better off than the usual run of Italian Marxist composers. (*The Crystal Bucket*, Jonathan Cape, 1981.)

The failure of the working class to live up to middle-class leftists' hopes had been disguised for decades by, first, the struggle against fascism in Europe and then by various campaigns, including anticolonialism and the struggle for civil rights. All were noble causes and all largely prevailed by the end of the 1960s. But rather than return to the once all-important struggle of the workers (whose demands for Ford Cortinas and clothes dryers were so distressing), they invented "new proletariats" that they could control, either external (as in campaigns for entities less likely to answer back such as children's rights and animal rights) or internal (members of the middle-class left themselves, albeit wearing various different badges: gays, women, disabled people, transgender, and so on).

For the New Olympians, this displacement activity by the left was highly convenient, since it coincided with the end of the golden age of postwar social democracy in the early 1970s. Progressive parties lost their nerve, gradually distancing themselves from economic reform in favor of identity politics and social engineering combined with a broad acceptance that the message of the financial Olympians was not only right but might not go far enough.

The left's new distaste for working-class affluence led it into strange company. Let us ponder what, in practice, was the difference between this statement:

> Late industrial society has increased rather than reduced the need for parasitical and alienated functions. . . . Advertising, public relations, indoctrination, planned obsolescence are no longer unproductive overhead costs but rather elements of basic production costs . . . a rising standard of living is the almost unavoidable by-product of the politic ally manipulated industrial society . . . there is no reason to insist on self-determination if the administered life is the comfortable and even the "good" life.

And this one:

> What is nowadays meant by prosperity . . . [is] that the working classes will have more of everything they like: fish fingers, over-cooked meats, transistor wirelesses to take out of doors with them, caravans and motor cruisers to fasten behind their cars.

In terms of the utter contempt for the materialist aspirations of working people there is little to choose between the first author, much travelled radical professor Herbert Marcuse (*One Dimensional Man*, Routledge & Kegan Paul, 1964), and the second, the often splenetic conservative journalist Auberon Waugh. (*Another Voice*, Firethorn, 1986)

Nick Cohen has written of "the nagging feeling that not all the bourgeois reformers' efforts to improve the lot of the masses had gone as planned, including "the failure of the masses to pass muster in Bohemia" (*What's Left: How Liberals Lost Their Way*, Fourth Estate, 2007).

While some leftist commentators proclaimed the death of the working class, others "accepted that the working class lived on, but were obsessed by identity politics" (Cohen, *What's Left*). Concludes Cohen, "From the theorists in the universities to the pundits in Canary Wharf [home of many British national newspapers], the intellectuals weren't interested in the working class and the working class wasn't interested in the intellectuals. You could not have found a more lethal way to kill left-wing politics if you had tried."

And as the middle-class left snubbed the working class, the compliment was returned. The economic and social turmoil at the end of the 1960s saw the beginning of a decades-long trend in which blue-collar voters not only felt free to abandon center-left parties but also to leapfrog contemptuously over traditional center-right politicians into the arms of right-wingers with both a much harder policy edge and an ability to assure working people that their background and culture was nothing about which to be ashamed. While apologizing in advance to any of those who take offense at being grouped with some of the others, we would list among these new right "working-class heroes" George Wallace and Ronald Reagan in the United States, Ian Paisley in Northern Ireland, Margaret Thatcher and Norman Tebbit in Great Britain, and John Howard and Pauline Hanson in Australia. We stress, it is simply the hard policy edge and the affirming stance toward blue-collar attitudes and lifestyles that links these and other figures. We are not suggesting, for example, that John Howard is the same as the segregationist George Wallace. By the mid-1970s, with the fall of Edward Heath in Britain and Gerald Ford in the States, it was becoming clear that moderate conservatives could not expect to be the beneficiaries of the crisis in postwar social democracy.

But then, the middle-class left may have been past caring. Cohen mentions in passing, and in a different context, a remarkable play by Trevor Griffiths, first staged at the National Theatre in London against a real-life background of crisis in December 1973. *The Party* is set during the upheavals in Paris in 1968. A group of metropolitan London leftists have gathered to discuss what the rioting is all about. They are joined by the genuine article, a traditional revolutionary socialist called John Tagg. Having heard his hosts' analysis of the situation, heavy on identity politics, Tagg lets fly:

> You say: The working class has been assimilated, corrupted, demoralised. You point to his car and his house and his pension scheme and his respectability, and you write him off . . . then you start backing the field: blacks, students, homosexuals, terrorist groupings, Mao, Che Guevara, anybody, just so long as they represent some repressed minority still capable of anger and the need for self-assertion. (Pause) Well. Which work-

ers have you spoken with recently? And for how long? How do you know they're not as frustrated as you are?' (Faber & Faber, 1974.)

Tagg was right but missed the point. Not only had the middle-class left found substitutes (including its own members) for the working class, but it was in the process of turning this newly invented proletariat into a source of lucrative career opportunities mainly, although not exclusively, in the public sector. A new type of public servant would be created, one concerned not with providing any actual services (nursing, for example, or teaching), but with changing people's attitudes and lifestyles.

According to the center-right think tank Reform, there were 4,945,000 people in the public sector in 1998; this had risen to 5,454,000 by 2003. In addition, according to Reform's Graeme Leach,

> Not all of the increase in public sector employment is accounted for by 'front-line workers' such as doctors, nurses, teachers and police officers. . . . [We] have shown that between 1997 and 2003, the number of doctors, nurses, teachers and police officers in the UK increased by 131,000. Assuming the same rate of increase in the numbers of each profession, between 2003 and 2006, the increase would be of the order of 70,000.
>
> Alternatively, assuming teachers, doctors, nurses and police officers remain the same proportion of public sector employment, the increase would be around 100,000.

Leach compares these figures to the 84,150 civil service jobs scheduled to be cut between 2004 and 2008. "[For] every one 'head office' civil service job cut, another four new public sector employees will be recruited, of which just one will be a doctor, teacher, nurse or police officer."

As Leach notes, Conservative front bench MP Oliver Letwin calculated that, even when midwives and prison officers were added to the recruitment of these four groups of professions, "only 45 percent of the growth in public sector employment would be composed of 'front-line staff'" (*Costing Britain: Falling Productivity in the Public Sector*, Reform, 2004).

The others will include those recruited to fill the so-called joke jobs: the outreach coordinators and healthy living strategists, the breast-feeding advisers and the tobacco control officers.

Most desirable of all, from the perspective of the post-1968 middle-class left, was a job in the burgeoning equality (or "equalities," to use the modish word) industry. Given that they themselves (wearing the various badges of approved victim groups) had become a dominant chunk of the new "proletariat," nothing could be more convenient than that they should staff the bureaucracies set up to "tackle" (a suitably vague bureaucratic word) the injustices from which they suffered. In some cases, these bureaucracies were established inside large private companies in order to keep the management on the right side of an expanding volume of laws and guidelines aimed at addressing the various grievances of these victim groups.

The growth of this new class of functionaries has caused a huge shift in the balance of power on the left. Nearly twenty-five years after the 1984–1985 miners' strike, the outcome of that dispute looks increasingly like the best possible news for the white-collar public sector masses, whatever they might have thought at the time.

Defeat for the miners cleared the way for the downsizing and ultimately the sale of coal, steel, electricity, water, car, and aircraft manufacturing and the railways. With these entities now largely off the government's books, cash was available for the steady expansion of state sector positions not only of dubious utility, to put it mildly, but often actively involved in social engineering projects aimed squarely at members of the traditional working class, whether assaults on their diet or lack of exercise or attempts to change their attitudes (or "thoughts," to put it less coyly). In July 2007, a lawyer reported a bookshop in St. Albans for selling *Tintin in the Congo*, first published in 1931 and full of offensive depictions of African people. As Hertfordshire police confirmed they were treating it as a "racial incident," David Sexton was bemused in the *London Evening Standard:* "What protests does the utterly dreadful state of the Congo itself occasion? None. But finding an anachronistic Tintin book on sale in St Albans—now that's completely intolerable" (July 13, 2007).

In an eerie parallel with the liberation of financial speculators from postwar controls, the middle-class left was now free of working people. It was self-sufficient, supplying from its own ranks both the new downtrodden masses and the personnel who would end their misery (not too quickly, however, lest all those jobs disappear). These new functionaries were a sort of mirror image of the New Olympians, united in two things: an ability to talk in terms unintelligible to the ordinary person and a disdain for those self-same people. True, the former group enjoyed smaller pay packets than those of the latter group; on the other hand, there were very many more functionaries than Olympians.

In the process, of course, any notion of greater income equality for ordinary working people took a backseat.

Thus at the 2007 Conservative Party conference, Barclays Bank sponsored an event entitled Absolutely Equal. Given that the £1 million pay packet of Barclays' chief executive John Varley was something like forty times the national average, one might have guessed that this absolute equality had nothing to do with money or wealth and everything to do with middle-class "identity issues." One would have been right.

To Cap It All: The Olympians Rattle the Begging Bowl

Does any of the following sound familiar? World markets are in turmoil, pulled down by a sinking dollar. In Britain, the crisis is particularly acute in the case of one institution amid a clamor for government help. After insisting that no help will be forthcoming, the authorities give way and the Bank of England is sent into the breach. As events unfold, interest rates are cut on both sides of the Atlantic as a determined effort gets under way to reflate shares.

That was October 1987, during the stock market crash that followed the Great Storm of the night of October 16. Unknown at the time, it became the model for everything that has followed. Then it was shares rather than bank deposits that were falling and the troubled institution was not Northern Rock but the energy group British Petroleum, whose open market share price had dropped below the "bargain" level at which the final government stake was to be sold to the public. This meant banks in London and on Wall Street, which had underwritten the surefire share offer believing that the fees involved would be money for nothing, faced huge losses. These exemplars of free enterprise insisted the government get them off the hook, which it did, arranging for the Bank to put a floor under the share price.

In retrospect, everyone was remarkably polite about the BP debacle. Chancellor Nigel Lawson, a self-styled "Tory radical," was required to spend little time explaining why subsidies for the recently defeated coal miners or the shrinking British car industry were pointless and wasteful, while subsidies (albeit of a stand-by nature) for investment banks were rational and fruitful. This question was especially piquant in light of the fact that these banks were being asked to do only what they had contracted to do as underwriters.

But in what was to become the soothing muzak of all such bailouts, the public was told that "market stability" and the "smooth functioning of the system" were the key issues, along with the "restoration of confidence." This was not a subsidy to any particular institution or group of institutions. Perish the thought.

Twenty years later, in the Northern Rock debacle, not a dot, not a comma is different. All that has changed, over the years, is that everyone involved has become rather more blatant.

In September 1998, the Federal Reserve Board, America's central bank, made little secret of the fact that it had arranged a bailout for the Long Term Capital Management hedge fund, which despite (or perhaps because of) being staffed by incredibly brainy New Olympians, had taken up sufficient bad market positions to cause an international financial crisis were it allowed to go bust. No nonsense there about not helping a specific institution. But at least that bailout involved the funds of other major U.S. banks, rather than of U.S. taxpayers.

Nine years on from that episode, and the summer storms of 2007 saw bankers and financiers in Britain and America demanding either public money or lower interest rates—or both—with all the nonchalance of young women in the swinging London of the 1960s insisting their fuddy-duddy general practitioners put them on the Pill. Indeed, the language used by one anonymous City bigwig to the *Daily Telegraph* on September 4—suggesting the Bank of England harbored a "Victorian" reluctance to provide support—was eerily reminiscent of the sort of accusation aimed by the love generation at its square elders.

But this was mild stuff compared to the outburst on August 20, 2007, from U.S. stock market guru Jim Cramer on the business channel CNBC. Like a desperate junkie begging for one more hit, Cramer demanded the Federal Reserve Board bail out Wall Street. This is just part of his rant:

> And Bill Poole [president of the Federal Reserve Bank of St. Louis]? [He] has no idea what it's like out there! My people have been in this game for twenty-five years. And they are losing their jobs and these firms are going to go out of business, and he's nuts! They're nuts! They know nothing! We have Armageddon. In the fixed income markets, we have Armageddon.

Irish commentator Gene Kerrigan was merciless: "This was the genuine voice of big capital. Whining, hysterical, demanding that the state grabs its chestnuts out of the fire. . . . Isn't high finance great gas altogether!" ("Chestnuts Roasting on Melting Markets," *Sunday Independent*, September 2, 2007).

Avinash Persaud, founder and chairman of London advisory group Intelligence Capital, was a little more measured in remarks on January 3, 2008:

> It is interesting that while by day bankers justify the egregious compensation packages they pay colleagues on the basis that they are forced to do so by the cold ruthlessness of the marketplace they inhabit, by night, when things go wrong, they are bailed out by easy money from local central banks, regulatory forebearance and fresh capital from government investment agencies. Bankers would appear to take a market view of rewards but a public welfare view on risks.

In extremis, or even in cases of mild discomfort, bankers, brokers, investment managers, and speculators forget their free-market principles in the blink of an eye. Many would have cheered support for journalist Ambrose Evans-Pritchard, who commented:

> US Treasury Secretary Hank Paulson can be forgiven for pushing through a rescue plan last week that amounts to a flagrant abuse of contract law and capitalist principles. . . . Would free marketeers rather see the whole edifice of capitalism burned to the ground to make their point?

He concluded, "The strategic failure of a whole generation of economists, bankers and policymakers has been so enormous that it may now take a strong draught of socialism to save the western democracies" (*Daily Telegraph*, December 10, 2007).

Philip Larkin once wrote of hippy-ish youths whose "Oriental contempt for 'the bread'" was matched only by their voracious appetite for it (*Required Writing*, Faber & Faber, 1983). Much the same attitude would seem to link high finance and public subsidies, as seen in the Bear Stearns bailout.

The New Olympians' failure to meet their basic boast—that they need no public money because their operations mirror the "natural" workings of the market—may appear to be the fundamental flaw in the system. In fact, it is the symptom of all the other failings. They have to borrow money from the public purse because their system does not work.

Debt is the key to the new economic order. Because British industry has been largely wiped out by new Olympian economic policies, we need to borrow from countries such as China to buy their goods. The United States is in a similar position, but on a larger scale. This debt is then bundled up in different ways by financial institutions to produce a profit. The institutions themselves, as we saw with Northern Rock, are heavy borrowers, and their debt, in turn, can be traded on the open market.

It is the central belief of New Olympians that any asset—a mortgage, a loan, a title deed—can be made more valuable by cutting it into different-shaped pieces and trading it to different institutions. This was the thinking behind collateralized debt obligations and remains the thinking behind complex derivatives that supposedly make two and two equal five. They had every reason to believe this, of course. All these fancy-sounding financial products meant they could maximize their profits from the Anglo-American debt binge of the last decade.

Not for nothing were the early New Olympians children of the 1960s. In their dreamy way, they and their successors are rebelling against The Man—the conventional banker or financier, the member of parliament or finance minister. They believe reserve requirements, loan ratios, mark-to-market rules, and all the rest are just obstacles to a financial nirvana. They want to take advantage of the beautiful new world of internationalism and technology. What is so wrong with that?

Apart from the fact that they have brought our economy to the brink of collapse, nothing whatsoever.

CHAPTER 4

—

Sunday, Monday, Happy Days
The Goldilocks Economy

All is for the best in the best of possible worlds.

—VOLTAIRE, *Candide*

My idea was that as the world absorbed information technology and learned to put it to work, we had entered what would prove to be a protracted period of lower inflation, lower interest rates, increased productivity and full employment. "I've been looking at business cycles since the late 1940s," I said. "There has been nothing like this."

—ALAN GREENSPAN,
The Age of Turbulence

There's a lake of gin we can both jump in, and the handouts grow on bushes. In the new-mown hay we can sleep all day, and the bars all have free lunches.

—HARRY McCLINTOCK,
"Big Rock Candy Mountain"

Right up to the moment she was awoken, Goldilocks had been sleeping peacefully. Deep in the forest, miles from home and totally lost, Goldilocks dreamed of unlimited quantities of the most delicious porridge she had ever tasted, sweet and toothsome and—

crucially—neither too hot nor too cold. In her dream, Goldilocks saw herself living in this little cottage with flowers round the door forever.

Then the three bears arrived back home.

Strange though it may seem, the hard-nosed men and women managing the world's financial markets are devout believers in fairy stories. Just like Zeus and Hera, the New Olympians like nothing better than to hear tales of their derring-do. Pressures of work may mean that they have to subcontract the job of reading bedtime stories to their children to an army of nannies and au pairs, but this has not made them any less susceptible to a charming tale in which everybody lives happily ever after (albeit with some living just a bit more happily than others).

For the past fifteen years, the idea of the Goldilocks economy has been the prevailing metaphor for the fairy-tale enthusiasts of the global economy. After the inflationary decade of the 1970s and the bust-boom decade of the 1980s, there would be porridge on offer in ever increasing quantities and at ever lower prices. The global economy would be neither too hot nor too cold but just right because the New Olympians were in control of policymaking not only at a national level (important though that was), but at supranational and subnational levels as well. The key New Olympian organizations were independent central banks, international bodies such as the International Monetary Fund, the World Bank, the European Commission, the World Trade Organization, and the International Court of Justice. On the face of it, these were disparate bodies with different spheres of influence and different constituencies; in practice they were linked by two threads: all wielded extraordinary power and all could do so while paying lip service to the democratically elected governments they were supposed to serve. If they listened to anyone, the New Olympian policymakers paid heed to their brothers in arms— the men and women running international banks and multinational companies. And at home, the lack of patience, even contempt, for democracy meant the growth of the new quangocracy—bodies of public sector "heroes" who could be relied on to put New Olympian thinking into practice at a local level. Providing the link between the two was a burgeoning army of management consultants, steeped in the same ideology of labor market flexibility, privatization, cuts in taxation, and the paring back of welfare states.

The Magic Mountain: Dressing Down in Davos

The key date on the New Olympian calendar is the week in late January when the entire tribe gathered in conclave in the Swiss ski resort of Davos, 5,000 feet up in the Alps and just down the valley from the fictional lair of Blofeld in the Ian Fleming novel *On Her Majesty's Secret Service*. For many years, antiglobalization protesters tried but failed to do what 007 managed in the book, to breach the defenses thrown around the annual meeting of the World Economic Forum. Here it was that the New Olympians were encouraged to bring their trophy wives, to replace the business suit with a Lacoste polo shirt and chinos, and to solve the problems of a globalized world. High up above the clouds, Bill Gates could chew the fat with the governor of the European Central Bank, Jean-Claude Trichet. Pascal Lamy, the director general of the World Trade Organization, would gather a cabal of trade ministers to press for action in the Doha Round of trade liberalization, each year warning that those of a protectionist bent were "drinking in the last chance saloon" or some similar cliché. A smattering of trade unionists and officials from the less extreme development-based nongovernmental organizations were meant to give Davos a patina of accessibility and openness. In truth, however, the days when mere mortals were given some say in the way things should be managed were long gone. Coming up with the formula for the Goldilocks economy had been painstaking work; the New Olympians were in no mood to allow electorates to mess around with the ingredients, let alone the self-appointed guardians of civil society.

Yet some were concerned about the safety of Goldilocks as she tripped happily through the forest. We count ourselves among their number. Their warnings were ignored, not least because it seemed—for a while—that the New Olympians did indeed have the Midas touch.

The origins of the Goldilocks economy go back to the late 1970s and the early 1980s. We have already described how our heroes had planned their return to Mount Olympus after the humiliations heaped on them in the 1930s and 1940s. When the postwar Keynesian order collapsed after the oil shocks of 1973 and 1979, there was an opportunity to try out all the potions that the wizards of high finance had been brewing up in secret. All the separate cadres that made up the New Olympian class played their part in bringing about the new order.

Central bankers were the first into the fray. Germany, Switzerland, and the Netherlands had been the countries least badly affected by the inflationary surge of the 1970s, and these countries' central banks were not run by meddling politicians with an eye on the next election. Instead, they were managed by fiercely independent technocrats trustworthy enough to look beyond the need to boost growth in the short term in order to win votes. For central banks, the timing was perfect. By the time the banks became viewed as the only check on the inflationary impulses of democratically elected politicians, the price shocks of the 1970s were actually abating, making the job of achieving price stability much easier. Looking back from early 2008, a clear pattern emerges of an inflationary earthquake in 1973–1974 followed by a series of aftershocks of diminishing force. In the United Kingdom, inflation peaked at 27 percent in 1975, falling to 20 percent in 1980, 11 percent in 1990, and just 3 percent in early 2007. This should come as little surprise, since low inflation has been the norm for capitalism ever since the dawn of the industrial age 250 years ago. True, there have been pulses of inflation, but these have tended to be confined to wartime, when monetary prudence is less important than defense of the realm. The Napoleonic War was a period when inflationary pressures were strong; the First World War was another. But in the ninety-nine years between the battle of Waterloo and the assassination of Archduke Franz Ferdinand at Sarajevo, prices fell. For the baby boomers born in the fifteen years after the Second World War, high inflation may have appeared to be the norm; in the context of the economic history of the past 250 years, the peacetime explosion of the cost of living in the 1970s was very much the exception.

Central banks, unsurprisingly perhaps, credit themselves with bringing about this change. Those involved in pay talks or in setting prices in company boardrooms no longer believe, as they did in the bad old days of the 1960s and 1970s, that soft-hearted politicians will pump money into the economy every time there is the merest threat that growth will slow and unemployment rise. Central banks use technical phrases such as "managing inflation expectations," but what they really mean is that the huddled masses are petrified that a recessionary thunderbolt will come thudding down from Mount Olympus if they get too uppity. The governor of the Bank of England, Mervyn King, believes that the pound's traumatic expulsion from the exchange rate mechanism on Black Wednesday in September 1992 was a turning point for monetary policy in Britain, since it resulted in the government setting a clear target for inflation that policymakers were expected to meet. For the previous fifteen years, the Treasury and the Bank had targeted the level of public borrowing, various measures of the money supply, and pegged the pound to the German mark in an attempt to find a way of keeping inflation low. After Black Wednesday they gave up on the idea of finding a proxy for inflation and simply targeted inflation itself. Full independence for the Bank to set interest rates—the first big initiative of Tony Blair's government in May 1997—strengthened the anti-inflation regime, according to King, and helped ensure that in the years since, the annual increase in the cost of living in the UK has run at only a tenth of the levels seen at its peak in the 1970s. Under the terms of the Bank's mandate, the governor is required to write a letter to the chancellor of the exchequer should inflation deviate by more than a percentage point from its 2 percent target; only one such epistle has so far been penned.

The idea that independent central banks deserve the credit for putting Western economies back on the straight and narrow after the inflationary excesses of the late Keynesian era does not convince everybody. Brian Henry, a UK economist of many years experience, wrote a paper at the end of 2007 in which he argued that the Bank of England happened to be in the right place at the right time and received kudos for something that was happening anyway. Henry argues that the trade-off between unemployment and inflation was improving of its own accord after the blows to the economy of the 1970s and early 1980s, but it took policymakers time to work out what had happened. "The major movements in unemployment and inflation heralded by some as due to the regime of inflation targeting and central bank independence can instead be accounted for by a mixture of external shocks and a slow process of recognition of the effects of these by the authorities" (Brian Henry, *Monetary Policy, Unemployment, and Inflation: Evidence from the UK*, National Institute for Economic and Social Research, January 2008).

Another British economist, Paul Ormerod, agrees, saying that the hallmark of industrial capitalism has been intense competition. Pressure from the marketplace has prevented prices from rising too fast (Ormerod, conversations with one of the authors). What differentiated the golden era of postwar prosperity from both earlier and later epochs of capitalism was the array of curbs on market forces—tariffs, nationalized industries, strong trade unions, full employment policies, and the absence from the global capitalist economy of the world's two most populous nations—China and India. Changes wrought over the past quarter of a century—tamed trade unions, privatization, falling trade barriers, the emergence of price stability as the ultimate economic policy goal, and the widening of the global economy to include new low-cost sources of production—have meant that the world of 2008 is more akin to that of 1908 than 1958.

Of all these factors, the most crucial for the creation of the Goldilocks economy has been the spread of the market around the world. China's post-Mao embrace of capitalism, the collapse of the Soviet Union in 1991, and the decision by India in the same year to abandon its autarkic economic strategy have vastly increased the potential to supply goods and services at low cost. Between them, China and India account for almost half the world's population, and the sudden increase in the global supply of labor has had a profound impact on prices in the West.

If the notion that hard-nosed central bankers will take no risks with inflation has been insufficient to "discipline" Western workforces, the prospect of jobs disappearing to Shanghai and Bangalore has normally done the trick. Trade unions that once might have responded to calls for pay restraint with industrial militancy have had to think twice about striking for better terms and conditions. That is not to say a more emollient approach has worked any better, particularly for trade unions with members working in traditional manufacturing. The difference in labor and social costs between employing someone in a textile mill in China, Vietnam, or Bangladesh and employing the same person in Yorkshire or North Carolina has meant that production has shifted eastward. Every country in the West has seen the share of its working population employed in manufacturing fall over the past quarter of a century, although some have seen sharper falls than others. In America, for example, sunrise industries such as computers and biotechnology and spending on defense have meant that the size of the industrial workforce remained unchanged. In the UK, by contrast, it was cut by half.

Taking the Waiting Out of Wanting: Finance Is Set Free

The final ingredient for the Goldilocks economy has been financial deregulation. Demolishing the controls on free movement of capital imposed in the 1930s and 1940s allowed the trade surpluses amassed by the newly industrializing countries of the Pacific Rim to be recycled into the West. Central banks, despite their role as guarantors of low inflation, strongly supported these changes, although normally taking a backseat role while politicians and banks made the case for reform. The politicians, egged on by the Mont Pelerin crowd, saw controls on capital as an intolerable curb on liberty and symbolic of the postwar welfare culture they despised so much. For the commercial bankers, it was a question of the bottom line. While hardly on their uppers during the 1950s and 1960s, they saw the ability to extend more credit and to move capital around the world at will as leading to higher profits. This, of course, was not the way change was dressed up for public consumption. When it came to the intellectual argument, the case centered on the efficiency of markets. Putting impediments in the way of free movement of finance—exchange controls, quantitative limits on credit growth, mortgage rationing—meant capital was being misallocated. Removing restrictions would mean that capital would go to where it could be most efficiently used. There was some truth in this argument, since the financial system that existed, certainly in the UK, at the end of the 1970s was riddled with restrictive commercial practices and discouraged innovation.

A simpler explanation of the need for change was made to consumers: removing capital controls would make credit easier and cheaper to obtain. Queuing for mortgages was unpopular, conjuring up images of rationing during the Second World War and the austerity era that followed it. A more liberal approach to credit also chimed with the post-1960s mood of personal freedom, although it did sit oddly with the Victorian values of thrift and self-restraint that Mrs. Thatcher also promulgated. There was a ready-made demand for higher borrowing, since one of the more popular measures of Thatcher's first term had been selling council homes to tenants at discount prices. Financial deregulation—it could be argued—was the logical next step to this process, allowing those on low incomes or living on relatively tight budgets to get their foot on the housing ladder. The argument that financial deregulation was really a giant leap forward for democracy is still regularly deployed. Extending mortgages to those without regular incomes or savings in the United States was not about a bunch of financial sharks preying on the weak and vulnerable. Instead, it was an attempt to spread home ownership to those at the bottom of the pile—African Americans, native Americans, Latinos, poor whites. This was not about banks picking up fat commissions for all sorts of live-now, pay-later loans to people who could not afford them; it was proof that the American dream was alive and well.

Perhaps unsurprisingly, Alan Greenspan was keen to promote this version of events in his memoirs:

Since 1994, the proportion of American householders who became homeowners had accelerated. By 2006, nearly 69 percent of households owned their own home, up from 64 percent in 1994 and 44 percent in 1940. The gains were especially dramatic among Hispanics and blacks, as increasing affluence as well as government encouragement of subprime mortgage programs enabled many members of minority groups to become first-time home buyers. This expansion of ownership gave more people a stake in the future and boded well for the cohesion of the nation, I thought. (*The Age of Turbulence*, Penguin, 2007.)

Faced with this combination of political will, financial sector muscle, and consumer demand, resistance to reform was easily defeated and change was swift. Within a decade of Thatcher's abolition of foreign exchange controls (again, sold to the public as allowing people to take more currency out of the country on their foreign holidays rather than as the green light for the City and Wall Street to move capital around the world unhindered), there were no more mortgage queues, building societies no longer had to rely on savings from individual depositors, and foreign banks and investment houses controlled much of the City of London. Many building societies ceased to be owned by their customers, changing themselves into publicly quoted banks where managers ceased to be figures of chilly probity and instead became salesman for debt. Whereas an invitation to visit the bank manager at the end of the 1970s was the grown-up version of a summons to the headmaster's study, a decade later the job of the bank manager was to entice, encourage, and cajole customers into taking out loans. The new mood was aptly summed up by a billboard advertisement for the Halifax, Britain's biggest mortgage lender and one of the building societies that had demutualized. Under a photograph of the Taj Mahal, the bank made it clear that it was now perfectly acceptable to take out an unsecured loan for a holiday. The slogan was, Your girlfriend out for a curry.

This was the heyday of American credit management guru Abe Walking Bear Sanchez, a big draw at corporate conferences. His message to companies was simple: "Is all bad debt bad? No." For firms with a high level of fixed costs, whether people or machinery, he argued, it makes sense to sign up riskier borrowers because even with their naturally higher rate of default, those who do pay will have generated juicier profits from unused capacity in the firm. "Learn how to control bad debt, not run scared of it."

This assumes that the level of default among the new, riskier customers can be predicted and managed, yet history suggests this is far from always being the case. To be fair, Sanchez made clear in his presentations the need for active management of debt, but his overall message was that old notions of business credit were old hat: "Many companies still operate their credit departments as they did in the

1950s. Times have moved on. . . . Credit should be no exception. It is no longer a privilege. It is a way of securing profitable sales that would otherwise be lost" (*Corporate Wizardry: Turning Credit into Cash*, Atradius, 2004).

Some questioned the wisdom of these changes, particularly since the borrowing free-for-all that inevitably followed financial deregulation led to the excesses of the late 1980s, when a colossal boom in house prices ended with punitive increases in interest rates that led to record numbers of homes being foreclosed. Having allowed the beast out of the cage, policymakers could no longer fall back on the controls they had once used to regulate credit; they had only the blunt instrument of interest rates. Writing in the late 1990s (*Debt and Delusion*, Penguin, 1999), Peter Warburton said:

> The negative aspects (of deregulation) include the commitment of extra financial capital to lending activities (which presumes a rapid expansion in personal and corporate borrowing), and the likelihood that bank and non-bank diversification into unfamiliar business areas will bring an increased incidence of failure. While central banks cannot be held responsible for the enthusiasm with which western governments have embraced financial deregulation, they must surely have recognised that the task of monitoring a de-regulated credit system would become far more difficult.

Apparently not.

Warburton's remarks are eerily prescient from the perspective of 2008. But for more than two decades, the risks inherent in the "new environment" were either ignored by the New Olympians, dismissed as a small price to pay for a more efficient global economy, or simply swept under the carpet.

There were good reasons for this, not least that the policies underpinning the Goldilocks economy allowed the New Olympians to grab a bigger share of porridge for themselves. The history of the past three decades is of a profound change in the balance of power, with capital gaining a bigger share of the proceeds of growth at the expense of labor. Labor's diminished share increasingly captured by those on the highest incomes at the expense of the unskilled; management increasing its control in the workplace at the expense of trade unions; and finance replacing manufacturing as the hub of Western economies. In his book on the postwar history of the global economy (*Capitalism Unleashed*, Oxford, 2006), Andrew Glyn, who died early in 2008, notes that in the early 1970s it looked, as far as the British variant of capitalism was concerned, that "this time the wolf is really at the door." The response was a ferocious struggle to combat the strengthening of labor and the squeeze on profits in the golden age.

> We now know that the outcome of this struggle was the radical weakening of the labour movement, macroeconomic stabilisation and domination of free market ideas. It was the comprehensive victory of capital in the struggle with labour—not just in developed western countries but in those parts of the world formerly under communist rule—that fostered the belief that mankind had reached "the end of history."

This was a world that had initial appeal to wage earners and salaried staff who were not trade unionists, many of whom had been repelled by the labor militancy of the 1960s and 1970s. As time went on, however, it became clear that every stratum of Western society (bar the New Olympians) had something to fear, even something to lose, from the new order. There was the risk that the burgeoning, unfettered, and ever more complex financial system would blow up; there was the threat not just to blue-collar but also to white-collar jobs; and there was the mounting pressure on welfare states (from which the middle classes had always gained as much as low-income workers).

The leading developing countries realized that in times of trouble, the New Olympians would ensure—partly through the brute force power of capital flight and partly through the agency of the IMF—that it would be poor people in poor countries who bore the heaviest brunt of the "adjustment" and not the Wall Street banks that had lent them money to finance unsustainable booms. Eventually, it became clear—even to some of the New Olympians themselves—that the unshackling of the financial markets had sent a Frankenstein's monster rampaging around the globe. Mervyn King, the governor of the Bank of England, argued that the message from the Latin American debt crisis of 1982, the Mexican peso crisis of 1994–1995, and the Asian financial crisis of 1997–1998 was that the West would always engineer a bailout for Goldman Sachs, Morgan Stanley, and Citigroup, even if it meant austerity packages for Thailand and Indonesia that had a real impact—death—on those deprived of life-saving drugs as a result of health cutbacks. King was not alone in his criticism. Joseph Stiglitz, eased out of his job as chief economist of the World Bank by the then U.S. Treasury Secretary Larry Summers for being too critical of the Washington consensus, took his revenge in a hatchet job on the IMF in the *New Republic*, calling those at the Fund responsible for the policies imposed on poor countries in 1997–1998 third-class brains from first-class universities. "These economists frequently lack extensive knowledge in the country; they are more likely to have firsthand knowledge of its five-star hotels than of the villages that dot the countryside," Stiglitz noted, adding that the Fund likes to go about its business in the shadows. "In theory, the Fund supports democratic institutions in the nations it assists, in practice, it undermines the democratic process by imposing policies" ("What I Saw at the Devaluation," *New Republic*, April 2000).

The Stiglitz article was a seminal work. Published precisely as the dot-com boom of the late 1990s was in its final, frenetic stages, the piece not only castigated the unholy troika of Wall Street, the U.S. Treasury, and the IMF for imposing recessionary policies on Asian countries, but also highlighted the coup d'état mounted by the New Olympians.

> Since the end of the Cold War tremendous power has flowed to the people entrusted to bring the gospel of the market to the far corners of the globe. These economists, bureaucrats and officials act in the name of the United States and the other advanced industrial countries, and yet they speak a language that few average citizens understand and that few policymakers bother to translate. Economic policy is today the most important part of America's interaction with the rest of the world.

And yet the culture of international economic policy in the world's most powerful democracy is not democratic.

The New Olympians saw Stiglitz's attack as an act of treachery. He was, after all, one of them—a former economic adviser to Bill Clinton before moving to the World Bank. New Olympians were supposed to stick together; by going public with his critique Stiglitz had betrayed his own class. It would, however, take more than half a decade for Americans to wake up to the fact that Stiglitz was right and that there were profound implications for themselves from the triumph of the New Olympians. In the meantime, the lessons of 1997 and 1998 were immediately digested by millions of poor people in East and Southeast Asia. One lesson was that the nations that had been at best agnostic about the gospel of financial market deregulation preached by the New Olympians—China and India—had avoided the recession that swept across the region. A second was that Malaysia, which imposed strict curbs on capital movements during the summer of 1997, saw its economy suffer far less grievously than Thailand, which followed the policies demanded by the Fund to the letter. A third lesson was that the fast-growing nations of Asia should never again be at the mercy of the Washington consensus. And when the Washington consensus strangled at birth an attempt by Asian countries to develop their own Asian Monetary Fund to rival the IMF, the region used its fast-growing export industries to build up a war chest of foreign exchange reserves big enough to burn the fingers of speculators and so make the Fund redundant.

Asian countries had, up until the crisis of 1997, been hefty borrowers on the world's capital markets. After 1997, that borrowing became taboo and Asian countries became lenders instead. As Brian Reading of Lombard Street Research put it, "They have no wish to repeat the wrenching 1997–8 recessions that followed the switch from currency inflows to outflows." Instead, they watched as the United States became a debtor nation, with all the vulnerability that entailed to a sudden flight of capital.

What happened was this. Asian countries had massive trade surpluses, which meant that they were saving—in the parlance of the

economics profession—more than they invested. They could have expanded domestic spending to soak up the glut of savings, but that
would have deprived them of the funds to build up their reserves. Instead, they allowed America and to a lesser extent Britain to solve the
problem for them by spending (investing) more than they produced
(saved). The process had four stages. First, manufacturing was already
being moved progressively to low-cost countries, leading to a hollowing-out of industry in the West, lowering potential productive capacity and leading to trade deficits. Second, people in Western deficit
countries were called on to spend more than their income in order to
prevent the savings glut in the East from tipping the world into recession. Central bankers like Alan Greenspan in the United States
and Lord George in the UK cut interest rates to stimulate spending,
fearing that the alternative would be recession. Lord George admitted that this meant the UK economy was unbalanced but said unbalanced growth was better than no growth. Up to a point, Greenspan
and Lord George were right. At a global level, savings and investment have to balance each other out, so if the East was saving more
(building up current account surpluses) the West had to spend more
than it was saving (run current account deficits) or risk a global recession caused by a lack of demand for the goods being supplied by
the world economy.

Third, the recycling of the Asian current account surpluses into
the West pushed up asset prices—shares, bonds, and property—and
made people in deficit countries feel wealthier. Fourth, the flows of
capital tended to find their way to countries with sophisticated financial systems, who by chance also happened to be those countries running the biggest current account deficits. For the New Olympians
this seemed to be a case of porridge all round. The part of the economy where they were most heavily concentrated—the financial sector—was thriving. The flow of capital from the East pushed up asset
prices, and they held more lucrative assets than anybody else. And
their income and wealth went further than it did before because
goods from the East were not only cheap but made cheaper still because all the hot money flooding into London and New York pushed
up the value of the pound and the dollar, making imports even less ex-

pensive (but making life even more difficult for those exporting man-ufactured goods and services).

This, then, was the Goldilocks economy. Strictly speaking, it was not a Goldilocks economy at all, since half the bowl of porridge was too hot and the other half was too cold, but for many years that did not seem to matter. Low inflation meant low interest rates, which in turn meant high levels of consumption and increases in asset values, which in turn brought a new pulse of hot money into Western economies. But if it all looked too good to be true, that is because it most certainly was.

The Asian crisis of 1997 was followed a year later by the Russian debt default and the collapse of the New York–based hedge fund Long Term Capital Management, run by two Nobel Prize–winning economists, Myron Scholes and Robert Merton, who claimed to have found the financial market equivalent of a perpetual motion machine. In September 1998, it emerged that Scholes and Merton might have been somewhat hubristic with their foolproof plan for valuing options when LTCM went bust and threatened to bring a host of the top names on Wall Street and the City down with it. Greenspan cut in-terest rates to boost confidence and the markets picked up again. Goldilocks slept on.

Dancing with Bears: The End of the Party

It took time, however, for the arrival of the three bears to disrupt the slumber of our heroine. Baby Bear arrived in the shape of rising com-modity prices. At the end of the 1990s, oil prices were below $10 a barrel and were hovering just above $20 a barrel when George Bush and Tony Blair were planning to invade Iraq in the early months of 2003. As Alan Greenspan admitted in 2007, once he had retired from the Federal Reserve, the war against Saddam Hussein was linked to the fact that Iraq's reserves are currently second only to those of Saudi Arabia. But if the aim was to provide America with cheap and secure supplies of crude oil from the Middle East, the war was a spectacular failure. It had a more prolonged impact on Iraq's oil production than expected, and also helped to create a risk of terrorist attacks on oil installations in the region, thus pushing up prices. An even bigger factor in quadrupling the cost of crude oil to a record level in the early months of 2008 was the heavy demand for oil—and other commodities—from China, India, and other rapidly industrializing Asian countries. Oil prices rose above $103 a barrel in the February, despite signs of recession in the U.S., comfortably the highest ever in nominal terms but also breaking the previous inflation-adjusted peak reached during the outbreak of the Iran-Iraq war in 1980. Ominously, bullion prices were also rising, traditionally a sign of trouble ahead as investors sought the fabled protection against inflation offered by precious metal. By the end of March 2008, gold had topped $1,000 a troy ounce, a twenty-eight-year high. Inflationary pressures had started to reappear back in 2004 and built up a head of steam in the years that followed, but Goldilocks had slept on.

Mother Bear arrived in the shape of booming real estate prices. We shall have more to say about this in later chapters, but suffice it to say here that interest rate cuts sanctioned by the Fed and the Bank of England led to property prices rising rapidly in both the U.S. and the UK. In America, Greenspan's determination to make the recession that followed the collapse of the dot-com bubble a short-lived one resulted in interest rates being cut to 1 percent—a level not seen since the late 1950s—and thus ensured that the solution to one popped bubble was to inflate another one. By the time the U.S. was experiencing the most pronounced real estate bubble in its history, even the New Olympians started to get concerned, and Greenspan proceeded to raise interest rates by a quarter point at seventeen successive meetings of the Fed's Open Market Committee. The ratcheting up of borrowing costs made mortgages less affordable, speculation riskier, and consumers less happy about borrowing money against the value of their homes. Mother Bear roared but Goldilocks slept on.

The failure of central banks—particularly the U.S. Federal Reserve—to comprehend that the Goldilocks economy might be polluted with contaminated ingredients was all the more surprising given that the umbrella body for central banks, the Bank for International Settlements, was well aware of the risks that were involved. Bill White, chief economist at the BIS, could hardly have been blunter.

While noting the benefits of reducing inflation from its previous high levels, White added, "At the same time, history also teaches that the stability of consumer prices might not be sufficient to ensure macro-economic stability. Past experience is replete with examples of major economic and financial crises that were not preceded by inflationary pressures." The lesson from history that seemed to concern White was the period from 1929 to 1932, when a financial and economic crisis was spawned by an era characterized by low inflation but massive speculation and excessive debt. "We are increasingly distant from the highly regulated period following the Great Depression and the Second World War, when our current policy frameworks were developed. Indeed, the structural landscape looks more and more like that seen in the 1920s and the decades prior to World War 1. It would not seem implausible, in the light of this underlying change, that our policy frameworks might also need revision" (William White, "Is Price Stability Enough?" BIS Working Paper no. 205, April 2006).

Less than six months later the BIS issued a fresh warning. A paper written by Claudio Borio ("Monetary and Prudential Policies at a Crossroads? New Challenges in the New Century," BIS Working Paper no. 216, September 2006) noted that

> the establishment of credible anti-inflation monetary policies and (real-side) globalisation have resulted in subtle but profound changes in the dynamics of the economy and in the challenges faced by policymakers. In the new environment which has gradually been taking shape, the main 'structural risk' may not be so much runaway inflation. Rather, it may be the damage caused by the unwinding of financial imbalances that occasionally build up over the longer expansion phases of the economy, typically spanning more than one higher-frequency business cycle. Depending on its intensity, the unwinding can lead to economic weakness, unwelcome disinflation and possibly financial strains.

The BIS, apparently concerned that Goldilocks was not just sleeping but had ingested a mind-bending drug, decided that it was time to be even more blunt. In its annual report of June 2007, it described the four main features of the Goldilocks economy: unusually

high levels of real growth; unusually low levels of inflation; unchar-
acteristically low real interest rates and risk premiums for buying
what would once have been considered less safe assets; and the fact
that record trade imbalances had so far been easily financed with exchange rates remaining quite stable. "In isolation, each of these outcomes might be welcomed without further reflection. However, the
combination of developments is so extraordinary that it must raise
questions about the source and, closely related, the sustainability of
all this good fortune."

This was the equivalent of the BIS stooping down to bellow,
"Wake up, Goldilocks! We've warned you time and again, you stupid
girl, but the three bears are now plodding up the garden path."

That was June 24, 2007. Just over two weeks later, as we saw earlier, Chuck Prince, the chairman and chief executive of Citigroup, the
world's biggest bank, made it clear that he thought the BIS was being
a bit of a drama queen. "When the music stops, in terms of liquidity,
things will be complicated. But as long as the music is playing, you've
got to get up and dance. We're still dancing."

At this point Father Bear arrived home. He came in the shape of a
crisis in the financial system itself. The palace on Olympus found itself under the sort of attack its inhabitants had always claimed was impossible. Low inflation and low interest rates had bred complacency,
the notion that the good times were permanent rather than cyclical
and that therefore what were once risky bets were now surefire suc-
cesses. Pension funds and other institutional investors avidly lapped
up this message. With people living longer and annuity rates falling
because of lower interest rates, they were looking for punts that offered higher returns than they could expect on government bonds.
Globalized financial markets duly obliged them with an array of
product lines such as the yen "carry trade," which allowed speculators
to borrow money in Japan, where interest rates were virtually zero,
and reinvest it in jurisdictions such as New Zealand and the UK
where interest rates were higher. The impact of this, of course, was to
push up the value of the New Zealand dollar and sterling, making exports from those countries still pricier and making the global imbalances still worse. A second product line involved derivatives based on

mortgages granted to U.S. borrowers with less than marvelous track records. We shall look at the travails of subprime lenders in the United States in a later chapter. Suffice it to say here, though, that these derivatives were as toxic as the products associated with every get-rich-quick scheme dating back to Dutch tulips and the South Sea bubble. Within a month of Prince putting on his dancing shoes, Father Bear roared and Goldilocks finally woke up.

The rest of this book is devoted to seeing whether our fairy story has a happy ending. Some say that Goldilocks was lucky and escaped in the nick of time. Others say that a five-year-old girl, lost in a deep and impenetrable wood, was no match for three ferocious bears, who were desperately cross at having no breakfast on the table when they returned home so ate Goldilocks instead. If it helps, Prince was fired three months later. Citigroup had stopped dancing. Its executives were too busy counting their losses on subprime mortgages.

CHAPTER 5

The Rainy Season
Middle America Feels the Squeeze

Living in America, I am constantly being surprised by how good the crowd's chances are, and by the square deal which the average American gets from the system.

— D. W. BROGAN, "Never on Saturday"

Sherman's father had always taken the subway to Wall Street, even when he was chief executive officer of Dunning Sponget & Leach. . . . It was a matter of principle. . . . But to the new breed, the young breed, the masterful breed, Sherman's breed, there was no such principle. Insulation! That was the ticket.

— TOM WOLFE,
The Bonfire of the Vanities

You're not at the bottom yet. There is a lot further you can fall.

— MARTIN AMIS, *Success*

For Middle America, 2008 ought to have been the best of times. As the year opened, there seemed every chance that the economic squalls of the previous year would prove to have been just that—a period of temporary turbulence that would join the 1997 Far Eastern financial meltdown, the 1998 Russian debt default, and the 2000 bursting of the high-tech stock market bubble on the honor board of the country's central bank, the Federal Reserve, as yet another crisis that had been overcome. Had Fed chairman Ben Bernanke and his colleagues not been feted for their prompt handling of the banking implosion that had followed the financial coronary triggered by the credit crunch, in contrast to the behavior of central bankers in less happy lands?

Better still, a presidential election was due, one in which, for the first time since 1952, neither an incumbent president nor vice president was standing for office. This meant that no candidate was duty-bound to support the outgoing Bush administration's military strategies in Afghanistan and Iraq, or even to support these wars at all (that some candidates did so is a different matter). More intriguing was the fact that all the candidates were free to oppose the economic orthodoxy of the previous thirty years, the so-called Washington consensus of tax cuts, business deregulation, interest rates set to suit Wall Street not Main Street, balanced budgets, privatization of public services, free trade, and hostility to organized labor (Hillary Clinton was a partial exception, given that her husband Bill, as president, had proved an enthusiast for the above-mentioned consensus).

By the late summer, and the emergence of the two successful candidates of the two main parties, matters on the political front ought to have looked more promising still for Middle America. Both parties had chosen, as their standard-bearers, men who were openly running as outsiders, promising a break with the past. Both seemed authentically to represent different types of ordinary Middle Americans. Few doubted that Republican John McCain really enjoyed eating health-threatening deep-fried hot dogs or that the Democrat candidate Barack Obama was equally fond of the more cerebral foodstuff arugula (a green plant known as "rocket" in British English).

Both, and Senator Obama in particular, had made some encouraging noises about defying the orthodoxy in order to get Middle America back on its feet, and been scolded for doing so by economically orthodox sections of the media. And both would have been well aware of the need to crank up their economic rhetoric.

Because outside the convention centers, these were not the best of times for Middle America.

The events of August 29, 2008, threw into vivid relief the discon-
nection between the political world and life as lived by tens of millions of Americans.

In Denver, Colorado, Senator Obama's speech accepting the nom-
ination generated, as may have been expected, a wave of emotion
among delegates. It followed high-profile pledges of support earlier
in the convention from both Bill and Hillary Clinton and Senator Edward Kennedy.

Meanwhile, 1,110 miles away in Dayton, Ohio, Senator McCain
pulled a campaign surprise with the announcement that his running
mate would be Sarah Palin, Republican governor of Alaska. While
high-brow commentators chewed over whether this was a bold gambit
to win over women voters disappointed at the Democrats' rejection of
Senator Clinton's offer of service, the less high-minded regaled the
public with the news that she was a former beauty queen who enjoyed
hunting with a rifle.

In the outside world, on that same day, the news for American
families was bad.

Official figures showed U.S. personal income had fallen in July by
0.7 percent, according to the Commerce Department, the sharpest
fall since one of 2.3 percent in August 2005, in the wake of Hurricane
Katrina. Analysts had expected income to remain unchanged.

According to the Reuters Washington bureau, "A big jump in
prices in July pushed inflation to a 17-year high, eroding what little
spending power consumers had. Consumer spending, which accounts
for about two-thirds of economic activity, rose 0.2 percent as expected, the slimmest gain since February, and inflation-adjusted
spending fell 0.4 percent, the biggest drop since June 2004 and the
second straight monthly decline."

The report contained the apparent good news that consumer confidence was at a five-month high, according to a survey Reuters carried
out in tandem with the University of Michigan. But even this silver
lining had a cloud attached: "For a record third straight month, a majority of consumers said their financial situation had worsened."

Perhaps some of those consumers toiled in the lower rungs that archetypal aspirational middle-class profession, investment banking. In

which case, they may have heard that their job was about to disappear from under them:

> Wall Street's losses are quickly becoming India's gain. Belt-tightening is pushing banks to re-examine what jobs really need to be in expensive cities like New York, London and Hong Kong and to relocate them to cheaper areas, either in their own divisions or through third parties. . . . After outsourcing much of their back-office operations to India, these banks are now examining some of the data-intensive banking jobs with gruelling hours that are traditionally given to fresh-faced business school graduates—research associates and junior bankers on deal-making teams . . . it means one thing: Wall Street is learning that lower-level investment banking jobs no longer need to be located in financial capitals. (Heather Timmons, "Wall St. Banks Bolster Wary Embrace of India As Jobs Move," *International Herald Tribune*, August 12, 2008.)

By July 2008, U.S. unemployment was up to 5.7 percent of the workforce, from 5.5 percent in June. It was to rise to 6.1 percent shortly thereafter.

Figures from the U.S. Department of Labor showed the total numbers employed falling from 147,315,000,000 in July 2007 to 146,867,000,000, a fall of 0.3 percent, while total numbers registered as unemployed rose over the same period from 7,556,000 to 9,433,000, a rise of 24.8 percent.

Within these grand totals, the sort of employment that has traditionally been the backbone of Middle America fared equally badly and, on some measures, worse than did the workforce as a whole.

Thus the sales and office occupations category divides into two subsections. The first, sales and related occupations, recorded a drop in numbers employed between July 2007 and July 2008 from 16,804,000 to 15,995,000 (4.8 percent) and a rise over the same period in numbers registered as unemployed from 918,000 to 1,055,000 (14.9 percent).

The other subsection, office and administrative support occupations, recorded a fall in employment from 19,604,000 in July 2007 to 19,102,000 in July 2008 (2.6 percent). Meanwhile, over the same period, numbers registered as unemployed rose from 874,000 to 1,088,000 (24.5 percent).

Interestingly, the production occupations category showed U.S. factory workers also suffering from the downturn, but not to an appreciably greater extent than those in the sales and office categories. In part, the nation's manufacturing workers had benefited from the decline in the value of the dollar, which made goods easier to export. Those registered as unemployed rose by 28.5 percent over the year, more than for either the sales or office workers, while the 4.2 percent fall in employment was greater than that for office workers but a little less than that for sales employees.

True, the construction and extraction category, traditionally very sensitive to an economic chill, did far worse than any of the above, with employment dropping 7 percent and numbers registered as unemployed rising by 33 percent.

While sales and office workers grappled with the downturn, the top end jobs to which many Middle Americans aspire seemed safe enough—for now.

The management, business, and financial operations category recorded a brisk 4 percent rise in numbers employed over the twelve months, taking the total to 22,596,000, while the sister category of professional and related occupations saw a 2.7 percent rise in numbers employed to 30,059,000.

Unfortunately, unemployment in both categories had also risen. In the case of management, business, and financial operations, the rise was a whopping 54 percent since July 2007 to 593,000, and for the professional occupations it rose by a more modest 6.6 percent, albeit to the higher figure of 992,000. These figures suggested, at the very least, that life in the higher ranks of the U.S. workforce left something to be desired in terms of job security.

And as the economic squeeze took hold, the response of the authorities depended very much on who you were and where you worked. On August 9, 2008, *The Economist* cast a dolorous eye over America's onetime industrial heartland and former byword for the sort of skilled and responsible supervisory jobs that ought to be the bedrock of Middle America. All was not well in the Motor City:

With each successive month the plight of Detroit's Big Three manufacturers—General Motors (GM), Ford and Chrysler—becomes a little more desperate and their eventual fate less certain. . . . July's wretched sales figures came hard on the heels of shocking losses announced first by Ford and then, a few days later, by GM. . . . Chrysler, which is privately held, does not release financial data, but was forced by growing rumours of impending bankruptcy to issue a statement saying that despite the market turmoil, it was running ahead of its operational plan and had plenty of cash to see it through—a claim met with some scepticism. ("Detroit's Race Against Time.")

Funnily enough, the same edition of the same magazine looked at a different industry—banking. In an article entitled "Mission Creep at the Fed: The Credit Crunch One Year On," it reported thus:

When he was still in academia, Ben Bernanke [Fed chairman] once argued that Franklin Roosevelt's greatest contribution to ending the Great Depression was not a specific policy, but his "willingness to be aggressive and to experiment . . . to do whatever it took to get the country moving again." That would fairly describe how Mr Bernanke has battled perhaps the biggest financial crisis since FDR's time, which erupted one year ago this week.

The chairman of the Federal Reserve has cast aside any notion that central bankers should be boring. He has slashed interest rates; rolled out a dizzying array of new lending programmes; backed the debt of Bear Stearns, a failing investment bank; agreed to lend to Fannie Mae and Freddie Mac, America's troubled, quasi-private mortgage agencies; argued for fiscal stimulus and mortgage write-downs; and proposed an expansion of the Fed's regulatory domain.

All well and good for the banks at the receiving end of his "dizzying array" of new lending programs. But this hyperactivity on behalf of senior executives and their wealthy shareholders was in sharp contrast to official lethargy in relation to the problems of the real economy. Would Ford or General Motors be considered "too big to fail," or was that a privilege attaching only to financial institutions? This skewed picture makes the Roosevelt reference more than a little ironic: it is hard to image the late president seeking to end the Great Depression by doing little else than prop up bankers, never, it seems, his favorite people.

Senator Obama seemed to grasp this as his race for the presidency entered its last laps. His program was replete with pledges to create 5 million new jobs through green technologies, to "fight for fair trade," to support manufacturing industry, end tax breaks for companies that send U.S. jobs overseas, give workers the freedom to join unions, create a national infrastructure reinvestment bank, and give working Americans a tax cut.

On the face of it, the candidate whose trim suits and boyish good looks seemed consciously to recall the late Senator Robert Kennedy was planning to revive the successful formula of postwar U.S. economic growth and social solidarity, the era whose ending in the 1970s was presaged by Kennedy's assassination in 1968. And such an optimistic reading could well be bolstered by comparing the Obama program with that of John McCain, which scarcely mentioned manufacturing, which promised to "create millions of good American jobs" without saying how, and whose centerpiece was a summer "gas tax holiday" to help hard-pressed motorists, a departure from economic orthodoxy, for sure, but not a particularly inspiring one.

True, both candidates made great play of supporting small businesses, something that ought to have sounded at least a faint alarm bell for those who hoped either man may be the one to restore the fortunes of Middle America. Support for small business is, as we shall see later, a type of post-1970s, postindustrial "industrial strategy" that has dubious ideological roots. Senator Obama seemed to be worryingly attached to it.

But aside from this, the signs were that both candidates would, if elected, come under intense pressure to drop any aspect of old style (i.e., postwar) economic activism and revert to the Washington consensus. Here was the European edition of the *Wall Street Journal* on August 28, 2008, scolding Senator Obama during his party convention:

> In Denver . . . the only reform idea for education is a tepid call for teacher testing. Free trade is in disrepute, with Barack Obama bowing to union wishes to rewrite Nafta [North American Free Trade Agreement], even unilaterally if Mexico and Canada don't bend. The party platform includes a passing reference to reviving the Doha Round of global trade talks, but nothing about the trade promotion authority that would be needed to pass more trade deals.
>
> More tellingly, rewriting federal law to promote union organizing is now near the top of the Democratic agenda.
>
> The paper added that the resources devoted by the unions to supporting the Democrats "have simply overwhelmed the 1990s New Democrat movement that tried to tug the party toward freer trade and public sector reform." ("Big Labor's Comeback.")

Aside from the interesting suggestion that having both main parties supporting the Washington consensus, rather than just one of them, is the ideal state of affairs, there was no sign Senator McCain would escape such strictures were he to stray from economic orthodoxy. "On economics, Mr McCain's record has been pretty sensible. He has favoured free trade, low taxes, light regulation and fiscal responsibility" ("Briefing: John McCain," *The Economist*, August 30, 2008).

The implicit message was that he had better keep it that way. In the same publication, on August 23, 2008, it was suggested that Senator Obama was likely to turn out pretty sensible too, if elected:

> The anti-Obama argument is that the Illinois senator is a "stealth liberal": a man who talks inclusive talk but is bent on advancing hard-core "progressive" policies. Mr Obama is a disciple of Saul Alinsky, an activist who expanded the labour movement's agenda to include a wide range of grievances beyond the workplace. . . . This ignores Mr Obama's essential pragmatism. At every stage of his career he has calibrated the balance of political forces and adjusted his behaviour accordingly. ("Briefing: Barack Obama.")

In other words, don't worry—he may not mean it.

That would have been bad news in the eyes of those who, for many years, had been concerned about the prospects for Middle America. The above-mentioned squeeze on middle-class jobs came after many years of increasing pressure:

> Over the past few decades, American workers powered the economy to new heights. Between 1973 and 2006, the size of the economy on a per person basis—real gross domestic product (GDP) per capita— increased by more than 85 percent. Productivity—a measure of the amount that workers produce per hour on average—increased by almost 50 percent. During the decades following World War II, similar increases in economic growth and productivity helped to strengthen and expand the middle class, and reduce the economic distance between Americans in different income classes. By contrast, the gains in growth and productivity since the 1970s have not contributed to greater economic security for all, and inequality has returned to levels not seen since the years before the Great Depression. Recent polls show that the usually optimistic American public has become increasingly concerned about the future of the American middle class. (Shawn Fremstad et al., *Movin' On Up: Reforming America's Social Contract to Provide a Bridge to the Middle Class*, Center for Economic and Policy Research, 2008.)

The authors add:

> There is no standard definition of the middle class. For our research we adopt a minimal definition of the middle class that equates it with basic income and health security. Under this definition, a middle-class standard of living means having sufficient income to afford housing, health care, and other necessities that enable one to live at a decent and basic level, a level that is above mere subsistence, but modest compared to that of families securely in the middle class.

Thus the two parts of the middle class as defined above—basic and secure—are both identifiable and both parts, the basic part in particular, have been having a hard time of it. But the great irony is that it has been precisely during the years of which the CEPR report is writing, the years since 1973, that politicians, the media, and others have spoken more and more vociferously in support of the middle class. Either they are talking about a different group of people altogether, or this highly vocal support is a sort of cover for their inability or unwillingness to do anything more concrete.

As we shall see, the answer is: a bit of each.

The Race to the Center: Dreaming up a New Type of American

In the modern United States, no campaign speech or policy proposal is complete without a reference to the middle class, sometimes coupled with working families to describe a constituency that embraces a large part of the American population.

It is easy to forget how recent is this easy, routine use of class descriptions. In 1959, journalist and social commentator Vance Packard wrote thus, "Since class boundaries are contrary to the American dream, Americans generally are uncomfortable when the subject of their existence arises . . . [there is a] widespread assumption that the recent general rise in available spending money in this country is making everybody equal" (*The Status Seekers*, Longmans, 1960).

The emergence of the middle class, as an overlapping but slightly different construct to Middle America, tends to be dated to the late 1960s or early 1970s, and the breakup of the postwar consensus. In particular, the blame tends, consciously or not, to be pinned on Richard Nixon (president from 1969 to 1974) and his strategists, who are assumed to have sought electoral advantage by playing up class and other divisions in American society and to have explicitly rejected the apparent unspoken pact whereby the Republican Party remained, at heart, a high-minded club of budget-balancing East Coast lawyers and bankers, resigned to taking power only under nonpartisan figures such as Dwight Eisenhower (president from 1952 to 1960). Until Nixon, this pact appeared to state that on no account were the Republicans to fish in the psephological pools of the white South, despite the yawning and widening incongruity between the position of

Democratic Party national leaders on racial and other questions and those of its southern establishment.

It is not our intention directly to challenge this view, put most recently and eloquently in *Nixonland: The Rise of a President and the Fracturing of America*, by Rick Perlstein (Scribner, 2008). However, there is at least some evidence that, certainly to begin with, Nixon retained the notion of America as a diamond-shaped society (the middle of which was nearly all-embracing and the points at the top and the bottom were insignificant), and consequently to describe this middle as a middle class would be supremely pointless. Here, in this vast central region, was where the "real America" was to be found. Thus Nixon on May 14, 1969, discussing with colleagues the prospects for small shopkeepers: "Does it means that Mom and Pop stores are on the way out—and supermarkets are all we'll have? . . . supermarkets may be able to sell Wheaties at a cent less, but I just don't think we want a nation of supermarkets" (Richard Reeves, *President Nixon*, Simon & Schuster, 2001).

Furthermore, the new president's inaugural address in January 1969 spoke of "the need for full employment and better housing, the rebuilding of the nation's cities, protection of the environment—all issues his predecessor had made central to his presidency" (Stephen Graubard, *The Presidents*, Penguin, 2006).

By suspending the gold convertibility of the dollar in August 1971 and introducing wage and price controls, Nixon, it can be argued, was trying to save the postwar system of "classless" prosperity. It was in 1971 that Nixon declared "we are all Keynesians now."

His successor, Gerald Ford was, broadly speaking, in the same mold. His tendency to assume that what was good for the motor industry was good for America arose not from any resurgent class consciousness but, more likely, from the fact that he had represented Michigan in the Congress. As the economic crises of the mid-1970s tightened their grip, Ford became tangled in contradictory appeals for personal frugality (to "whip inflation") and increased spending to boost demand. Not until the 1976 election did a new tone enter the public debate, a suggestion that Middle America could be defined in sharp opposition to both an insider class and to that class's client groups:

We must give top priority to a drastic and thorough revision of the federal bureaucracy, to its budgeting system, and to the procedures for constantly analyzing the effectiveness of its many varied services. Tight businesslike management and planning techniques must be instituted and maintained. . . . This is no job for the fainthearted. It will be met with violent opposition from those who now enjoy a special privilege, those who prefer to work in the dark, or those whose private fiefdoms are threatened.

We must abolish and consolidate hundreds of obsolete and unnecessary federal programs and agencies. (Jimmy Carter; *Why Not the Best?* Broadman, 1975.)

Added the future president:

Steps like these can insure a full return on our hard-earned tax dollars. . . . There are about 25 million Americans who are classified as poor, two-thirds of whom happen to be white, and half of whom receive welfare benefits. At least ten percent of these are able to work. A massive bureaucracy of two million employees at all levels of government is attempting to administer more than 100 different programs of bewildering complexity. . . . Often it is financially profitable not to work and even to have a family disrupted by forcing the father to leave home. Some combined welfare payments exceed the average working family's income, while other needy families have difficulty obtaining a bare subsistence. (Carter, *Why Not the Best?*)

Intriguingly, this thinly veiled critique of Lyndon Johnson's Great Society programs came from a fellow Democrat. But if Middle America or an American middle class, or both, as overlapping entities, were starting to emerge as political entities, it was an open question as to who exactly were its members. Middle managers, the great army of corporation men and women, were far from assured a place in this new grouping. President Carter made an early attempt to deprive ordinary businesspeople and middle-ranking executives of one of the long-standing perks of their position—the three Martini lunch. British writer Keith Waterhouse took up the tale:

What he [Carter] said was: "When a business executive can charge off a $55 luncheon on a tax return and a truck driver cannot deduct a $1.50 sandwich, then we need basic tax reform."

All hell broke loose. . . . "Deductibility of business entertainment," thundered the Hotel and Restaurant Employees and Bartenders' Union, "is a human rights issue. Half a million workers could lose their jobs if tax deductions were disallowed." (*Rhurbarb, Rhubarb*, Michael Joseph, 1979.)

All of which may have seemed amusing and little more, but it did indicate that the new era for middle-class America was not taking the shape some may have expected. If the blue-collar masses of Detroit and Pittsburgh were to be "restructured," so too were their white-collar counterparts.

Take banking, a quintessentially middle-class career the world over and nowhere more so than in America, where strict controls on the industry and on both the size of banks and on their ability to operate across state borders had ensured the survival of a dense undergrowth of small institutions serving their communities.

Here is a description of such banks more than twenty years ago, as seen through the eyes of an examiner working for the regulator, the Office of the Comptroller of the Currency:

To have a career as a bank examiner in a place like Oklahoma is to endure many character-building episodes in which the key props are a small town, a little bank, a chicken-fried-steak-and-yellow-gravy lunch well before noon in the genial company of a small-town little-bank president, and, after dark, a cinder-block motel, Wild Turkey [whiskey] and tap water, and a television set full of *Kojak* reruns. (Mark Singer, *Funny Money*, Knopf, 1985.)

Banking deregulation in the 1990s led to a headlong shrinkage in the number of U.S. banks as a wave of mergers reduced considerably the openings for anyone wishing to be a "little-bank president." Nor was the potential demise of the three martini lunch the only worry for the suburban executive, in many ways the archetypal figure of postwar

U.S. prosperity. In the new climate, managers boasted at having "stripped out layers of management" and "taking costs [i.e., jobs] out of the businesses."

Of this process there was no greater exponent than Jack Welch, chairman and chief executive officer of General Electric from 1981 to 2001. His views were unexceptional by the time he shared them with British viewers in an interview with Sir David Frost:

> Frost: Now one of things you did that you were famous for was getting rid of the lowest performing ten percent within the company on an annual basis, people, managers had to produce their list and category c had to go and so on, and that led, within five years, to 100,000 people losing their jobs and you say in the book here, any organisation that thinks it can guarantee job security is going down a dead-end, only satisfied customers can give people job security, not companies?
>
> Welch: Absolutely true, in fact vital companies, strong winning companies are the only answer to job security, some fuzzy paternalism is not the answer because in the end a sound, viable company gives back to its community, its employees are assured, self-confident, they mentor people in the inner city, they pay taxes, they do all these things and now you're seeing all over the papers as you see the recession come, you're seeing sacks here, sacks there people that weren't competitive, so the only real . . . no one likes to take anybody out but why, David, this ten percent thing gets a lot of action, the facts are, why would you all of a sudden-in grade school you're graded, in college you make the team or you don't, you graduate or you don't. People are graded all along why at age 22 when you quit school should you stop being evaluated? It's nonsense. (*BBC Breakfast with Frost*, October 7, 2001.)

The new suspicion of middle managers was, of course, amplified many times over if they worked in the public sector. "They have been labelled by Irving Kristol in the USA as the 'new class.' They are activists. They work for the public interest, work for others, define the poor and work out ways to help them. They are middle-class and altruistic" (David Graham and Peter Clarke; *The New Enlightenment: The Rebirth of Liberalism*, Macmillan/Channel Four, 1986).

Kristol, a key neoconservative thinker, had identified salaried public sector administrators as a sort of mutant middle class. Quoted
again in *The New Enlightenment*, he said:

> What created doubts for us in the Great Society programs of Lyndon
> Johnson was the fact that they were so very ambitious and seemed to have
> such a utopian vision of human nature. Most of us in the neo-conservative
> group had come from either working-class or lower-middle-class fami-
> lies. Most of the people who went into the Great Society programs came
> from upper-middle-class families, most of them were Harvard graduates.
> . . . They thought abolishing poverty was easy, that it could be done
> simply by devising the right program.

Not that Kristol was suggesting that the free market successor to the
Great Society ought to be somehow classless. Far from it: "We are
bourgeois," says Kristol. "It is bourgeois society that produces the kinds
of people who make a free market work and who makes capitalism acceptable. . . . The first job of a civilisation is to produce a certain kind
of person" (quoted in Graham and Clarke, *New Enlightenment*).

But what kind, exactly? The American middle class as tentatively
defined by Carter was made up of tax payers rather than tax consumers—either in the sense of being on welfare, of administering
welfare schemes, or of being private sector employees expecting a tax
break for their booze-laden lunching habits. Welch took this notion
further, identifying time-serving corporate salaried staff as a dead
weight to be disposed of at the earliest opportunity. Yet if the white-
collar masses of neither the public nor private sector were at the heart
of this new class, who was?

Funnily enough, in 1959 Vance Packard inadvertently identified
the future hero class for the free marketeers when he bemoaned "the
shrinkage in the number of small entrepreneurs and self-employed
people. Such independent entrepreneurs originally constituted a true
middle class in the United States. They found economic security by
commanding their own destinies, however small. In Jefferson's day,
nearly four-fifths of all Americans were self-employed enterprisers.
By 1940, only a fifth remained. And today the number has shrunk to

approximately 13 percent. . . . We have become an employee society" (Packard, *Status Seekers*).

His complaint would not be answered for a good twenty years, and that answer may well have been far removed from the sort of thing Packard had in mind. The entrepreneurs who emerged in the late 1970s and have been lauded ever since have proved rather less the bedrock of a virtuous society described immediately above and rather more like the familiar mixture of asset strippers, speculators, and wealthy corporate executives, albeit ones who could claim entrepreneur status on the ground of having bought the company concerned (usually with borrowed money) rather than simply worked for it.

Nevertheless, entrepreneurialism provided valuable ideological cover for the squeeze on Middle America from the 1970s onward. First, it justified the widening gap between the earnings of corporate bosses and the middle strata of society; the executives were entrepreneurs who had taken risks, thus deserving of their good fortune.

Second, it provided an ideal version of the middle class to which the real middle class was forever being told it ought to aspire. Job and retirement insecurity, inability to afford good housing or health care could all be blamed on a lack of entrepreneurial spirit. Indeed, seeking these benefits could also be cited as evidence of a lack of entrepreneurialism, because no genuine entrepreneur would worry overmuch about such things (that the real-life "risk takers" were inordinately keen on their salaries, health plans, homes, and pensions was another matter). Like the "shock workers" of the old communist bloc, entrepreneurs, however vaguely defined, were heroes of the new economy. Indeed, one of their foremost cheerleaders said exactly that: "They overthrow establishments rather than establish equilibrium. They are the heroes of economic life" (George Gilder, *The Spirit of Enterprise*, Simon & Schuster, 1984).

A side effect of George Gilder's romantic view of entrepreneurship was to give the political right an alternative role model or at least an alternative public face. Instead of the high-minded Republican lawyer, banker, or soldier, with a stiff-necked rectitude about balanced budgets and national security, conservatism now had, in the entrepreneur, an edgy, fashionable loner: "Society is always in deep debt to the entrepreneurs who sustain it and rarely consume by themselves more than the smallest share of what they give society. . . . There is nothing abstract or predictable about them or what they do. Some are scientists, some are artists, some are craftsmen; most are in business. Although they act as individual men and women, they are nearly always driven by familial roles and obligations" (Gilder, *Spirit of Enterprise*).

The hint of frugality in this paragraph suggests that, on top of all its other virtues, the entrepreneurial middle class was fairly indifferent to money and other rewards. Again, the mythical figure of the Soviet era shock worker comes to mind: dedicated, selfless, more interested in achievement than rewards. The shock workers exceeded their production norms; the entrepreneur heroes unleashed shareholder value.

Not everyone was convinced. One writer, at least, saw in all this not so much a new middle class as the reemergence of one of the oldest of social groups—the very rich.

In the language of nineteenth century producerism, "labor" and "capital" did not mean what they mean to us. The term "capitalist" was reserved for those who, producing nothing, lived off speculative profits, while the "laboring class," as a Democratic party broadside explained, referred to "the producer of wealth; the yeomanry who till the soil; mechanics, manufacturers, operatives, traders, whose labor sustains the state." Whigs no less than Jacksonian Democrats took an expansive view of the "working classes," defined by Levi Lincoln as the "practical agriculturalist and husbandman, the manufacturer, and the mechanic." Rufus Choate considered it appropriate to speak of the "laborious, trading and business portions of the community" in the same breath. Daniel Webster claimed that "nine tenths of the whole people belong to the laborious, industrious, and productive classes." They typically owned a little capital, he said, but not so much "as to render them independent without personal labor." Those who "combine capital with their labor" were referred to interchangeably as working-class and middle-class. (Christopher Lasch, *The Revolt of the Elites and the Betrayal of Democracy*, Norton, 1995.)

But that was then and this now. Lasch went on to describe the disintegration of this real, tangible Middle America and its replacement with something very different: "In our time . . . the democratization of abundance—the expectation that each generation would enjoy a standard of living beyond the reach of its predecessors—has given way to a reversal in which age-old inequalities are beginning to reestablish themselves, sometimes at a frightening rate, sometimes so gradually as to escape notice."

The changing class structure of the United States presents us, sometimes in exaggerated form, with changes that are taking place all over the industrial world. People in the upper 20 percent of the income structure now control half the country's wealth. In the last 20 years they alone have experienced a net gain in the family income. In the brief years of the Reagan administration alone, their share of the national income rose from 41.6 percent to 44 percent. The middle class, generously defined as those with incomes ranging from $15,000 to $50,000 a year, declined from 65 percent of the population in 1970 to 58 percent in 1985. These figures convey only a partial, imperfect impression of momentous changes that have taken place in a remarkably short period of time. The steady growth of unemployment, now expanded to include white-collar workers, is more revealing. So is the growth of the "contingent labor force." The number of part-time jobs has doubled since 1980 and now amounts to a quarter of available jobs. No doubt this massive growth of part-time employment helps to explain why the number of workers covered by retirement plans, which rose from 22 percent to 45 percent between 1950 and 1980, slipped back to 42.6 percent by 1986. It also helps to explain the decline of union membership and the steady erosion of union influence. All these developments, in turn, reflect the loss of manufacturing jobs and the shift to an economy increasingly based on information and services.

Thus behind all the blather about "enterprise" and "Middle America," the real Middle America was being hollowed out. Job security and union-negotiated social benefits were as much a target for the new asset strippers as plant, machinery, and land. It is true that the image of the rebellious entrepreneur pervaded twenty-first-century corporate America. No advertisement for a business school or MBA course was complete without a line or two declaring that conformists need not apply and that the institution or course in question produced nothing but free thinkers. Often this would be illustrated with a grainy photograph of a Native American or other ethnic minority, just to emphasize the nonconformity of the students.

Mysteriously, on graduation, they would almost without exception turn into Jack Welch clones, "stripping costs [i.e., jobs] out of the business" and banging on about "shareholder value."

Thomas Frank, in his very funny book *One Market under God* (Secker & Warburg, 2001), looks at the other side of the mythical coin from the "rebellious" entrepreneur beloved of George Gilder— the new middle class "liberated" by entrepreneurial financial providers to join in the fun on Wall Street:

> In the fall of 1994, Joseph Nocera, the financial journalist . . . published *A Piece of the Action: How the Middle Class Joined the Money Class*, an account of the rise of all the consumer financial instruments of the previous 30 years—credit cards, money market accounts, mutual funds. For Nocera, each and every one market yet another advance for the common man, another step toward "financial democracy," another opportunity for "the middle class" to use "all the financial tools that had previously been available only to the rich." At the end of that long road, naturally, lay the bull market of the 1990s, which differed from all other booms, Nocera asserted (the 1920s boom was considered only in passing), in that it was enriching the regular people rather than the bloated aristocrats of Wall Street. Nocera never offered much of a definition of the "middle class," but still he claimed for it an inherent and awesome virtuosity.

Frank adds:

> But here, as in so many market populist texts, it is the repugnant elitism of the old-time financial industry and the rise of the more democratic new generation that is the really important narrative. Nocera's populist

financiers . . . affirmed the wisdom of the People. . . . Traditional authority figures—journalists, congressmen, and the like—are said to
doubt (snobbishly, arrogantly) the intelligence of the people, to seek to
protect "us" from ourselves. . . . On the other side were the people's financiers whose quiet, noble determination to let "us" control "our"
own lives made them fantastically rich.

Time was when this notion of the entrepreneur acting to em-
power those around him was a rarity. In neither America nor Britain
in the immediate postwar decades was there seen to be anything particularly desirable (or indeed undesirable) in self-employment or
starting a business. Packard's comment, quoted above, that "we have
become an employee society," applied equally to Britain, if not more
so. From the serried ranks of corporate America to the burgeoning
battalions of the British civil service, the word "entrepreneur" carried little weight.

Ironically, an early enthusiast for the ideology of entrepreneurship
was an American who tried to sell the idea to the British in a book entitled, simply, *The British*. Thus journalist Drew Middleton is the
ideal link to a discussion of the travails of the middle class on the
other side of the Atlantic.

Soaking the Yeomanry: Rising Damp in Middle Britain

The British (Martin Secker & Warburg, 1957) dwelled at some length
on the new postwar working class and its "paramount emphasis on security." He understood why, after years of poverty, British workers
felt this way. But he could not approve: "There is no great admiration
for individual enterprise, for risk or sacrifice. Among the many men I
have talked to in the New Towns [postwar British communities sited
away from big cities], I never met one who was interested in saving
enough money to buy his own small business, to strike out for himself. . . . Yet this is a nation that desperately needs the imaginative, in-
ventive mind if it is to overcome its economic difficulties."

Three decades later, and the process of encouraging just this type
of salty, independent class was well under way.

How? Well, today there is a fairly conventional narrative as to the construction of the modern middle British majority. You can read it in newspaper and news magazine think pieces, catch it on television or radio whenever one of those three-part series about the way we live now is being aired or you can read it in chunky books of the type that get serialized in the press.

Here it is, in a nutshell. Thirty years ago, large parts of our social infrastructure were not working: housing, the nationalized industries, the public utilities. Margaret Thatcher broke them into small pieces and sold them to the people who had allegedly owned them all along—the British public. In the case of council houses, this was a direct sale of the asset concerned. In other cases, the sale was of shares in the organization in question. Large numbers of people thought this could not work and that the whole idea was crazy. They were to be proved wrong. Whatever one's original position on this question, whatever one's current position on the political spectrum, it has to be admitted that, broadly speaking, three great benefits have flowed from this social revolution.

First, the ranks of what may loosely be described as the middle class (what we in this book call Middle Britain) have been greatly swelled, by the simple fact of the extension of the ownership of assets to millions more people. Second, some of the sold-off entities were previously state monopolies, a status denied them in the private sector. This is excellent news for Middle Britain, because it now has a choice of products and suppliers where previously there was none. To take one small example, until 1980 the only permitted supplier of telephone answering machines was the state-owned British Telecom. Third, asset ownership and the newly competitive nature of the privatized industries gave people a new self-respect and self-reliance; no longer dependent on council housing officials, surly telephone engineers, tardy British Gas employees, or similar personnel, they could move to a different house, switch their business to other suppliers, and generally behave with the sort of blithe disregard for time-serving, foot-dragging, rule-book bound employees that had previously been the prerogative of only the chilliest of upper-middle-class housewives.

On this reckoning, the real story of the last quarter century has been the emergence not of the New Olympians of whom we write, whether in finance and banking or in central banks and governmental and quasi-governmental organizations, but this "New Yeomanry" of independent, resourceful, and property-owning Middle Britons.

Of course, from the start, three decades ago, this new Middle Britain was defined to a considerable extent in contrast to the losers in the new economic order. "So long as success and ability are rewarded—as they must be if we are not all to become paupers—there will be classes, as there are even in Soviet Russia. And how can it be in the general interest to encourage envy and hatred of ability and success?" (Conservative Central Office, *The Right Approach*, 1976).

Sometimes losers and winners could be divided within industrial groups, with a "winner" group that could expect success in the new economic order being split from the hinterland of losers. Sometimes winner status related to higher levels of skills, as with the toolmakers in the breakaway United Craft Organisation at the British Leyland vehicle maker in the late 1970s. Sometimes it was merely that the prospects of the winners looked better than those of their fellows, as with the Nottinghamshire miners, who refused to join the miners' strike of 1984–1985.

Furthermore, if the need for losers in the new economic paradigm is rarely mentioned, there is even less acknowledgment that this "free market model" is also in need of enormous quantities of public money. Council house sales, for example, have left Britain with a bill for housing benefit of about £15 billion in 2006–2007, equivalent to more than 1 percent of gross domestic product (GDP), in part the price Britain pays for having sold all that social housing. Furthermore, such housing is having to be partly reinvented at some expense, with the government trying to provide lower-cost homes for "key workers" in London and the southeast. Rail privatization has involved governments paying about double the subsidy received during the British Rail era for a similar level of service. The savings products that define Middle Britain (chiefly pension schemes and individual savings accounts) come complete with tax breaks. Many, perhaps most, of the privatized industries had to be stuffed like Strasbourg geese full of taxpayer money to ensure the sale got away; either that, or the sale had to be ludicrously underpriced, which is a subsidy by another name.

Meanwhile, the same turbo-charged, liberalized finance that was said to be helping bring this New Yeomanry into existence was simultaneously threatening the career paths and job security of Middle Britain. By the autumn of 2008, plans were well advanced to allow corporations to own law firms, medical clinics, and accounting firms, in defiance of all principles of good sense and professional independence. In a move beyond parody, in January 2008 the British government announced plans to allow companies including McDonald's and the train track operator Network Rail to issue nationally recognized qualifications based on their own workplace training schemes.

While career prospects darkened, so did the immediate financial outlook. As in the United States, sliding house prices, soaring inflation, and tightening credit markets put the squeeze on the New Yeomanry. We believe the current cold climate in Middle Britain is no accident, but part of the inevitable working out of the New Olympian system. For nations such as Britain that took the free market road from the 1980s onward, the early benefits, of the sort that would have been enjoyed by the middle earners in society, seemed to be just fine—an end to mortgage rationing, easier credit, the scrapping of restrictions on taking currency abroad, and a wider range of consumer products and services. Only by the mid-1990s would the truth be dawning that the "reform" or "adjustment" process was still under way, that it would never really end, and that cherished entities such as local hospitals, post offices, transport services, and schools were under threat—not to mention the career prospects of the middle class. All had to be asset-stripped to feed the maw of the New Olympians and their appetite for deals and profits.

To sum up, on both sides of the Atlantic it would seem that the more the middle class is discussed, the gloomier its prospects become. Indeed, the creation of the "heroic" entrepreneurial middle class has provided ideological cover for the rooking of the real Middle America and Middle Britain. It is perfectly true, as free market critics have alleged, that a middle class is, to an extent, a social construct, relying not only on custom and practice but on the tolerance and even encouragement of a series of protective enclaves across society, whether in terms of small-scale retailing and farming or in professional "closed shops" in the law, banking, and elsewhere. But, as Irving Kristol is happy to admit, that the new "entrepreneurial" class is also largely a product of the society in which it operates.

Middle America and Middle Britain were sold the idea that they would be better off without their traditional postwar allies in the pursuit of the good life—organized labor and the welfare state (however rudimentary the U.S. version of the latter may have been). Like the out-of-towner mysteriously separated from his friends and befriended by apparently warmhearted types who, after a while, suggest an innocent card game, the Anglo-American middle classes have been had by shady characters who promised them a good time and then picked their pockets. It is interesting that this pocket-picking was perfected first in Britain and then exported to the United States, an inversion of the usual chain of events.

The urgent need now is to find themselves some real friends in place of these false ones. Long forgotten pals may be a good place to start.

CHAPTER 6

The Odd Couple

Alan Greenspan, Gordon Brown, and the World's Biggest Bubble

Rain or shine, you won't shake me,
I don't mind, where you take me,
Spend my time following you around.

— SYLVAN MASON, "Following You Around"

You know something? You two deserve each other. Make nice. You two are partners.

—*Starsky & Hutch*

Brown and Blair trekked into my office at the Federal Reserve. As we exchanged greetings it appeared to me that Brown was the senior person. Blair stayed in the background while Brown did most of the talking.

—ALAN GREENSPAN,
The Age of Turbulence

Kirkaldy tends to be off the beaten track for American visitors to Scotland. Golfers sometimes take the slow road on their pilgrimage to St. Andrews a bit farther around the coast, but most are too busy contemplating the delights of the Old Course to make a detour to the ancient capital of the kingdom of Fife. Even fewer of them make the journey in winter, when the days are short and a bitter wind howls into the Firth of Forth from the North Sea.

It was, however, to this unprepossessing town of austere granite buildings that one of the most celebrated Americans of his generation, Alan Greenspan, arrived with something of a spring in his septuagenarian step on February 6, 2005, to pay homage to Kirkcaldy's favorite son, Adam Smith.

Smith was the author of *The Wealth of Nations*, the foundation stone for classical free market economics published in the same year as the Declaration of Independence. Greenspan, viewed by many commentators as the second most important man in America after President George W. Bush, had been invited to give a lecture on Smith by Gordon Brown, the most powerful politician in Britain after Prime Minister Tony Blair.

Both Greenspan and Brown were at the height of their powers and greatly esteemed by the financial markets on both sides of the Atlantic. Chairman of the Federal Reserve Board for almost eighteen years, Greenspan was credited with a magician's touch for his handling of the U.S. economy, engineering its transformation from the creaking leviathan of the 1980s to the world-beating pioneer of new technologies in the 1990s. When disaster had threatened, first with the Russian debt default of 1998, and then again with the combination of a collapse in the dot-com bubble and the terrorist attacks on September 11, 2001, Greenspan had steered the U.S. economy into much calmer seas than those he could see as his car drove round the coast to Kirkcaldy that raw winter's day. Greenspan, in the eyes of his many admirers, was the central banker who had seen it all and done it all. Truly he was, in the words of one of them, the maestro.

Brown, in whose constituency Kirkcaldy stood, had been chancellor of the exchequer since Labour's general election victory in 1997. He and Tony Blair had been rivals for the leadership of the Labour Party when the job had fallen vacant in 1994 and Brown still bitterly resented losing out to a man he considered his intellectual inferior. The two men struck a deal: Brown would give Blair a free run for the

Labour Party leadership in return for being allowed to set the agenda for economic and social policy.

In the three years leading up to the 1997 election, Brown and his chief adviser, Ed Balls, had visited the U.S. many times. Balls had studied in the U.S., and Brown took his summer holidays on Cape Cod; both men were convinced that the left in Britain should look across the Atlantic for policy inspiration rather than across the English Channel to what they saw as the moribund economies of Western Europe. As a result, it was decided that the next Labour government would have a welfare-to-work program, its own version of the Earned Income Tax Credit to boost the incomes of the working poor, and an independent central bank. Brown and Balls struck up a close working relationship with Greenspan, taking advice on what they should do to ensure that the day-to-day decisions of a newly liberated Bank of England were unencumbered by political meddling. In his memoirs, Greenspan noted that when Blair and Brown had first visited him together in 1994, it had been the latter who had created the stronger impression, an assessment that no doubt flattered the chancellor of the exchequer's eggshell-thin ego.

Greenspan continued to hold Brown in high regard as the British economy continued the long period of sustained, low inflationary growth it had enjoyed since Black Wednesday, the day in September 1992 when George Soros and other speculators had forced the pound out of the European exchange rate mechanism. Previous Labour governments had quickly found themselves destabilized by financial crises: Blair by contrast was able to win a second general election landslide in 2001 on Brown's management of the economy. In February 2005, another general election was only three months away and despite the political unpopularity caused by Britain's part in the invasion of Iraq there was little doubt that the feel-good factor would work for Labour once again. Brown had played the Greenspan card deftly throughout his time at the Treasury. He arranged for the Queen to give the Fed chairman the rare privilege of an honorary knighthood in 2002; Greenspan duly praised the chancellor as "without peer among the world's economic policymakers."

Now Brown was keen for Greenspan to play a part in the rehabilitation of Smith as a "progressive" rather than as a philosopher king of the free market right. There was, however, more to it than that. In the 1960s and 1970s, the relationship between Britain and America when it came to economic and financial matters was a servile one: Britain would, with depressing regularity, have to go cap in hand to Washington for a line of credit or a loan to see it through a crisis. The not so subliminal message for British voters as they weighed up the options for the 2005 election was that the United States and Britain were forging ahead together due, in no small part, to the fact that the world's greatest central banker and the world's greatest finance minister were joined at the hip.

Greenspan and Brown had indeed been following broadly similar policies in their respective countries. These policies had resulted in strong growth, a recovery in stock markets after the dot-com bust, and soaring house prices. They were, sad to say, also misguided and wholly delusional since the prosperity was bought with counterfeit money. Three years on from the love-in on Firth of Forth, Greenspan was increasingly seen as the man whose solution to one bubble was to create another, even bigger one. Brown, who finally fulfilled his ambition to become prime minister, found that as with another Scottish grandee, Macbeth, it was as well to be careful what you wished—and plotted for. By the end of 2008, the real estate markets in both countries were broken-backed. Foreclosures and repossessions were rising. Banks on both sides of the Atlantic had either gone bust or had had to be bailed out by the Fed and the Bank of England. The losses amassed as a result of the speculation in subprime mortgage lending meant easy credit was a thing of the past. Inflation was going up as house prices were coming down. Greenspan was no longer the maestro but the sorcerer who had beguiled the public with almost two decades of bubble economics and had dealt his hapless successor, Ben Bernanke, an almost unplayable hand. As the sorcerer's apprentice, Brown's honeymoon as prime minister had been painfully short; there were plots against him in his own party as Labour MPs sought to save themselves from electoral disaster by ditching the man blamed for pushing Britain to the brink of its first recession in sixteen years.

Predictably, neither man thought he was to blame. Greenspan used a global book tour in late 2007 to publicize his self-regarding memoir to deny that he was either responsible for the subprime crisis or could have acted in any other way than he did. Brown had spent the past decade boasting about how the wisdom of his policies—independence for the Bank of England, new rules to govern taxation and government spending, the injection of greater competition into markets—had abolished Britain's tendency to lurch from boom to bust. Now the mantra was that the queues of customers outside Northern Rock and the unmistakable sound of air leaking out of the real estate bubble had nothing to do with any failings on the part of the Labour government. Britain, Brown said, was caught up in a global downturn caused by problems in the American subprime mortgage market but was "well placed" to come through the difficult times.

The unwillingness of either man to accept responsibility jarred. Greenspan had personally directed U.S. economic policy for nigh on twenty years; not just deciding the Fed's interest rate strategy but having a wider influence on the economic policy direction of successive administrations, especially that of Bill Clinton. It had been Greenspan who in the years before he became Fed chairman in 1987 had lobbied hard for the deregulation of the savings and loan institutions, only to find that they abused their freedom through a mixture of incompetence and fraud. A thousand failed in the late 1980s in what John Kenneth Galbraith (*The Culture of Contentment*, Houghton Mifflin, 1992) called "the largest and costliest venture in public misfeasance, malfeasance and larceny of all time." Up to that point, at least.

It was Greenspan too who noted in December 1996 that stock markets were suffering from "irrational exuberance" and then, by a series of ill timed and needless cuts in interest rates, convinced investors that the Fed would always underwrite share prices if times got tough. The so-called Greenspan put acted as a backstop for Wall Street during the equity bubble of the 1990s, a period when Paul Volcker, the previous chairman of the Fed, cast doubt on the theory, swallowed hook, line, and sinker by his successor, that the U.S. was gripped by a new economic paradigm. "The fate of the world economy," Volcker noted caustically as dot-com mania gripped America in May 1999, "is now totally dependent on the growth of the U.S. economy, which is now dependent on the stock market, whose growth is dependent on about fifty stocks, half of which have never reported any earnings."

The relationship between Blair and Brown was sometimes compared to that between Winston Churchill and his deputy, Clement Attlee, during the Second World War: Blair was the foreign policy supremo who fought the wars and tended Britain's "special relationship" with America; Brown was there to keep the home fires burning and it was his view that he was keeping the fires burning very brightly indeed. In March 2005, a month after Greenspan's Adam Smith lecture, Brown boasted that Britain was "experiencing the longest period of sustained economic growth since records began in the year 1701."

When Greenspan arrived in Britain in early October 2007, Brown still behaved like a star-struck groupie. "Alan Greenspan is a towering figure in the international financial community who combines the qualities of outstanding leadership, extraordinary insight, absolute integrity and a strong sense of social responsibility and internationalism," he said. It was not the prime minister's last misjudgment that month, nor the most serious. Labour had a comfortable opinion poll lead over the main opposition party, the Conservatives, and Brown was being urged by his advisers to take advantage of the constitutional right of a prime minister to call a general election at the time of his own choosing. Despite being warned that the already evident slowdown in U.S. growth was certain to spread across the Atlantic to affect Britain in 2008, Brown first allowed his aides to whip up a frenzy of speculation that an election would be held in November, then changed his mind at the last minute. Fears about the contagion effect from the U.S. proved to be well-founded. Greenspan's legacy to his disciple was a crisis centered on the City of London and the real estate market—the twin engines on which the British economy had been kept aloft for the past decade. Contrary to Brown's attempts at reassurance, Britain was spectacularly badly placed to withstand a global downturn and its chronic weaknesses—heavily indebted consumers, a twin trade and budget deficit to match that of the U.S., a shrunken manufacturing base—were painfully exposed by Greenspan's follies.

Since it is probably fair to assume that Greenspan will not be invited to a comeback lecture in Kirkcaldy, it is worth recalling what he said in his paean to Adam Smith in February 2005. There was a touch of awe from the central banker who, according to his reputation, digested vast quantities of economic data to assess what was happening in the world's biggest economy. Smith, he said, did it differently on "remarkably little formal empirical evidence" to draw his inferences about the beauty of the free market's invisible hand. It was clear to Greenspan, though, that Smith would have entirely approved of the New Olympian project for the United States that was pursued with such vigor in the 1980s and 1990s, since it provided a boost to competition, productivity, and living standards. "By the 1980s, the success of that strategy in the U.S. confirmed the earlier views (of Smith and other classical economists) that a loosening of regulatory restraint on business would improve the flexibility of our economies. Enhanced flexibility has the advantage of enabling market economies to adjust automatically and not having to rest on policymakers' initiatives, which often come too late or are misguided."

This last comment was made without irony, as was Greenspan's apparently innocent observation that Smith was an outspoken critic of just the sort of commercial abuse then being perpetrated by the sharks of the subprime mortgage market. "Smith's sanction, however, was directed to the freedom of markets and trade, not to the new business elite, many of whose business practices Smith severely deprecated."

Not that Greenspan saw anything to worry about. "One could hardly imagine that today's awesome array of international transactions would produce the relative economic stability that we experience daily if they were not led by some international version of Smith's invisible hand. The inference is not that people always act rationally in commercial transactions. The periodic bubbles in product and financial markets prove otherwise. But, by and large, the description of economic process that Smith developed, and others have since extended, does appear to adequately describe today's determinants of world commerce and the wealth of nations."

Here you have the New Olympian creed boiled down to one short paragraph. The "awesome array" of transactions in the financial markets creates stability, not instability.

Bubbles happen, but only rarely, and when they do it is the invisible hand that sorts out the problem and not the willingness of policymakers to use vast quantities of taxpayer money to save the gods and goddesses of Wall Street from the consequences of their own folly.

Charge It! Building a Mountain Range of Debt

Two months after his Smith lecture, Greenspan made another speech, this time on consumer finance. Technological advance and innovation in the financial services industry had led to a plethora of new products such as subprime mortgages. More sophisticated credit scoring methods had allowed loans to be provided for those who previously would not have got them. On leaving office, the former Fed chairman admitted that he had no idea of the downside risks involved in questionable lending practices. "While I was aware a lot of these practices were going on, I had no notion of how significant they had become until very late. I really didn't get it until very late in 2005 and 2006" (*60 Minutes*, September 16, 2007). It was, of course, all a bit late by then.

Mind you, this was the same Greenspan who in January 1973, just as higher inflation was about to bring the long postwar boom to an abrupt end, told investors in the stock market that "it is very rare that you can be as unqualifiedly bullish as you can now." The window of opportunity for the bulls was relatively short, as it turned out. Wall Street peaked four days later and subsequently lost 46 percent of its value. It was the self-same Greenspan who in 1994 proudly announced that timely action by the Fed in the spring of 1994 had "defused a significant part of the bubble which had previously built up," only to assert on leaving the Fed that it was "very difficult to definitively identify a bubble until after the fact—that is when its bursting confirmed its existence." As William Fleckenstein notes (*Greenspan's*

Bubbles, McGraw-Hill, 2008), "I'm sure it's a great comfort to folks to know that after a bubble collapses and they have lost money, the Fed will be able to recognise that there *had* been a bubble."

Greenspan, like Brown, believed that he was presiding over a true re-naissance in the economy built on the solid foundations of improved productivity, a new wave of technological innovation, the unleashing of the animal spirits of entrepreneurs, and the free markets lionized by Adam Smith. As far as Britain was concerned, this was always a fantasy, since the age-old problems of spending more than the coun-try produced were only temporarily disguised by low-cost imports from China and the rest of the developing world. In the United States, with its formidable, if diminished, industrial base and its world leadership in sectors such as aerospace and computer hardware, there was a kernel of truth to the grand narrative sketched out by Greenspan. In both countries, however, the pivotal role of debt in boosting growth artificially was brushed under the carpet.

Personal sector debt in the U.S. had increased by more than 150 percent in the decade that followed the shock to the world's financial markets caused by the crisis in Asia in the summer of 1997. At the start of this period, average Americans had debts of slightly less than their annual income—93.4 percent. Ten years on, this had risen to 139 percent.

The British addiction to debt was even stronger. When Tony Blair became prime minister in 1997, the total debt held by individuals stood at £570 billion. When he stood down in 2007, it had more than doubled to £1.5 trillion. Incomes rose as well, but not nearly as fast as debt. By the time Brown achieved his long-held ambition and clam-bered to the top of what Benjamin Disraeli called the "greasy pole" of British politics, the debt to income ratio stood at 173.1 percent—up from 101.6 percent in 1997, the highest of any developed country.

But why worry? Debt was only going up because it cost more and more to buy a home, and so long as asset prices kept going up there was no need for concern. In the United States, house prices doubled between 1997 and the peak of the boom in 2006; in the UK they rose even more spectacularly, trebling between 1997 and 2007. When concerns were raised about these rising levels of personal debt, policy-makers on both sides of the Atlantic shrugged them off. It was important, they said, to look at both sides of the balance sheet rather than just liabilities. Rising house prices meant the personal sector's balance sheet was strong.

There was a precedent for this line of argument, although not an especially encouraging one. The Bank of Japan and Tokyo's Ministry of Finance had taken the same relaxed approach to the rising debt levels seen at the end of the 1980s. These too were justified by the booming asset prices that, according to one unsubstantiated (and almost certainly apocryphal) report, meant that the real estate value of the imperial palace was greater than the whole of California. But the argument only held for as long as asset prices kept rising, and the Japanese experience showed quite clearly that when the bubble burst—as it always does in the end—the value of the asset collapsed but the value of the debt did not.

The plunging housing market in the U.S. during 2007 and 2008 inevitably led to comparisons with the Japanese experience. Greenspan's successor, Ben Bernanke, insisted that Americans need not fear a repetition of the Japanese experience. Drawing on his own academic research into the Great Depression, Bernanke cut interest rates aggressively in an attempt to ensure that there was not a prolonged period of debt deflation. But as some commentators noted, consumers in the U.S. (and the UK) were in a more exposed position than their Japanese counterparts at the end of the 1980s, since year after year of borrowing had left them with nothing to fall back on in hard times.

"The US is not Japan a decade ago. It is much, much worse," said Albert Edwards of Société Générale. "The Japanese household savings rate was a lofty 15 percent when their bubble burst in 1990 and a reduction over the last decade (to only 3 percent currently) helped prop up household consumption in the face of massive income headwinds. With savings ratios close to zero, no such cushion now exists in the two primary Ponzi economies, namely the US and the UK. Desperately weak economic data has left no doubt that the UK has extended its special relationship with the US to joining it as it sways on the window ledge above oblivion. Both the US and the UK have enjoyed housing-backed economic bubbles.' He added: 'We are now paying the price for unbelievable incompetence from both the Fed and the Bank of England for allowing these excesses to build.'"

The bubble in the real estate market was Greenspan's solution to the collapse of the bubble in dot-com shares—a bubble he had been responsible for inflating. As economist Paul Krugman noted back in 2002, the recession of 2001 was not a typical postwar U.S. downturn where higher inflation prompted the Fed to raise interest rates and where cheaper borrowing led to a resumption in growth once prices had been brought back under control. Instead, Krugman noted, 2001 was like pre–Second World War recessions, where America was left with a crashing hangover brought on by irrational exuberance (*The Great Unraveling*, 2003). "To fight this recession the Fed needs more than a snapback; it needs soaring household spending to offset moribund business investment. And to do this . . . Alan Greenspan needs to create a housing bubble to replace the Nasdaq bubble."

At the time, the Fed was in the middle of a sustained period of thirteen interest rate cuts. Greenspan reduced the federal funds rate to 1 percent by the middle of 2003 and held it there until the middle of 2004. Real interest rates in the U.S.—adjusted for the level of inflation—were negative from October 2002 to April 2005, a thirty-one-month period matched surpassed only once since the Second World War, the thirty-seven months between September 1974 and September 1977, when the Fed was losing the battle against inflation. Judged as a means of steering the economy out of recession, the policy was a success. The three years from 2002 to 2005 saw a marked increase in homeownership and was the time when real estate prices rose the fastest.

The expert on bubbles, Robert Shiller, argues (*The Subprime Solution*, Princeton University Press, 2008) that the effects of cheap money were amplified by the large numbers of adjustable rate mortgages pumped out after 2000, particularly to subprime borrowers, since these loans became easier to service as the Fed cut interest rates. "Adjustable rate mortgages were common because those who had been influenced by bubble thinking and wanted to get into real estate investments as heavily as possible were demanding them. The mere fact that interest payments would be going up soon did not deter them. They expected to be compensated by rapidly increasing home prices, and they believed that those higher prices would permit them to refinance at a lower rate."

Unfortunately, this process was less a case of miraculous escape than of out of the frying pan and into the fire. In the past, bear markets on Wall Street had led to falls in real estate prices. This time they were up, and at the peak of the boom were rising at an annual rate in excess of 20 percent. In previous downturns, debt burdens had fallen, but from 2000 onward mortgage lending responded to low interest rates and its growth peaked at just under 15 percent in late 2003. It continued to rise by 10 percent a year until 2006. Between 2003 and 2005 mortgage debt grew by $3.7 trillion. In just three years mortgage debt rose by as much as it had in the 214 years between the Declaration of Independence and the decision by President George H. W. Bush to send troops in 1990 to remove Saddam Hussein from Kuwait.

Debt servicing costs—the slice of income needed to pay the interest on a home loan—rose from 15.5 percent in 2000 to 18.2 percent of disposable income in the United States, and there was a similar trend in the UK. This tells only part of the story, however, since these figures include only interest payments and not the need to pay the original capital sum borrowed. This was going up as house prices rose, resulting in many borrowers opting for interest-only loans in the hope that they would be able to pay back the original loan from the capital gain on their home.

On the surface, the recovery looked impressive, although it was not as strong as those that had followed recessions in the past. Again, however, things were not quite what they seemed. Consumers were certainly spending more, but only thanks to equity withdrawal on an epic scale. People borrowed against the rising value of their homes and were, in effect, using them as ATMs. By the middle of the current decade, 10 percent of personal disposable income was coming from equity withdrawal.

It was a similar story for employment, where there was a boom in demand for construction workers, mortgage processors, and real estate agents. In all, 40 percent of new jobs in the U.S. between 2003 and 2006 were related to the property market.

Greenspan saw no problems with any of this. Giving testimony to Congress on April 17, 2002, he explained patiently why there was no chance of the dot-com bubble being replaced by a real estate bubble.

Sales in real estate incurred substantial costs. When most houses were sold the vendor had to move out. Arbitrage opportunities were more limited and while there might be bubbles they would only affect specific parts of the country. "Even if a bubble were to develop in a local market, it would not necessarily have implications for the nation as a whole."

What's more, the chairman of the Fed suggested that homeowners should stop being so timid and instead embrace the wonderful new products being dreamed up by the financial services industry. Homeowners had lost money over the past decade, by having fixed rate mortgages rather than floating rate loans, he said in a speech on "Understanding Household Debt Obligations" in February 2004. "American consumers might benefit if lenders provided greater mortgage product alternatives to the traditional fixed-rate mortgage."

Greenspan's reputation was at its zenith and so, according to one commentator, was the bubble mentality in the housing market. "The year 2004 was to the housing bubble what 1998 was to the 1990s stock market bubble: the moment in time when participants started to feel truly invincible and behaved accordingly" (William Fleckenstein, *Greenspan's Bubbles*, McGraw-Hill, 2008).

It must therefore be assumed that those who took out floating rate mortgages in 2004 did so in the belief that they were a surefire bet, since they came with the blessing of the maestro. Yet there had rarely, if ever, been a better time in the U.S. to take out fixed-rate mortgages, then at their lowest level in fifty years. Nor did mortgage payers know that Greenspan was going to make adjustable rate loans much more expensive by starting a process whereby the Fed would ratchet up interest rates in quarter-point steps at each of its next seventeen meetings.

Rising debt levels in Britain resulted in house prices tripling in the decade after 1997. As in the U.S., consumers borrowed freely against the rising value of their homes and helped spawn a rapid increase in jobs related to the housing sector. One early sign of problems ahead was that first-time buyers were priced out of the market, since they couldn't afford the high prices demanded by vendors even with the new, lax standards applied by mortgage lenders. London and the southeast, where the prices were highest, saw the most difficult conditions.

Brown's response to the housing boom in the UK was to commission a report by an outside expert. Brown was keen on reports by experts, since they allowed him to say that the decisions he was making were uninfluenced by political dogma. The reality was that most of these "independent reports" were loaded from the start. The outside "experts" were left in no doubt as to the conclusion they were supposed to reach, and if they failed to respond to the nods and winks from the Treasury, the report would quietly gather dust.

The remit for Barker's study gave the game away. She was to "conduct a review of issues underlying the lack of supply and responsiveness of housing in the UK." Brown did not want a report that might have blamed the easy availability of credit, financial deregulation, property speculation, or Britain's system of tax breaks for market pressures. He wanted a report that said the problem was caused by the barriers that planners, environmentalists, and the UK's green belt regulations, which strictly limit development around London and other big cities. Unsurprisingly, that is what Barker duly delivered.

"In the UK, the rapid growth in buy-to-let investors was playing a key role in preventing individuals trying to get on to the first rung of the property ladder. A proliferation of mortgage products geared specifically towards landlords saw the number of buy-to-let mortgages soar from 58,500 in 1998 to more than a million by 2007. Total buy-to-let lending had climbed to £122.1 billion or 10.3 percent of all mortgages outstanding. Capital-rich landlords were scooping up houses, fuelling a virtuous cycle of rising prices, falling supply and inevitably a plentiful supply of tenants, from those forced by a rising market to rent" (Graham Turner, *The Credit Crunch*, Pluto, 2008). The numbers of people living in their own homes in the UK have been falling since 2005.

The Road Not Taken: Imagining a Bubble-Free World

It is worth pausing for a moment to examine what would have happened to the U.S. and British economies in the absence of what one economist (Edward Wolff, Levy Economics Institute Working Paper no. 502) has called this "explosion of household debt." There was, of course, a simultaneous increase in public debt in both the U.S. and the UK, but a study (Turner, *Credit Crunch*) using an economic model employed by UK consultancy group Oxford Economic Forecasting found that the impact was considerable even when private sector debt alone was considered.

OEF assumed a rise in debt to disposable income levels a quarter of the increase actually seen; in the U.S., it assumed it was just under a third as big. In Britain, consumer spending would have been reduced by 8.9 percent over the decade to 2007; in the U.S. it would have been cut by 6.2 percent. Consumer prices would have been much weaker—12.5 percent lower in Britain, 17.1 percent in the U.S. Inflation would have averaged just 0.2 percent in Britain—with actual falls in the price level in some years—while in the U.S. it would have averaged 0.7 percent.

Wages would have 12.5 percent lower in the UK and 21.4 percent lower in the U.S. In Britain, property prices would have risen by a third of the increase seen; in the U.S. real estate would have risen by just over a quarter. "These numbers show quite conclusively that debt was a major factor in driving the property market, not a lack of supply, or strong economic growth per se" (Turner, *Credit Crunch*).

The increase in debt levels was not just the result of financial deregulation or policy errors. Rather, it was inextricably linked with two other strands of the New Olympian agenda—the taming of organized labor and free trade. Both the U.S. and the UK have been running increasing trade deficits over the past decade as imports from low-cost countries have jumped. In 1993, the year the U.S. signed the NAFTA treaty with Mexico and Canada, it ran a small trade surplus of $4.4 billion with its southern neighbor. By 2007, this had turned into a deficit of $75 billion. This, though, was less than a third of America's $250 billion trade deficit with China. Britain's trade deficit with China has risen from £2 billion to £14 billion in the past decade; there have also been hefty increases in imports from cheap plants set up in Eastern European countries such as the Czech Republic and Slovakia following the collapse of communism. Every category of manufacturing employment has fallen since Labour came to power, but overall employment has risen thanks to the expansion of jobs in the service sector.

The exporting of manufacturing jobs in both Britain and America has boosted profits but kept wages in check. Cheap imports have come flooding in to both countries but what Greenspan once called "the flattening of wage compensation" meant they would be left on the shelves unless consumers had a way of paying for them. There was a "squeeze on the middle classes" (Wolff, Working Paper) and if they couldn't consume more as a result of increases in their wages then the only alternative was to get them to borrow more money. By 2005, the average credit card debt of a low- and middle-income indebted households in the U.S. stood at $8,650, while one-third of families had debts in excess of $10,000. Nor was the borrowing incurred only to finance luxury items; two decades of barely rising earnings meant 71 percent of those with incomes in the lowest 20 percent of Americans said they were using plastic to buy basic living essentials or to deal with unexpected financial emergencies such as health care (Center for Responsible Lending, *The Plastic Safety Net*, October 2005).

This level of borrowing was possible not only because the New Olympians smelled a business opportunity (although they did) but also because the Chinese, the Japanese, and the Koreans had to do something with their trade surpluses. They invested the money in financial assets in the West, driving down interest rates and making borrowing cheaper and easier, at least for a while.

Greenspan, Bernanke, Brown, and Paulson were all dedicated free traders. They apparently saw no link between the investment in low-cost production and the debt bubbles that have developed in their countries. Instead, they have blamed new technology for any dislocation caused to their economies, insisting that this will be only short-term provided workers become better educated and equip themselves with new skills. In the real world, the squeeze on wages created the conditions for the asset booms in both Britain and the United States.

Retailers in the U.S. did well out of this process. Between 2001 and 2007, the U.S. economy grew by 40 percent, but the profits of retailers rose by 110 percent. Outsourcing meant that 10 percent of goods sold in Wal-Mart were from China. In the bad old days of strong unions and rising real wages, workers were able to buy the goods they produced. Outsourcing made the financial and housing bubbles necessary because generating fantasy wealth was the only way Americans and Britons could afford to maintain their spending habits.

But the ability of the U.S. and the UK to borrow was dependent on the willingness of creditor countries to lend, and eventually the appetite of foreign investors for U.S. and British assets started to wane. The dollar fell sharply in 2007, particularly after the financial crisis began, and this led to a pickup of inflationary pressure as imports became dearer. Higher inflation made it harder for policymakers to cut interest rates, and this added to the pressure on borrowers.

As Turner put it, "The great globalisation story had come full circle. Cheap imports had been a major selling point of the free trade agreements that had proliferated under the World Trade Organisation. They had been a major factor keeping inflation under control and allowing central banks to keep interest rates low, to fuel the housing bubble. Import costs were now soaring, threatening to undermine the Federal Reserve's ability to cushion the fallout from runaway house prices. Outsourcing was not quite the free lunch its proponents had suggested" (Credit Crunch).

The U.S. had been here before. There were parallels with the late 1920s, when overinvestment triggered a crisis in which workers did not earn enough to buy all the goods—radio sets, cars, vacuum cleaners—that the American economy was producing. Borrowing filled the gap. Between 1925 and 1929, U.S. consumer debt doubled. But as with the bubble of the first decade of the twenty-first century, there was little inflationary pressure in the early stages of the boom. Prices of furniture and household durables fell by 5.65 percent between 1925 and 1929.

Franklin Roosevelt's New Deal programs of the 1930s were the response to the bubble years of the 1920s, and an attempt to prevent a return to irresponsible lending. As we have shown elsewhere in this book, the New Olympians spent the first few decades after the Second World War planning their counterattack, and eventually the stagflation of the mid-1970s provided them with the perfect opportunity to strike. As William Greider noted in his book on the Federal Reserve (*Secrets of the Temple*, Simon & Schuster, 1987), the Democrats were so demoralized by the high inflation of the Jimmy Carter presidency that they supported the deregulation of banking in 1980. Greider says rightly that the Depository Institutions and Monetary Control Act proved "to be an appropriate prelude to the 1980s. The politics of deregulation accurately forecast the political preferences that would prevail in the new decade, which interests would be served and which would be pushed aside. The free-market terms established by the measure cleared the way for finance; unregulated interest rates allowed an era of unprecedented prosperity to unfold for the owners of financial wealth. Other sectors, the ones most dependent on borrowed money, housing agriculture, industrial production and labor, consumers, would absorb the consequences."

Shiller notes that the scrapping of state usury laws in 1980s made effective oversight over the subprime market crucial, since it was now possible for the originators of loans to charge high enough interest rates to cover the increase in defaults and foreclosures made inevitable by looser lending standards. "Yet the expanded regulation never came, and over time during the 1990s and into the 2000s, a 'shadow banking system' of nonbank mortgage originators was allowed to develop without anything like the regulation to which banks are subject" (*Subprime Solution*).

For a time, this did not seem to matter. In America, the baby boomer generation bought the liberation mantra peddled by a troika of policy makers, Wall Street, and bubblevision TV stations such as CNBC, where bulls were twenty times as likely to be invited to air their views as were bears. Technology also played its part, since the new breed of day traders could sit hunched over their computer screens, confident in the belief that they were fully in command of their own financial destiny. There was a cauldron of bubbling ingredients ready to come to the boil. William McChesney Martin, one of Greenspan's predecessors as Fed chairman in the 1950s and 1960s, once argued that it was the duty of the central bank to take away the punch bowl just at the moment the party was starting to swing; Greenspan's approach was to add a few extra jiggers of high-grade hooch and give the punch bowl a vigorous stir.

Fleckenstein is particularly scathing about the emergency cut in interest rates in October 1998. This was a period when Russia's debt default had led to the enforced Fed-orchestrated bailout of the hedge fund Long Term Capital Management. The Fed had already cut rates by a quarter point the previous month and the stock market, despite its declines since July, was up on the year by 3.5 percent. The minutes of the meeting show that no convincing case was put for action, but at Greenspan's behest the FOMC cut rates anyway. The "Greenspan put," the notion that the Fed would place a floor under the stock market whenever it ran into trouble, was born. Fleckstein calls this decision "one of the most irresponsible acts in the history of the Federal Reserve."

Greenspan ruled out actions by the Fed that might have stopped the bubble inflating. The Fed had the power, under the 1934 Securities and Exchange Act, to regulate broker loans—or margin debt—that were used to buy shares. Speculators were able to borrow up to 50 percent of the value of their stock purchases, and by early 2000 it stood at $265 billion—an increase of 45 percent in four months and its highest since the Wall Street crash of 1929. Greenspan insisted in testimony to Congress that tightening margin requirements would have no impact on share prices.

Such masterly inactivity was, of course, entirely consistent with Greenspan's lop-sided logic that nothing could or should be done to dampen Wall Street's spirits in the good times, but it was then the duty of the central bank to act as a grand soup kitchen to high finance when the bubbles burst. The stock market collapse of 2000 brought inflation down sharply and the Fed, fearing that America faced a period of deflation similar to that seen in Japan in the 1990s, panicked.

It cut interest rates a total of thirteen times, bringing them down in successive steps from 6.5 percent to 1 percent. Even *The Economist*, the house journal of the New Olympians, was censorious. In September 2002 the magazine criticized Greenspan for acting as cheerleader for the new economy. "Even if some of the increase in productivity growth was real, his enthusiasm contributed to investors' euphoria. Ironically, Mr Greenspan was among the first to give warning of a bubble in 1996, drawing attention to the market's irrational exuberance. What a pity he failed to put America's monetary policy where his mouth (briefly) was."

Brown's oft repeated repugnance for the economics of boom and bust obviously did not extend to what his mentor was doing in the U.S. The thirteen interest rate cuts were the answer to the destruction of paper wealth equivalent to more than the annual disposable income of the U.S. The seventeen increases in the Fed funds rate—started by Greenspan and completed by Bernanke—were necessary to control the bubble in the housing market that resulted from all the cheap money sloshing round the economy. And just as the bubble in the housing market was even bigger than the bubble in the stock market, so the bust was bigger too.

James Galbraith noted (Milton Friedman Distinguished Lecture, Marietta College, Ohio, March 2008) that in August 2007 the Fed was at the crest of an "aggressive tightening" under way since late 2004, aimed at the increasingly problematical task of preempting inflation while averting recession.

Crisis '07: The Bursting of Bubble World

Back in the summer of 2006, Bernanke was clear that his priority was to prevent the debt-financed expansion from pushing up the cost of living. "The recent rise in inflation is of concern to the FOMC [the Fed's open market committee]. . . . The Federal Reserve must guard against the emergence of an inflationary psychology that could impart greater persistence to what would otherwise be a transitory increase in inflation."

By February 2007 he was warming to his theme, noting, "The FOMC again indicated that its predominant policy concern is the risk that inflation will fail to ease as expected." Less than a month before "Debtonation Day" on August 9, 2007, he noted (July 19, 2007): "With the level of resource utilization relatively high and with a sustained moderation in inflation pressures yet to be convincingly demonstrated, the FOMC has consistently stated that upside risks to inflation are its predominant policy concern."

Like Greenspan, Bernanke was gung-ho for developments in the financial sector. "Technological advances have dramatically transformed the provision of financial services in our economy. Notably, increasingly sophisticated information technologies enable lenders to collect and process data necessary to evaluate and price risk much more efficiently than in the past."

This was May 23, 2006, when mortgage brokers were crisscrossing America in search for a new wave of suckers ready to take out a "liar" or a "Ninja" loan (famously so called because the borrower had no income, no job, and no assets). The chairman of the Fed was blissfully unaware of what was happening, noting in the authentic voice of the classic New Olympian, "Market competition among financial providers for the business of informed consumers is, in my judgment, the best mechanism for promoting the provision of better, lower cost financial products." No need, obviously, for all those tiresome New Deal regulations that might throw sand in the wheels of the market. Education for consumers rather than control over lenders was Bernanke's answer to those who worried that some subprime borrowers might be getting in over their heads.

On February 14, Bernanke said, "Despite the ongoing adjustments in the housing sector, overall economic prospects remain good. Overall, the U.S. economy seems likely to expand at a moderate pace this year and next, with growth strengthening somewhat as the drag from housing diminishes."

By late March he was less bullish, but only slightly. "Delinquency rates on variable-interest loans to subprime borrowers, which account for a bit less than 10 percent of all mortgages outstanding, have climbed sharply in recent months." But not to worry, because "at this juncture, however, the impact on the broader economy and financial markets of the problems in the subprime market seems likely to be constrained."

Eventually Bernanke started to realize that something might be happening outside the temple. On July 19, 2007, he noted that "in recent weeks, we have also seen increased concerns about credit risks on some other types of financial instruments." To take a military analogy, this is a bit like the Russians failing to work out that Hitler was about to invade in June 1941 until they heard the Panzers revving up on the other side of the border.

And when it did become clear what was happening, the New Olympian policymakers reacted with precisely the same mixture of horror, anger, and disbelief displayed by Stalin when he found that he had been betrayed by his supposed ally and taken for a sucker. For them there was the belated realization that the strong growth they had enjoyed for so long was in large part an optical illusion. The freeing of the financial interest had unleashed a tidal bore of asset stripping and "creative destruction" ("destructive destruction" would be closer to the mark) on productive economic assets. But the plunge in living standards that would normally be associated with this pillaging and ransacking could be held at bay by the very same financial interests extending large amounts of credit to the public, much of it secured on houses. In this way, a country can live well beyond its means (as seen in the current account figures for both the U.S. and the UK), as can its government (as seen in the figures for the budget deficit), because tax revenue is inflated by debt-generated economic activity.

High home prices were essential to maintaining this illusion of prosperity, particularly as growth in earnings had been subdued for years. But as storm clouds were gathering over the housing market, a climatic depression had already settled on growth in the standard of living. In the U.S., the biannual State of Working America (Economic Policy Institute, September 2008) concluded that the business cycle which started in 2001 had proved to be a record breaker for all the wrong reasons. For the first time on record, middle-class families were at the end of a recovery without having regained the ground they lost during the previous recession. "Gross domestic product and historically high productivity growth should have raised paychecks up and down the income ladder, but instead the benefits of that growth have bypassed most of the people who made it possible."

For the rich, life had not been as good since the 1920s. Three-quarters of the gains from Greenspan's last hurrah went to 1 percent of taxpayers. They saw 11 percent real income growth, while the other 99 percent got less than 1 percent, massive debts, and real estate crashing in value. As *The Economist* noted (July 2008), a Gallup poll found that nearly seven out of ten Americans thought wealth should be distributed more evenly, the highest fraction since the question was first asked in 1984. There was good reason for this: real median household income had fallen since 1999 and labor's share of the national cake had got smaller.

It was a similar story in Britain. Earnings had long been under downward pressure, but consumer borrowing had taken up the slack, borrowing often fueled by rising house prices. At this stage, those uninitiated in the double-speak (and, indeed, treble-speak) of the "miracle economy" seen in the United States and Britain in the 1990s and the 2000s may have spotted that the "stability" so prized by Greenspan and Brown relied on a number of highly unstable factors all supporting each other.

Thus the economy depended to a large extent on consumer spending, which in turn depended on consumer borrowing. That borrowing was underpinned by high house prices, which allowed homeowners to raise money against the part of their property's value that was unencumbered by a mortgage.

Obviously this slice of the value grew with the growth of house prices generally, which in turn depended on high levels of mortgage borrowing. So one type of borrowing essential to economic growth, mortgage equity withdrawal, ultimately depended on another type of borrowing, mortgages raised for house purchase. The same people tend to be engaged in both sorts of borrowing, and the borrowing has to be officially encouraged because otherwise the economy would shudder to a halt. But, as with the tightrope walker, the indebted public must never be allowed to look down, and infusions of cheap money were intended to ensure that they did not. Nor must there be much by way of questioning the thinking behind this self-validating spiral of mortgage and consumer debt. Any answer was likely to run along the lines that consumer borrowing is "secured on home equity withdrawal" and that home equity withdrawal was itself made possible by higher house prices. As, indeed, are high levels of mortgage borrowing; these were "secured on the asset side," that is, on the same inflated prices that the "secured" mortgage borrowing made possible in the first place.

In other words, the circularity of the whole business was rather like the fabled perpetual motion machine of yesteryear. Rising asset prices supported increased borrowing, which supported economic growth and rising asset prices. These rising asset prices supported yet more borrowing, which supported more economic growth and even higher house prices. Everything ran smoothly as long as consumers kept borrowing ever more money against ever more expensive houses while spending some part of the notional real estate profits on goods and services. Before long the average property would cost dizzying multiples of the average wage, so to keep people buying at ever higher prices required even lower interest rates.

Liberalized finance packaged up the fact of subdued earnings and unfulfilled aspirations into a booming mortgage and consumer finance industry. For some time, this giant extension of credit to the general public provided a substitute for real prosperity. Politicians, for whom a sense of history is, like reading, very much an optional extra these days, concluded that financial liberalization had "worked." They slapped their thighs in merriment at the recollection of how things used to be, when governments tried to control capital.

Everyone was better off now. The proof of the pudding, surely, is in the eating? Wall Street and the City did not disabuse them. But like any drug, liberalized finance wreaked more damage with every dose. Thus easy credit sucked in more cheap imports. It inflated the value of property, thus bloating this "asset class" at the expense of productive investment. It made vast amounts of money available for "private equity" operations (asset stripping), damaging further the productive sector of the economy. Above all, the financial sector insisted that economic policy in general and monetary policy in particular remained geared to its own needs, with interest rates always supportive of inflated asset prices.

Politicians, convinced that all this "prosperity" was the fruit of their own foresight in freeing the financial interests, have it drummed into them (not that it would seem to need much drumming) that the worst thing they could do would be to tamper with the New Olympians of Lower Manhattan and London's Canary Wharf.

From the summer of 2007, the Fed under Bernanke tried to get the perpetual motion machine working again. Fed fund rates were brought down from 5.25 percent to 2 percent between the fall of 2007 and the spring of 2008 in an attempt to revive borrowing and lending. The initial results were disappointing; the U.S. economy contracted in the fourth quarter of 2007 and only posted a recovery in the spring of 2008 because the weakness of the dollar helped exports and consumer spending was temporarily increased by $150 billion of tax cuts.

In the spring of 2008 there was a sharp fall in the growth of the U.S. money supply and of credit. "The demand for loans is not there, nor are banks willing to extend credit even if it were. If this weakness becomes entrenched over the Autumn, it is a clear signal of very weak US output growth in 2009" (Gabriel Stein, Lombard Street Research, August 18, 2008). "A slowdown caused by households and financial companies taking on too much debt cannot end by them taking on more debt. Both these sectors will have to go through a process of deleveraging before the economy will turn up again" (Stein, Lombard Street Research).

The spring and summer of 2008 also saw a marked increase in delinquency rates on both consumer and commercial loans as the financial crisis spread from the subprime sector to the rest of the economy. For a time, it appeared, consumers had sought to load extra debt onto their credit cards in order to maintain the spending habits built up over the previous fifteen years. But as one economist noted, this was not sustainable. "As consumers increasingly 'max out,' and with the fiscal stimulus package no longer supporting retail activity or confidence, a further slowdown in the real economy looks likely to intensify pressures on the US financial sector" (Rob Carnell, ING

Bank, August 21, 2008). If anything, the credit crunch was getting worse. The Fed conducts regular surveys of senior loan officers at lending institutions; the message in the summer of 2008 was that what had started as a squeeze on mortgages had spread to all forms of household and corporate borrowing.

The Bank of England took a somewhat tougher line in the UK, allowing small reductions in its policy rate when the financial markets were at their most jittery in the winter of 2007–2008 but then holding steady in the face of rising inflationary pressure. The upshot was, however, similar in both countries: a collapsing housing bubble, debt deflation, and recession.

The one member of the Bank of England's Monetary Policy Committee to call the UK economy correctly was David Blanchflower, who commuted from his home in New Hampshire for the meetings in London that set interest rates. Blanchflower, from an early stage in the financial crisis, warned that—just as with rock and roll, shopping malls, and drive-in fast food restaurants—Britain would get what America had, after a short delay. In the U.S., Blanchflower said, the problems in the subprime mortgage market had set off a four-phase chain reaction through the rest of the economy. The first phase of the crisis in the U.S. lasted from January 2006 to April 2007, a period that predated the August 2007 freezing up of financial markets but saw the housing market start to slow from its peak and monthly falls in house prices start to appear. In the second phase, between May and August 2007, there were bigger falls in real estate prices, and hefty declines in housing starts and permits to build. Consumer confidence weakened and jobs became harder to find.

By September 2007, average hourly earnings growth and consumption started to slow against a backdrop of even steeper declines in house prices and real estate activity. The start of 2008 saw a fourth phase, with the previous slowing in the rate of growth of nonfarm payrolls turning into falls in employment, retail sales, house prices, and spending on big-ticket items. Mortgage defaults and foreclosures rose rapidly.

"I believe there are a number of similarities between the UK and the United States which suggest that in the UK we are also going to see a substantial decline in growth, a pick-up in unemployment, little if any growth in real wages, declining consumption growth driven primarily by significant declines in house prices. The credit crunch is starting to hit and hit hard."

By the late summer of 2008, Blanchflower's fears appeared fully vindicated. The housing market had peaked in the summer of 2007, with small monthly rises in house prices turning into falls of well over 1 percent a month by the spring of 2008. Consumer confidence fell sharply and unemployment started to rise. Growth in the UK came to a halt in the second quarter of 2008, ending an uninterrupted period of expansion stretching back to 1992. The annual growth rate—a vigorous 3.3 percent in the summer of 2007—had slipped to 1.4 percent. As one economist (Paul Dales, Capital Economics, August 19, 2008) noted, on every occasion since 1955 when the UK economy had slowed to a growth rate of 1.5 percent or below, the next quarter had witnessed either a sharp recovery or an outright recession. Dales said the economy was like a jet aircraft: it needed to maintain a minimum air speed or it stalled.

This, then, was the legacy of Greenspan and Brown. The chancellor of the exchequer had arranged for the chairman of the U.S. central bank to be granted the freedom of the City of London in 2002, an honor dating back to the Middle Ages that conferred the privilege of herding sheep across London Bridge. There were those who argued that had Greenspan chosen to be a herdsman rather than a central banker, the U.S. would have gorged itself to death one year, starved the next. And all the time, of course, getting a little bit deeper into debt, a little more like Britain on its descent from pioneer of the Industrial Revolution to economic also-ran within half a century.

The risks were aptly summed up Paul Craig Roberts, assistant secretary of the Treasury under Ronald Reagan. Roberts compared America to Britain during the Second World War, when it was forced to borrow heavily to finance military spending. He accused the Bush administration of fiscal irresponsibility and said the nation's creditors saw a "deluded country that acts as if it is a privilege for foreigners to lend to it, and a deluded country that believes foreigners will continue to accumulate U.S. debt until the end of time. The fact of the matter is that the U.S. is bankrupt."

He cited a report to Congress from comptroller general David Walker that stated that the federal government did not maintain effective internal control over financial reporting (including safeguarding assets) and compliance with significant laws and regulations. "In everyday language, the U.S. government cannot pass an audit" (Peace and Justice Center, peaceandjustice.org).

CHAPTER 7

Here There Be Monsters

The Perils Lurking in the Uncharted Waters of the Financial Markets

Speculation is the romance of trade, and casts contempt upon all its sober realities. It renders the stock-jobber a magician, and the Exchange a region of enchantment. It elevates the merchant into a kind of knight-errant, or rather a commercial Quixote. The slow but sure gains of snug percentage become despicable in his eyes; no "operation" is thought worthy of attention that does not double or treble the investment. No business is worth following that does not promise an immediate fortune.

— WASHINGTON IRVING,
A Time of Unexampled Prosperity

"I'm in capital markets. I arrange swaps."

"Swaps?" The word reminded her of Basil when he was her kid brother, a gangling boy in scuffed shoes and a stained blazer, sorting conkers or gloating over his stamp collection.

"Yes. Suppose a corporate has borrowed x thousands at a fixed rate of interest. If they think that interest rates are going to fall, they could execute a swap transaction whereby we pay them a fixed rate and they pay us LIBOR, that's the London Interbank Offered Rate, which is variable."

— DAVID LODGE, *Nice Work*

Speculation is a round game: the players see little or nothing of their cards at first starting; gains may be great—and so may losses. The run of luck went against Mr Nickleby; a mania prevailed, a bubble burst, four stock brokers took villa residences at Florence, four hundred nobodies were ruined, and among them Mr Nickleby.

—CHARLES DICKENS, *Nicholas Nickleby*

With the benefit of hindsight, it is clear that the bubble went through four distinct phases. In the first phase, there was a change in the economic climate caused by financial innovation. Asset prices rose as a result, and with good reason. In the second phase, overseas speculators noticed what was happening and demanded a piece of the action, driving up prices still further. In the third phase, all ideas of basing investment decisions on economic rationality were dispensed with as buyers assumed they would always be able to sell for a higher price. Finally, and inevitably, there was a collapse caused by the unwinding of speculative positions prompted by the tightening of credit.

If it all seems familiar, then it also would have been to Isaac Newton, Daniel Defoe, and Robert Walpole. For this was how economic historians summed up the conditions that led to the South Sea bubble crisis of 1720. The story of the past three centuries is the story of how little life has changed. Financial markets are endlessly innovative, always coming up with new money-making ideas. The public is eternally credulous, suspicious only in the immediate aftermath of a crash, but soon convinced by those selling tulips, shares in railroads, dot-com stock, or real estate that "it is different this time."

Historians would counter that this is the triumph of hope over experience, and that financial markets eventually realize as much. One sure sign that a bubble is about to burst is when financial commentators start to warn that "it is different this time," the five most dangerous words in the lexicon of markets. At that point, they dust down their history books and find that futures trading was common in the tulip mania that convulsed the Netherlands in the first half of the seventeenth century, that financial engineering was key to the fortunes of the South Sea Company, and that widespread insider trading and crooked share tipping were revealed in the financial postmortem examination conducted after the Wall Street crash.

In the end, little changes. The coffee houses become Internet cafés, the powdered wigs become Armani suits, and the millions become trillions; but the song remains the same. Just like most of the companies that saw their shares ramped up in the dot-com boom of the late 1990s, the South Sea Company did little actual trading and made no profits. Like so much of the New Olympians' financial system, the South Sea bubble was inflated less by any sort of hardheaded analysis by investors as by a quasi-mystical faith. And as with most of the financial crises of the past quarter-century, the South Sea bubble had an international dimension: stock markets in Paris, Amsterdam, Lisbon, and Hamburg were affected when the shares collapsed. And just as with the buildup to the 2007–2008 credit crunch, the South Sea bubble originated in a novel form of financing—converting government debt into equity in the South Sea Company in return for a monopoly on trade with South America—that seemed to offer risk-free returns for all involved.

And, just as today, there was no shortage of commentators in eighteenth-century London who insisted that lessons needed to be learned from the speculative madness. This, for example, was Adam Anderson, the first historian of the South Sea bubble, writing in 1764. "The unaccountable frenzy in stocks and projects of this year 1720 may by some be thought to have taken up too much room in this work; but we are persuaded that others of superior judgement, will approve of the perpetuating . . . the remembrance thereof, as a warning to after ages" (quoted in Richard Dale, *The First Crash*, Princeton University Press, 2004).

Alan Greenspan expressed similar sentiments when he gave evidence to Congress following the collapse of the dot-com boom at the turn of the millennium. "At root was the rapid enlargement of stock-market capitalizations in the latter part of the 1990s that arguably engendered an outsized increase in opportunities for avarice. Our historical guardians of financial information were overwhelmed."

Warming to his theme, Greenspan sought to reassure senators by insisting that the weeds had been pulled up and that everything in the garden was rosy once again. "Perhaps the recent breakdown of protective barriers resulted from a once-in-a-generation frenzy of speculation that is now over. With profitable opportunities for malfeasance markedly diminished, far fewer questionable practices are likely to be initiated in the immediate future" (Alan Greenspan, testimony before the Senate Committee on Banking, Housing, and Urban Affairs, July 16, 2002).

Greenspan was wrong on two counts. First, the dot-com frenzy was far from a one-off. Since his arrival at the Federal Reserve there had been the global stock crash of 1987, the Japanese financial and real estate bubble of the early 1990s when, according to unsubstantiated reports, the land occupied by the imperial palace in Tokyo was worth more than the whole of California, and the various bubbles in the developing economies in the 1990s. These last had seen a speculative frenzy as foreign capital flooded into and then out of Thailand, Malaysia, South Korea, and elsewhere. In the UK, the boom of the late 1980s was reaching its peak just as Chairman Greenspan was getting his feet under the desk, marked by soaring prices for residential and commercial property, ludicrous overvaluation of business assets, and feverish demand for art, antiques, and collectibles. In the U.S., deregulation of the country's mortgage banks, the savings and loan institutions, in the 1980s paved the way for a disaster that cost the U.S. government about $200 billion. The S&Ls (or thrifts) had been hit by high interest rates and high inflation, both of which eroded the value of mortgages advanced in quieter times. "Reform" removed controls on interest rates and investments; stupidity and sometimes outright fraud were among the results.

For Greenspan, the words "once in a generation" appeared to have a different meaning from the dictionary definition. Unless, that is, Greenspan was referring to a more than averagely long-lived insect of some kind. For "once in a generation," read "every few years."

Even were a casuist to point out that the 1987 crash was not really the result of a bubble and that all the other examples of frenzied behavior had taken place beyond the shores of the United States, as he spoke to Congress in the summer of 2002, Greenspan's Fed was ensuring that the American housing market would see many "profitable opportunities for malfeasance."

Given that he has been a strong supporter of the deregulation of financial markets on his watch, it is perhaps unsurprising that Greenspan believes that crises are the result of individual wrongdoing rather than system failure. Not all chroniclers of bubbles agree with this interpretation, even in instances where there has been bountiful evidence of both cupidity and fraud. Historian Larry Neal (in *The Rise of Financial Capitalism: International Capital Markets in the Age of Reason*, Cambridge University Press, 1990) says the South Sea bubble appeared "to be a tale less about the perpetual folly of mankind and more about the continual difficulties of the adjustments of financial markets to an array of innovations." This book has much to say about the "perpetual folly of mankind" and also the dubious dealings of those who would exploit that folly. In this chapter, however, we will try to explain in simple language the "array of innovations" that made possible the 2007–2008 subprime mortgage crisis and liquidity crunch.

No housing market is ever entirely rational. In the absence of not only unlimited development land but of unlimited development land near places of employment and general amenity, there are bound to be short-run booms and busts. This is as true in a relatively empty country, such as the United States, as in a relatively crowded country, such as Britain. What ought to keep such a market in trim is a fairly steady supply of money for house purchase rationed out on a reasonably unchanging set of criteria, in terms of the multiples of salary the lenders are prepared to make available, the quality of property against which they are prepared to lend, and so forth. Those unable to obtain housing finance have traditionally departed that particular housing market, heading either for the rental sector, for accommodation with family or friends, or even for a cheaper area. This may sound harsh, but almost nobody in any country is living in their absolute first choice of house, or location—or both. And, as we shall see, the alternative was to prove less than impressive.

The selling of subprime mortgages was a classic New Olympian project that involved all the various chapters of the organization. Central banks, ratings agencies, investment banks, hedge funds, the financial media—all were fully implicated in the manufacture of the new products.

What happened was this. At the very start of the process, a family in the United States decided to buy a home and went looking for a mortgage. Some of these people were already homeowners and had mortgages that were small in relation to the value of their property. These people, most of whom were also in full-time, well-paid employment, are known as prime borrowers who are at very low risk of defaulting on their loans. Another group of prospective buyers were not so well placed financially; they tended to be first-time buyers and so had no equity in existing property. They were also more likely to be in part-time employment and often on low wages, even assuming they were in work at all. This group was known as subprime borrowers, and loans extended to this section of the public were obviously riskier than those provided to prime borrowers.

On the face of it, this presented a problem for the American real estate sector, since it needed a supply of first-time buyers to keep the market humming. Without first-time buyers, property markets seize up, because those higher up the ladder cannot move to new homes unless a new entrant forms the first rung in the chain. This, in turn, cools down the rise in house prices, which in turn shrinks the potential size of the assets on which the lending is secured, making such loans less attractive to lenders.

Fortunately help was at hand, in terms of throwing the gears of the housing market out of neutral or even reverse and into overdrive. The U.S. way of managing home-loan finance had moved on since the days when small town bankers had operated their 3-6-3 model (take in deposits at 3 percent, lend out on mortgages at 6 percent, hit the golf course by 3:00 P.M.). In the new world, the real estate industry would sign up a subprime borrower with an attractive-looking introductory offer and then sell the loan to an investment bank.

Investment banks were happy to do this, because they could bundle up mortgages of varying qualities into securities that could be traded in the financial markets. This was a process known as securitization, with the securities given the ugly name of collateralized debt obligations (CDOs). Everybody was a winner: the subprime borrowers got their mortgages and hence a foot on the housing ladder; the rest of the home-owning population saw the breakneck pace of activity in the real estate market maintained, with prices rising strongly as a result; the real estate brokers picked up fat commissions; and Wall Street found itself with a new and lucrative means of speculation ideal for an environment in which low interest rates had made returns on safe investments such as government bonds extremely low.

The International Monetary Fund, given the role of acting like the Oracle at Delphi for this new offering from the Olympian heroes, purred with pleasure, noting that deregulation and technological advances had revolutionized financial systems in the developed world.

"The changes that have occurred in financial systems have transformed the opportunities for borrowing and saving facing households and firms," it said in its October 2006 World Economic Outlook. Households now had a broader array of borrowing options to choose from and could invest in a wider range of financial instruments. Firms were no longer so dependent on banks for their financing because they were able to raise bonds on the world's capital markets. Banks too were changing the way they made their money, moving away from simply taking deposits and lending money to activities for which they could charge fees, such as the securitization of loans.

All this was one aspect of Washington economist Thomas Palley's financialization concept. In a paper in December 2007, he defined it thus:

> Financialization is a process whereby financial markets, financial institutions, and financial élites gain greater influence over economic policy and economic outcomes. Financialization transforms the functioning of economic systems at both the macro and micro levels.
>
> Its principal impacts are to (1) elevate the significance of the financial sector relative to the real sector, (2) transfer income from the real sector to the financial sector, and (3) increase income inequality and contribute to wage stagnation. Additionally, there are reasons to believe that financialization may put the economy at risk of debt deflation and prolonged recession.

> Financialization operates through three different conduits: changes in the structure and operation of financial markets, changes in the behaviour of non-financial corporations, and changes in economic policy. (*Financialization: What It Is and Why It Matters*, Levy Economics Institute and Economics for Democratic and Open Societies, 2007.)

A final sting in the tail of financialization—a final absurdity, in fact—has been the creation of financial instruments that give a creditor a vested interest in the failure of a company that owes them money. These are the credit default swaps (CDS), a type of insurance policy on a piece of lending, usually issued by a bank, which can be traded on the open market.

In any attempt to restructure a troubled company, most creditors will be prepared to write off some of what they are owed in order to get the firm back on its feet. But CDS holders are better off if the company goes bust, because this will trigger repayment of what is owed under the terms of the CDS. Alongside the CDS are more straightforward debt securities that give creditors first refusal of a company's assets in the event of a liquidation. As with the CDS, this can give a creditor an incentive to block a rescue and means a fifth column can be present at business restructuring meetings.

Tally-Ho! The Hunt for Yield

As is clear from the IMF's above-mentioned encomium to the new world financial order, subprime mortgages were merely one in a range of what were described as "innovative financial products" aimed at both households and companies. Since the creation of the Eurodollar market in London in the late 1960s—which took dollars held in sleepy accounts outside the U.S. and bundled them into higher-earning loans—the New Olympians had sought ways of making money "work harder," to use the cliché beloved of financial advertising. But by the early 2000s, there was a new urgency to their efforts. The joint effect of the dot-com crash, the September 11 attacks on New York and Washington, and the continuing doldrums in Japan was to predispose central bankers to keep official interest rates at very low levels. They were further encouraged to do so by the downward pressure on the price of consumer goods exerted by the exports of developing countries, chiefly China.

The Olympians may have preached price stability but they profited from high inflation. True, as Margaret Thatcher's Tories had pointed out in the 1970s, high inflation was bad for savings. According to the 2003 Barclays Equity Gilt Study from the eponymous bank, £100 parked with a building society in January 1975 would have shown a "real" (i.e., inflation-adjusted) value of just £92 by the end of December 1980. But it was much kinder to share prices and other paper assets. Over the same six years, £100 invested in shares would have risen in real terms to £132—and that figure includes all shares, the duds as well as the winners, so the higher-risk, higher-reward argument does not really apply.

Furthermore, even low-risk government stock outperformed savings; £100-worth of gilts in January 1975 would have become £108 by the end of 1980.

High inflation has the effect of silently redistributing wealth from some people and giving it to others. In the 1970s, members of those trade unions with powerful bargaining positions were held up as winners, and pensioners on fixed incomes as losers. Less noted was the "winner" status of those holding shares and other securities. In the opening years of the new century, however, the New Olympians were granted what they (or at least their apologists in academia and the media) had claimed they had wanted all along: low inflation and low interest rates.

The bubble of money puffed up by Alan Greenspan and his central bankers had to be invested somewhere. By keeping interest rates low and letting banks use their fractional reserve powers to create money out of thin air, central banks generated huge amounts of cash. This poured into safer investments, such as government securities, so returns, naturally, fell. Great rafts of capital roamed the world, looking for above-average rewards. What the Bank of England was to refer to repeatedly as "the search for yield," sometimes known as the "hunt for yield," was under way in earnest.

In many cases, companies that would have gone bust in normal times were able to refinance themselves, sometimes more than once.

It is a sobering thought that some of the high-profile casualties of the dot-com collapse, such as Clickmango or boo.com, might still be with us had they hit trouble a year or two later than they did. In some cases, the money bubble bankrolled "private equity investors" to take over and then asset-strip companies that had previously been listed on one or more stock markets. In other cases this flood of cheap money was bundled up into loans—for both consumer and house purchase purposes—to people who were quite likely to have difficulty in meeting the repayments. This was the infamous subprime lending.

What these and other investment types have in common is that they are, by definition, more risky than gilt-edged stock or blue-chip shares. In the hunt for yield, investors, such as fund managers or offshore hedge funds, could not be choosers. To top up their returns in a climate of very low yields, they needed to assume more risk. Indeed, the very act of making the higher-yielding investment would bring the risk into existence. For example, imagine a person with a poor credit history and a patchy employment record applying for a home loan in 1970, or 1980, or even 1995. As they would almost certainly be refused, the file would be closed and there would be no continuing implications for the lender.

But should this application be accepted, the lender is taking onto its books, along with the potential reward of this higher-yielding (because riskier) home loan, the potential risk of default. In an absolutely rational world, the overall financial position of the lender would be unchanged, because the default risk would cancel out the yield potential. Only when the home loan had run its course (or gone into default) would it be possible to figure out whether it had proved a good bet. Even then, assuming the lender made a very large number of such loans, the yield on these loans overall ought to adjust itself to the default risk.

Markets and prices are not, of course, absolutely (or even approximately) rational. In the real world, impaired borrowers of all types—corporate and individual—could probably be persuaded to pay even more above the odds than usual for the privilege of borrowing money, thus bolstering the lenders' real-term yields, at least until some sharp competitors turned up. This over-the-odds cost for poorer borrowers is not affected by the ultra-low rates on which many of them were tempted to take out subprime mortgages, as those rates applied only to the earlier part of the life of the loan. Over its whole life, the borrower would be expected to pay at least enough to reflect in full the risk that they represented.

That said, life would be a lot easier for the lenders if all that risk could simply be made to disappear. Happily, some of the brightest minds in the City, Wall Street, and elsewhere had been perfecting precisely this sort of disappearing trick for at least two decades.

Looked at from one angle, the whole history of financial institutions is that of trying to secure the rewards of a particular investment while passing the risk of that investment to someone else. Put another way, they pursue the rewards that come from risky position taking (of which declaring a buying or selling price is the preeminent example) with the security that comes from simply earning fees. You could call this a creative dynamic, or you could call it something less complimentary. For decades, the principal means of achieving this was the so-called greater fool method, whereby institutions would routinely sell overpriced assets either directly to individual investors or to pooled investment funds such as pension schemes, unit trusts, savings plans, and so forth. By the time the fruit reaches the general public, it has been pretty well sucked dry.

But from the 1980s onward, new, intricate forms of financial engineering seemed to promise something far less crude than this sort of pump-and-dump activity in terms of getting the risk to disappear while hanging on to the rewards. So-called derivative products had been available in the commodity markets for years, allowing producers such as farmers, mining firms, and oil companies to "hedge" their risks by selling future production at a price fixed in the present. By the early 1990s, however, homely and wholesome activity of this type was only about 2 percent or less of a derivatives market that had ballooned into a vast, speculative card game.

Derivatives come in two forms: futures (which confer the obligation to buy or sell a commodity or financial asset at a fixed point in the future) and options (which confer the right to buy or sell a commodity or financial asset at a fixed point in the future). Because options, unlike futures, allow holders simply to walk away should prices move against them, they are more expensive than futures. That said, in the overwhelming majority of cases neither futures nor options contracts ever run to actual delivery of the specified commodity or security; in the market there are enough equal and opposite contracts to cancel them out. It is simply gambling.

Collateralized debt obligations are not, strictly speaking, derivative products. But they emerged from the same financial-engineering industry and radiate the same reassuring sense that risk can be almost infinitely dissipated while the rewards can be pocketed. They, like derivatives, are premised on the idea that breaking something up into the right-shaped pieces or slices will increase its value and diminish its riskiness. CDOs are an example of the other great invention of the financial engineers—securitization.

This is one of those words that sounds reassuring, deriving as it does from the word "security." But it describes something that is anything but. It covers the process whereby a large number of IOUs, all of which are slightly different from one another, can be rolled up into one monster IOU and sold on the capital markets. One example is hire-purchase loans, the income stream of which can be sold to major investors, provided enough loans are aggregated to make the sums involved worthwhile.

Another example is mortgages. In the U.S., Salomon Brothers pioneered the trading of mortgage-backed securities. Thus Salomon was ideally placed when, in October 1981, a change in American law saw the country's savings and loan institutions (the so-called thrifts responsible for much mortgage lending) offload $1 trillion of home loans on the capital market. As former Salomon employee Michael Lewis recorded, the thrifts were in deep trouble after U.S. interest rates shot up in 1979 because the thrifts were restricted in the rates they themselves could charge. So Congress changed both the tax and accounting rules to allow them to offload their now unprofitable mortgages to Wall Street and other investors and to replace them with new ones, more profitably priced.

As Lewis noted, it "amounted to a massive subsidy to Wall Street from Congress. Long live motherhood and home ownership!" (*Liar's Poker*, Hodder & Stoughton, 1989).

Perhaps ironically, Salomon's top mortgage trader, Lewis Ranieri, became convinced his activities had something to do with spreading the benefits of home ownership, putting big finance on the side of the little person. He was not to be the last to plug this theme.

Lewie Ranieri, formerly of the Salomon Brothers' mail room and utility bond trading desk, had become the champion of the American homeowner. It was a far more appealing persona than that of the slick, profiteering Wall Street trader.

"Lewie had this spiel about building homes for America," says Bob Dall [a colleague at Salomon Brothers]. "When we'd come out of those meetings, I'd say, 'C'mon, you don't think anyone believes that crap do you?' But that was what made Ranieri so convincing. He believed that crap."

Ranieri was perhaps the first populist in the history of Wall Street. (Lewis, *Liar's Poker*.)

Alas, it was not long before the forerunner of the CDO financial engineers arrived. "The nature of the trader changed," says longtime mortgage bond salesman Samuel Sachs. "They wheeled in rocket scientists, who started to carve up mortgage securities into itty bitty pieces" (Lewis, *Liar's Poker*).

Yes, indeed.

Regardless of the source of the income stream—mortgages, hire-purchase debt, student loans, or, in one celebrated case, ten years' worth of revenues from the first twenty-five albums of the singer David Bowie—securitization involves taking the debt off the books of the originating institution (such as a mortgage lender), putting it together with a large number of similar debts, and selling it on to an institution or individual unconnected with the original transaction.

Securitization, according to the IMF, was a good thing. It allowed the "unbundling" of financial risks, which could be "repackaged" into portfolios of financial instruments and transferred to investors willing to assume such risks.

Here, in a nutshell, is the justification not only for CDOs and securitization, but also for derivatives and for most of the other exotic financial products that have proliferated in recent years. They are said to relieve workaday businesses of the risks involved in recovering what they are owed and transfer that risk to the broad shoulders of New Olympian investors and institutions only too happy to assume it, on the principle enunciated by Raymond Chandler's fictional private eye Philip Marlowe that "trouble is my business."

Sad to say, the current gathering storm of lawsuits from these institutions in relation to having been sold many of the flakier securities belies somewhat this notion of the hedge funds and the more buccaneering investment banks as the unflappable hard men of high finance.

Furthermore, it is far from clear that the most dangerous of the exotic financial instruments—whether CDOs or anything else—did in fact end up with these super-cool, ultra-professional investors. In 1997 Frank Partnoy, a former First Boston and Morgan Stanley derivatives trader, wrote of life on Wall Street. In one passage, Partnoy is asking an experienced derivatives salesman who actually buys First Boston's derivatives. Hedge funds?

> "No way. Are you kidding me?" It was a stupid question. The top hedge funds were much too sophisticated to buy this trade from First Boston. They could place such bets on their own.
>
> Mr Partnoy tries again. Other investment banks? No. Investment funds? No. Commercial banks? No.
>
> I was running out of choices.
>
> Finally, the salesman enlightens him.
>
> "State pension funds and insurance companies." "What?" I was shocked. He just smiled. (*Fiasco*, Penguin, 1997.)

Subprime Mortgages: Inside, Outside, USA . . .

In its modern form, securitization had its origins in the early 1970s with the first appearance of asset-backed securities (ABS), and had become a huge business by 2007. New issues of asset-backed securities amounted to $3.07 trillion in the United States alone in 2005.

As already noted, securitization takes the risk away from the originator of a piece of business, a car loan, for example, and transfers it to an individual or institution with an appetite for risk. Key to this is transforming an illiquid asset (i.e., not easily traded) and turning it into an asset that can be traded freely. This is achieved by taking individual financial transactions—mortgage debt, student loans, or aircraft leases, for example—and pooling them. The pool of assets produces a stream of income (e.g., the interest payments on mortgages) and the bank that created the pool can turn that stream of income into a lump sum by selling the rights to the income stream.

Leigh Skene of Lombard Street Research notes there is still a credit risk, but the bank seeks to remove that by setting up a structured investment vehicle (SIV), or a conduit, a type of what are known as special purpose vehicles (SPVs). He notes that securitization involves three key characteristics: the pooling of assets, the delinking of the credit risk of the pool of assets from the credit risk of the originating lender through a special purpose vehicle, and, finally, a trust that either passes the cash flow from the assets straight to investors or creates different tranches with different risks and returns.

> For instance, mortgage company X has originated $1 billion nominal value of mortgages from which it receives a cash flow. It can turn that income stream into a lump sum today by selling the rights to that cash flow to an SPV. The SPV puts the cash flow into a trust so it cannot be distributed to Company X's creditors if it goes into bankruptcy. The trust then pays for the rights to the mortgages by issuing bonds that receive the cash flow from the assets less administrative costs. (*Credit and Credibility*, Lombard Street Research, September 2007.)

If the average layman found all that esoteric, there was an added complexity. The next innovation was to leverage, to increase the potential profit (or loss) by slicing and dicing the asset-backed securities into tranches, some more risky than others. These financial instruments are the above-mentioned collateralized debt obligations (CDOs).

"The senior bonds have first claim on cash flows, and are usually rated AAA to A" (*Credit and Credibility*). "Mezzanine bonds have a subordinate claim on cash flows and are usually rated BBB to B. The equity class is the most junior, unrated and receives the residual proceeds of the collateral—but also absorbs the initial losses. The high risk of the equity class has led to allegations of mis-selling and commentators have called it 'Toxic Waste,' so the originator of the loans or the underwriter of the securities issued under the trust usually retains it."

In 2006 and early 2007 there was big money to be made from ASBs and CDOs. In the United States, around $6 trillion of the $10 trillion mortgages outstanding had been packaged into mortgage-backed securities, while the issuance of CDOs rose by almost 100 percent in 2006 to almost $1.2 trillion. As one commentator noted, this was an industrial-style process: raw materials (loans) were sent down the assembly line to be turned into an array of products (CDO tranches). The quality assurance department (rating agencies) inspected the goods, which were then shipped out. There were top-of-the-range products (AAA-rated tranches) for the pension funds and mutual funds, while the mezzanine tranches were snapped up by those with an appetite for something a bit riskier, such as hedge funds.

They often did so by treating an SPV as a glorified hedge fund, to take the toxic waste off the balance sheet of the parent bank (http://suddendebt.blogspot.com/2007/12/here-there-be-monsters.html).

That just left the toxic waste, where the manufacturing parallel broke down. When an industrial conglomerate is left with waste, it either recycles it into a new source of raw materials, finds somewhere to make it safe or harmless, or in the case of the more unscrupulous firms, dumps it in the environment. None of these options was open to the banks with their toxic waste; instead, they either had to find speculators willing to bear the high risks involved or keep the waste on site and hope that it did not contaminate the rest of the plant.

One of the reasons the credit crunch proved so serious was that nobody knows for sure how much toxic waste was produced, although one estimate for 2004 alone (before CDOs became popular in the markets) puts the total at $100 billion or more (http://suddendebt.blogspot.com/2007/12/here-there-be-monsters.html). "Trying to navigate through the terra incognita of structured finance holdings at banks and hedge funds is a near impossibility," says one Internet site specializing in CDOs. "They are so heavily annotated with Class 11 and Class 111 markings—plus unknown off-balance sheet exposures— as to be the equivalent of 'Here There Be Monsters' in old maps. It is little wonder that the credit market has seized: mariners are unwilling to steer by such maps; the few that do ask for pay commensurate to the risk" (Hellasious, December 14, 2007; http://suddendebt.blogspot .com/2007/12/here-there-be-monsters.html).

When times were good, it didn't matter much that the ship was being steered with incomplete maps, a dodgy compass, and a captain fond of his grog. So long as house prices were going up and mortgage defaults were low, the banks could make big money by selling toxic waste to their own special purpose vehicles.

Unlike, say, the sterling-dollar exchange rate or shares in Tesco, there was no readily available market price for CDOs. The banks, therefore, employed the very brightest mathematicians to construct fiendishly clever models that would enable them to put a price on the CDOs. In a rising market, the message from the models was that holding toxic waste was advantageous, since the lowest-rated tranches of the CDOs benefited disproportionately when asset prices were going up, because investors secured higher returns for the extra risk they were taking. These pricing models, therefore, marked up the value of the toxic waste, which the hedge funds and SPVs could use as collateral to buy still more toxic waste.

The story changed when asset prices turned down. First, banks found there was a big gap between the value of toxic waste according to their carefully constructed models and the actual price they could get for the waste from a buyer, even assuming they could find one. Second, the toxic waste tranches lost just as heavily on the way down as they had gained on the way up, leading to the banks that had lent to the hedge funds demanding extra collateral to compensate for the lower valuations. As had been the case with LTCM in 1998, the hedge funds were fully leveraged and could raise the additional collateral only through a fire sale of assets. To their horror, the lending banks found that they couldn't sell this collateral—much of which was in the form of highly rated bonds—at anything like the valuations put on it by the models. Within days, banks decided they were no longer happy with maps that merely indicated "Here there be monsters." On the contrary, they refused to leave port without assurances that they had the very latest charts on which all wrecks were marked, that the seas would remain calm for the foreseeable future, and that the government would act as underwriter for their voyage into the unknown.

And this was a global problem. The securitization process had increasingly taken on an international dimension, since the markets for mortgage-backed securities were attracting a significant number of foreign investors. Again, this had met with the approval of the IMF. As with all Delphic utterances, however, there was a sting in the tail. Yes, the Fund approved of securitization; that was hardly a surprise since it contained all the elements—financial liberalization, deregulation, and globalization—guaranteed to make the IMF happy. But policymakers had to remain vigilant, or there could be repercussions.

> The key question for policymakers is how to maximise the benefits of this continuing move toward financial systems that are more reliant on arm's length transactions, while minimising the downside risks. Financial and regulatory policies have to adapt to changing financial systems in order to maintain stability. The greater speed and flexibility with which transactions can be executed and the higher degree of leverage in the household sector in more arm's length systems could become sources of financial instability with macroeconomic consequences, if not adequately monitored. Supervisors and regulators will therefore need to continually assess and upgrade their policy tools to match financial systems. (IMF, World Economic Outlook.)

Well, yes—if regulators cannot or will not keep a close eye on the novelty products being cooked up in the City and on Wall Street, then the global economy could be in serious trouble. The Olympians had the deregulation they demanded. Now they prepared to blame the regulators for not having paid close enough attention. It is a fair bet that few of those involved in the buying and selling of CDOs in late 2006 and 2007 bothered to read what the IMF had to say about the possible risks of securitization, and that even those who did probably paid little heed to the warning. The IMF's soporific language cannot have helped. But there seems little evidence that the regulators managed to grasp what the IMF was saying.

This was an environment in which a prolonged period of low—and in the case of the Bank of Japan, zero—interest rates had led to a rapid increase in the amount of money available for speculation, because this plunge in the price of money made it much easier for borrowers to demand more, thus generating more credit in the system. It was a period when there was a search for high-yielding investments. It was a time when securitization, derivatives, and leverage could be used to bypass any remaining regulations on speculation. And it was a time when markets remained supremely confident that central banks would bail them out in the unlikely event that the economic skies darkened.

From the perspective of a hedge fund manager, it had made perfect sense to load up with CDOs, which had delivered profits for a while. The term "hedge fund" was inspired by Alfred Winslow Jones, a former editor of America's *Fortune* magazine, who decided that it was a good idea to take conflicting positions on pairs of stocks in order to limit his risk. Jones took a punt on stocks he considered cheap, but limited his exposure to the bet going wrong by gambling that a stock he considered overvalued would go down. This strategy was not foolproof (both the cheap and the expensive share could go the wrong way), but it held out the hope of small, incremental gains that would multiply over time.

Today's hedge funds are a far cry from the model Jones envisaged. As one writer put it, "Today's global macro funds are anything but hedged: they involve naked speculation, albeit extensively researched. Some are characterised by aggressive use of derivatives, such as swaps, futures and options which, like insurance contracts, require small down-payments for potentially big payouts" (Henry Tricks, "The Biggest Bets in the World," *Prospect*, December 2006).

Long-term capital management had shown how things can go wrong for hedge funds. The Russian debt default of August 1998 had led to a divergence in bond yields as investors took the view that some countries are less creditworthy than others. LTCM had bet that bond spreads would narrow and found that it had to start selling assets to cover losses. On paper it had $125 billion of assets, but $120 billion of them were backed by borrowed money. The inevitable fire sale of assets followed, prompting a bailout organized by the Federal Reserve as it became clear that the hedge fund would go bust.

But since neither LTCM or the much more serious dot-com collapse appeared to derail the global economy, hedge funds took the view that the combination of a benign macroeconomic backdrop and the availability of the new range of sophisticated financial products meant it really was "different this time." That view was reflected in credit spreads, the gap between the interest rates paid for rock-solid investments such as U.S. Treasury bonds and those payable on riskier assets such as the bonds issued by developing countries. When financial markets are cautious, these spreads are wide; in 2006 and early 2007, the spreads had narrowed even though the quality of some of the products being offered—subprime mortgages most notably— were of deeply dubious quality.

Up until midsummer 2007, that was the sort of talk few in the City or Wall Street wished to hear.

New Frontiers for the Olympians: The Global Imbalances

The boom in CDOs, derivatives, and other exotic instruments did not happen in isolation. True, Western central banks, such as the Federal Reserve Board and the Bank of England, pursued very lax monetary policies during most of the 2000s. But easy money alone is no guarantee of even illusory prosperity: ask the people of Zimbabwe. Rather, these exotic, and frequently toxic, instruments were bobbing like corks on the surface of a vast tide of money, most of which was flowing in the wrong direction, from poor, young countries to rich, aging ones.

Like the crumbling aristocrat forever borrowing from the butler to pay the gardener's wages, major Western economies have been borrowing money from developing countries in order to fund their purchases of goods from . . . developing countries. Figures published in the IMF's October 2007 World Economic Outlook make sobering reading. As a percentage of GDP, the U.S. current account deficit was calculated to move as follows, from 6.2 percent in 2006 to 5.7 percent in 2007 to 5.5 percent in 2008.

The figures for the UK are as follows: 3.2 percent, 3.5 percent, and 3.6 percent. Other so-called Anglo-Saxon miracle economies are performing even more badly. For Australia, the figures are 5.5 percent, 5.7 percent, and 5.6 percent, and for New Zealand they are 8.7 percent, 8.5 percent, and 8.6 percent.

Nor is this Rake's Progress confined to the Anglo-Saxon countries. True, the IMF notes healthy current account surpluses for both Germany and the Netherlands, but elsewhere in the Eurozone are some truly worrying figures. For Spain, the deficit is calculated to move from 8.6 percent of GDP in 2006 to 9.8 percent in 2007 and 10.2 percent in 2008. For Greece, the figures are 9.6 percent, 9.7 percent, and 9.6 percent; for Portugal, they are 9.4 percent, 9.2 percent, and 9.2 percent, and for the Republic of Ireland 4.2 percent, 4.4 percent, and 3.3 percent.

So these are some of the debtors. Who are the creditors?

China is one. The IMF has its surplus as moving from 9.4 percent of GDP in 2006 to 11.7 percent in 2007 and 12.2 percent in 2008. China has suffered famine within living memory and millions of its people are living in grinding poverty, yet China is lending money to people in Dorking, Surrey, and McLean, Virginia.

Malaysia is another. The IMF has its current account surplus moving from 17.2 percent of GDP in 2006 to 14.4 percent in 2007 and 13.3 percent in 2008. Malaysia may be an industrialization success story, but many of its people have yet to share fully in the fruits of that success and there are racial and other tensions below the surface of society. Yet Malaysia is lending money to people in Basildon, Essex, and Bantry, Co. Cork.

Then there is Singapore, where the numbers are 27.5 percent, 27 percent, and 25.4 percent; Taiwan, where the numbers are 6.8 percent, 6.8 percent, and 7.1 percent; Russia, where the numbers are a more modest 9.7 percent, 5.98 percent, and 3.3 percent; and Saudi

Arabia, where the numbers are 27.4 percent, 22.2 percent, and 20.1 percent.

These are what the IMF refers to delicately as the "global imbalances," the process whereby developing countries in need of capital end up exporting their own savings to the developed countries that ought, in classical capitalist economic theory, to be investing in the developing world. Not only, in classical theory, does this provide higher returns for the developing country investors (given their own, more mature companies are unlikely to be growing as quickly), but those returns provide an income stream from which to pay the pensions of the aging developed country population. Instead of this, the New Olympians have cheerfully sold to the developing countries vast quantities of assets, both paper securities, such as U.S. Treasury bills, and, more recently, tangible assets such as companies and property. In doing so, of course, the New Olympians have earned fat fees, apparently oblivious to the fact that, when the last share, factory, or acre of land has been sold, there will be no more of the "deal flow" on which the City and Wall Street rely.

Until that happens, however, the agreeable illusion is maintained that we can live beyond our means indefinitely, an illusion best summed up not by an economist but by the corrupt police chief played by Claude Rains in the film *Casablanca*, who explains thus his ability to drink for free at a local watering hole: "Please, Monsieur, it is a little game we play. They put it on the bill; I tear the bill up. It is very convenient."

Of course, the convenience of the West will ultimately prove to be a low priority of our creditors. Indeed, as senior British officials complain in private (and occasionally in public), we have an allegedly single global market that contains two incompatible systems, the free market in capital and goods beloved of the New Olympians, which reigns supreme in the developed world, and the nation-building system exemplified by China, which has constructed its economy using policies that have some similarities to those used by the West after the Second World War: capital controls, fixed exchange rates, industrial strategies. Furthermore, China and other Asian economies have been helped by the Olympian-inspired deindustrialization of the West and by the willingness of the New Olympians to pretend that Britain and the United States could permanently live beyond their means. In the autumn of 2007, a new battleground opened up between the Western system and the developing countries, the so-called sovereign wealth funds (SWF). These entities are precisely what their name suggests: government investment schemes that buy up assets around the world that are then held on behalf of the country concerned. The SWFs tend to be concentrated in the creditor countries and are looking to snap up assets in debtor countries. In the case of Norway, for example, such state-supervised investment is likely to be largely benign from the point of view of the country in which the investment has taken place. In the cases of Russia or China, those on the receiving end of their investments may wonder as to the likely extent of political interference.

As a rule, finance ministers of the Group of Seven rich nations fear and loathe SWFs, which they regard as an expression of primitive and uncivilized thinking, like cannibalism or widow burning. On the evening of October 19, 2007, in Washington, G7 finance ministers invited to dinner representatives of some of the SWF countries. There were suggestions that a code of conduct was to be drawn up under which SWFs would behave themselves when operating in Western countries and act as if they were ordinary commercial investors.

Ahead of a policy statement in February 27, 2008, Manuel Barroso, president of the European Commission, said that Brussels could not allow non-European funds "to be run in an opaque manner or used as an implement of geopolitical strategy."

The Americans have been holding talks with SWFs, and the IMF was expected to publish a voluntary code of conduct in time for the April 2008 spring meeting. And whereas the Davos meeting of the World Economic Forum in January 2007 had been dominated by shows of respect for the then ever present private equity firms, the meeting of 2008 saw SWFs under the spotlight. The U.S. was far more concerned about the activities of the latter (which it did not control) than of the former (most of which were American owned). But when the former Treasury secretary Larry Summers called on

SWFs to be more transparent and sign up to a code of conduct, he was rebuffed. The Saudis accused him of double standards, asking why there were calls for regulation of SWFs by Washington but no calls for the regulation of hedge funds. Russia, which has already used the financial clout from its oil and gas reserves to bully its near neighbors, was equally blunt. It said Summers's comments were "unhelpful," diplomat-speak for being out of order.

But given the imbalances—the sums owned by key rich nations to poorer ones—the G7 was in no position to lay down the law. As British officials made clear in private conversation with the authors, the rise of the SWFs was a symptom, not a cause, of the rise of economic power outside the G7. They could have added that these new economic actors were not only outside the G7, but did not share the G7 dogma of free trade, open markets, and unfettered capital market activity.

In the battle for ideas between the free traders and the nation builders, the underdeveloped countries were a critical strategic objective. Although the poorer countries were helped in the first years after decolonization by demand for their commodities in the long postwar boom, they were badly affected by the oil shocks of the 1970s, accumulating massive debts that they could not pay in an era of high interest rates. Many of the poorest nations found themselves trapped in a cycle of low growth, high indebtedness, and weak governance.

Come the 1980s and 1990s, and the New Olympians had an answer to the problems of the developing world. Unsurprisingly, they were the same answers as those being promoted domestically. The Washington consensus—the mind-set of a coalition of the U.S. Treasury, Wall Street, the World Bank, and the IMF—insisted that the least-developed nations open up their markets to foreign imports, scrap capital controls, cut public spending, and keep a tight rein on welfare projects. Precisely the opposite policies, in other words, to those used by every country in history that has developed successfully, including Britain, the United States, Germany, and Japan.

By and large, the Washington consensus did not travel well. Its failure to generate real benefits for poorer countries was summed up by Malawi's then trade minister Sam Mpasu, speaking at world trade talks in Cancun, Mexico, in September 2003: "We have opened our economy. That is why we are flat on our back."

But while many of those forced to swallow the New Olympian medicine in the 1980s and 1990s saw their economies go backward, those that ignored the Washington consensus, such as China and India, started to develop rapidly. True, they traded with other countries and, in some cases, dismantled capital controls, but they did so at their own speed and in their own way.

Professor Dani Rodrik, of Harvard University, wrote:

> What is striking about China, India and a few other Asian countries that have done well recently, is that they have played the globalisation game by the Bretton Woods rulebook rather than the current rulebook. These countries did not significantly liberalise their import regimes until well after their economies had taken off, and they continue to restrict short-term capital inflows. They have used industrial policies— many of them banned by the World Trade Organisation—strategically to restructure their economies and to enable them to better take advantage of world markets. (*Saving Globalisation?* Winter 2007.)

In less fortunate nations, the impact of failed policies has been twofold: it has proved to be a fertile breeding ground for terrorism and it has led to pressure for mass migration. In light of this, it is unsurprising that the assault on New Olympian policies came from the aid agencies and other nongovernmental organizations that called for debt relief, higher aid flows, the right for poor countries to industrialize behind tariff barriers (just as the rich ones had done), and for the relaxation of stringent conditions for economic assistance.

But even within the G7, bubble-type activity has been thriving, as seen in the phenomenon known as carry trading—the process whereby hedge funds and others exploit differences in interest rates in different countries, chiefly Japan. The Tokyo authorities, following the bursting of the country's bubble in the 1990s, had mandated extremely low official interest rates. The carry trade involved borrowing in Japan at low levels—about 1 percent on average—in order to lend in markets where interest rates were higher. Both New Zealand and the United Kingdom fell into this category, since they had interest rates of 5 percent or more. The annual return of some four percentage points could be multiplied by leverage—borrowing—while the increase in the value of the New Zealand dollar and sterling caused by the influx of "hot money" from overseas added to the profit from the carry trade.

The economic impact of the carry trade on a country like Britain was perverse; the size of the UK's trade deficit meant that the pound should have been depreciating in order to make imports dearer and exports cheaper, thus helping to bring the balance of payments into equilibrium. However, the profits from the carry trade were considerable and had the knock-on effect of bringing business into London's financial markets. The downside for the hedge funds was, of course, that the big returns also entailed big risks, since, as Leigh Skene of Lombard Street Research has noted, an unexpected movement in a currency triggered by an economic or political event can wipe out a year's profit within a week.

Furthermore, the New Olympians may have reflected that the carry trade proved that the foreign currency market—routinely championed as a superefficient Olympian institution—does not actually work properly. If it did, differences in interest rates would be cancelled out by differences in exchange rates, and there would be no profit.

They may have reflected that way. But in a world riven with imbalances, such reflections could be dangerous, in that they could lead to further reflection, and so on. Reflections on the nature of such a world, a place in which New Olympians have made fortunes from asset-stripping Western economies, and are making second fortunes from selling those assets to the gigantic pawn shop that is the developing world in return for our being able to buy goods from developing countries. Surfing the wave of money coming in (for now) from those developing countries, they became convinced of their ability to conjure up ever greater wealth through types of financial engineering that allow rewards to be pocketed and risk to be massaged away.

No self-respecting New Olympian could face the ghastly truth that they had grown fat on a fantastical type of food for the gods and their hero-servants, a deadly form of ambrosia.

Waiting for the Barbarians: The Last Helpings of Ambrosia

The yen carry trade was an early casualty of the credit crunch of 2007–2008, coming to a halt as soon as financial markets started to reassess risk. It was, however, merely a support act to the main event, the problems caused by an overly optimistic view of what securitization and other financial engineering could deliver.

According to the Bank of England's Financial Stability Review of October 2007, there was no single cause for the outbreak of market turbulence, but it said a key development was the impact of mounting expected losses in the American mortgage market on the toxic waste tranches of subprime residential mortgage-backed securities (RMBS). It had been clear for some time that the U.S. housing bubble was deflating; what changed in the summer was that financial markets realized that the more highly rated tranches of subprime CDOs also contained toxic waste. The banks had the same problem as that faced by a food manufacturer who knows that an infected carcass has contaminated one in ten thousand tins of corned beef but doesn't know which one. In the food business, all tins of corned beef are taken off the shelves; in the financial world the same happened to CDOs.

Falling prices of highly rated RMBS put pressure on investors who in their search for yield had highly leveraged positions in what they believed to be low-risk debt. Losses also began to appear in AA and AAA tranches of so-called mezzanine collateralised debt obligations. As a direct result, two leveraged funds of Bear Stearns collapsed in late June. As losses mounted and exposed funds tried to de-leverage, secondary market liquidity in RMBS evaporated and prices fell further, amplifying mark-to-market losses.

The Bank's report added that by the end of June 2007 financial vehicles that funded long-term investments with short-term debt had accumulated assets of almost $2 trillion but were finding it hard to finance their activities as key investors, including money market mutual funds, were concerned about the true state of their finances. Like everybody else, Threadneedle Street struggled to put a figure on the likely scale of the losses.

> The fundamental values of subprime RMBS depend on the prospective default losses on the mortgages to which they are linked. These appear particularly uncertain at present. It is unclear, for example, the extent to which weaker lending standards, increased fraud and the resetting of mortgage interest rates from teaser rates could raise the frequency of defaults. In addition, it is uncertain whether declining house prices could lead to lower recovery rates in the event of default.

Fittingly, it was left to *The Economist*, a cheerleader for the New Olympians and all their works, to provide the coda to the IMF's remarks about the potential perils of securitization. Writing in the autumn of 2007, hence with the immeasurable benefit of hindsight, the world's premier business magazine expressed surprise that anybody had been taken in by what was obviously such a flawed concept:

> Imagine a country where a fifth of all mortgages are taken out by the shakiest borrowers. About half of these loans are written by companies that are almost entirely unregulated. The mortgages, on average are worth almost 95% of the underlying house. Half of them demand no documentation of the borrower's income.
>
> These loans are then bundled and sliced into complicated debt instruments. The risk of these is gauged by credit-rating agencies which are paid by the very firms that created the securities and which make a lot of their money from advising on how to win the best ratings. Many of these structured debt instruments are bought by banks in other countries using off-balance sheet entities for which they make little capital provision and about which banking supervisors know virtually nothing. Financial supervisors tend to be sober and calm, but that tale ought to bring any half-competent regulator out in a cold sweat. ("Lessons from the Credit Crunch," October 20–26, 2007.)

The first crisis to test the new glittering world of high finance, said *The Economist*, had shown that markets were now so interconnected and so global that poison could spread across continents at dizzying speed. "It is a long way from the shabby hoardings of American sub-prime mortgages to the marbled halls of the European interbank market. It was as if the ambush of a few legionnaires in the forests of Germania had triggered a revolution in ancient Rome."

What *The Economist* could have added, of course, was that in the end the tribes lurking on other side of the Rhine and the Danube eventually swept down through Italy and brought Rome to its knees.

Nor is it clear that CDOs will be the last toxic security to poison world markets. Indeed, compared to some instruments, CDOs were—strange as it may seem—relatively straightforward. They may have ended up as the cause of instability, but they were not intended to be so. Some securities, however, would be almost certain to desta-bilize markets.

Frank Partnoy, whom we met earlier in this chapter, gives the ex-ample of one derivative product relating to the future level of the LIBOR (the rate at which banks lend to each other) cubed. Who, asks Partnoy, could possibly have Libor-cubed liabilities? The question answers itself. Such an instrument has lost contact with reality. It has been designed with one end in mind, to earn large fees. And, as Part-noy discovered, it is quite likely to be sold on to supposedly conserv-ative institutions such as pension funds.

It is bad enough when CDOs, derivatives, and other instruments are sold to such institutions in the process transferring risk from New Olympian operators to, in effect, the general public. But at least there was some risk to transfer in the first place, however wrongfully we may believe that risk was generated. But in this case, the risks against which it supposedly hedges do not exist. The product itself is the sole risk.

How many of these instruments are out there and what trigger will expose their real market value as being as badly impaired as that of the CDOs?

In summary, the New Olympians used financial deregulation from the 1970s onward to asset-strip countries such as Britain, whose long-term current account position deteriorated more or less consistently since the 1980s. With returns on our own productive assets and even on our service businesses and overseas investments inadequate in terms of paying our way in the world, borrowed money has poured in, in the expectation that our New Olympians will be able to generate higher than average returns. In order to do so, the Olympians have had to make very much riskier bets; effectively, they have turned the UK into a vast hedge fund. Having assumed all this risk, the Olympians then used financial engineering to make it disappear again, with the result that banks, pension funds, and others have found themselves stuffed with toxic securities.

Looked at in this light, the New Olympians' activities have been and continue to be absolutely terrifying, as are the already realized and the anticipated consequences.

CHAPTER 8

Last Tango on Wall Street

The Fall of the "American Miracle"

"Pay? It's a word I seldom use. I have a rule in life, never pay what you can talk your way out of."

—*Phil Silvers Show*

Whether a bubble or a froth, the party was winding down by late 2005, when first-time buyers began to find prices increasingly out of reach. . . . The heady days when buyers paid above offering price to bid away a house were over. Sellers' offering prices held up, but buyers pulled their bids. Sales volumes according fell sharply for both new and existing homes. The boom was over.

— ALAN GREENSPAN, *The Age of Turbulence*

Slam! So it wasn't a game?

— DAVID BOWIE, "Watch That Man"

In the film *Trading Places,* Randolph and Mortimer Duke are two elderly, crooked commodity brokers who, while seeking to fix the market for frozen orange juice, strike a bet that it would be possible for a small-time hustler from the ghetto to replace the obnoxious yuppie running their company.

What is interesting about the film today—apart from the absurdly low sums involved when the plan goes predictably awry—is that the

Dukes and their fellow financiers seem to spend more time lolling around in the wood-panelled luxury of their Philadelphia club than they do actually making decisions that might make them money. To the filmgoer of today, *Trading Places* may appear to represent a world that no longer exists. New Olympians get up early and go to bed late because they operate in 24/7 markets that never sleep. Their Black-Berrys are with them night and day, blinking out the command to an-swer an email that might make or break a deal. To be sure, they earn the sort of packages in a year that ordinary mortals could not dream of taking home in a lifetime, but the money is the reward for incisive decision making and sheer hard graft.

In fact, the New Olympians' response to the financial crisis of 2007 and 2008 suggests that not much has changed since Jon Landis made Eddie Murphy a star in his film more than two decades ago. Life was pretty much what it had been for Wall Street's leisured class a century before, as documented by magazines devoted to the glorifi-cation of conspicuous consumption. Life for New York's wealthy was as good as it had been since the days of Vanderbilt, Rockefeller, and Morgan. Where once the rich would not think twice about hiring a symphony orchestra to serenade a newborn baby, so today the New Olympians, eager to show that they are both hip and loaded rather than merely nouveau riche, may ring around to see if Elton John, per-haps even the Rolling Stones, care to earn $5 million by playing at a bash for their wife or daughter. Few, though, are prepared to castigate the scions of Wall Street in the way that Walt Whitman did when he called New York society "cankered, crude, superstitious, and rotten" (Walt Whitman; quoted by Walter Fuller Taylor, *The Economic Novel in America*, Octagon, 1964). After all, these men and women were the true descendants of the frontiersmen who had blazed their trails across the West in the nineteenth century. The covered wagon had been replaced by a dealing screen, but the pioneering spirit principle remained the same. These were the men and women who made the dollars that kept the economy ticking over. These were the men and women who worked hard and played hard, and were a shining exam-ple of intelligence, self-reliance, and doing things the American way. As it turned out, these were also men (not women, as it happens) who were driving their golf buggies across the manicured fairways of some of America's swankiest courses when the biggest financial crisis in their lifetime erupted in the summer of 2007.

Rewards for Failure: Food Fit for Heroes

The first big bank on Wall Street to come clean about its exposure to the subprime crisis was Bear Stearns, which admitted in July 2007 that it was facing big losses at two of its hedge funds. In June, the month leading up to the crisis, it could hardly be said that James Cayne, the chief executive of Bear Stearns, was burning the midnight oil to remedy the situation, since he managed to find time for thirteen rounds of golf. In August, when the credit markets froze up as banks refused to lend to each other, Cayne obviously found the idea of golf a bit too strenuous and repaired to Nashville, where by all accounts he thoroughly enjoyed himself at a bridge tournament. This bank was sold to J.P. Morgan Chase, in a U.S. government–sponsored rescue, in March 2008.

Cayne was not alone. Stan O'Neal, then the boss of Merrill Lynch, spent twenty days in the six weeks between the middle of August and the end of September honing his golf game. The bad news was that while O'Neal was away from the office, Merrill Lynch was sitting on losses from subprime loans of $3.7 billion. The good news was that the practice paid off, since O'Neal managed to reduce his handicap. The even better news was that this particular New Olympian would now have the time and the money to tinker with his swing and find his touch on the greens, since his reward for failure at Merrill Lynch was $160 million in payoffs and pensions.

Sad to say, for those struggling to pay their mortgages in the trailer parks of Las Vegas or the scruffier parts of Bakersfield, California, real life was not like the movies. As the prospect of foreclosure rose steadily there was no sugar daddy—no Randolph or Mortimer Duke—prepared to exchange their life on the wrong side of the tracks for one of chauffeur-driven limousines, jacuzzis, and five-star cuisine. As Cayne was preparing to ruff a trump in Nashville and O'Neal was splashing out of a bunker at the Vineyard golf club near

Martha's Vineyard, the collapse of the American real estate market was threatening more than 2 million families with foreclosure. The rest of this chapter will explain how loans provided to some of the poorest people in the United States spread a fast-moving form of financial dry rot through the world's markets. The story is essentially a simple one. For the past two decades, the United States has been living in a fantasy world, relying on an indulgent central bank to drop interest rates at the first sign of any discomfort and hence allow the economy to float along on a series of bubbles. One of Gordon Brown's favorite jokes is that there are only two types of chancellors of the exchequer: the ones who fail and the ones who get out in time. The same rule of thumb applies to chairmen of the Federal Reserve Board. Alan Greenspan, who presided over America's central bank for nigh on two decades, got out just as the unsustainable property boom he had engineered came to grief. Touring the world to publicize his self-regarding memoirs, Greenspan suddenly found that the miracle economy he was supposed to have created perhaps wasn't so perfect after all, and he proceeded to give Ben Bernanke, the man facing the unfortunate task of picking up the pieces, the benefit of his accumulated wisdom. In all truth, you did not need to be Adam Smith or John Maynard Keynes to work out what had gone wrong and why.

As the crisis unfolded, Greenspan's time at the Fed began to echo the tenure of U.S. Treasury secretary Andrew Mellon, who held that position at the time of the Wall Street crash. Just like Greenspan, Mellon in the late 1920s kept interest rates low, much to the delight of Wall Street. Like Greenspan, Mellon favored the rich, in his case through his tax policies. Just like Greenspan, Mellon presided over a boom in mergers and takeovers. And just like Greenspan, Mellon ignored signs of distress in the economy outside the investment houses of Lower Manhattan.

Bountiful supplies of cheap money provided by Greenspan allowed American consumers to borrow more money, which they used to buy real estate. Property prices rose rapidly, pushing home ownership out of the reach of many low-income families. The financial system decreed that this did not matter; ways could be found to provide these so-called subprime lenders to live the American dream. A modern version of the Wild West medicine show arrived in trailer park America, with real estate agents displaying the full range of hucksterism as they gulled the poor, the old, and the vulnerable with their once-in-a-lifetime, live-now-pay-later, special introductory offers. Where once the U.S. mortgage industry had been a staid, conservative affair, it was now at the cutting edge of financial innovation. At first there were "low doc" mortgages, where the normally high level of documentary proof that a borrower was financially sound was relaxed. When the next group of applicants was required to keep the boom going, "low doc" mortgages became "no doc" mortgages. The sin of omission became the sin of commission in the next stage of the real estate boom, with the advent of "liar loans" in which individuals were encouraged to falsify the details of their employment, wages, and savings. Those who lacked all three were offered "Ninja loans," which stood for no income, no job or assets. As with all bubbles as far back as Tulip Mania in seventeenth-century Holland, the real estate market was rife with sharp practice and, in some cases, outright illegality.

In the Wild West, snake oil salesmen might be run out on a rail. This time, though, they got clean away, helped by a rising real estate market which, for a time, made those who had taken out loans they couldn't really afford think that all would be well. Indeed, the U.S. mortgage industry resisted tightening the rules on lending, delaying their introduction during the last frenetic months of the boom between December 2005 and September 2006, on the grounds of avoiding "regulatory overreach" that would stifle innovation. Subprime loans in the United States were not a new phenomenon. What was different, however, about the spate of loans extended as the market reached its zenith in 2005 and early 2006 was the aggressive nature of the lending and the recklessness with which the real financial situation of many borrowers was treated. As a result, a subprime loan taken out in 2005 was twice as risky as one taken out in 2002. "Subprime loans originated in 2002 have a one-in-ten lifetime chance of foreclosing. For loans originated in 2005 and 2006, the probability shoots up to one in five" (Center for Responsible Lending, *Losing Ground*, December 2006).

There is hard evidence for our medicine show analogy. A recent study by three IMF economists for the Centre for Economic Policy Research in London (not connected with the similarly named Washington institution) concluded that fewer people had been denied home loans and that the decline in lending standards had been greatest where competition for business was strongest. The paper identified four factors that explained the change in lending standards.

> First, we find evidence that standards declined more where the credit boom was larger. This lends support to the assertions that rapid credit growth episodes tend to breed lax lending behaviour. Second, lower standards were associated with a past fast rate of house price appreciation, consistent with the notion that lenders were to some extent gambling on a continuing housing boom, relying on the fact that borrowers in default could always liquidate the collateral and repay the loan. Third, change in market structure mattered: lending standards declined more in regions where (large and aggressive) previously absent institutions entered the market. Finally, there is evidence that disintermediation played a role, with standards declining more in regions where larger portions of the lenders' loan portfolios were sold to third players. (Giovanni Dell'Ariccia, Deniz Igan, and Luc Laeven, "Credit Booms and Lending Standards: Evidence from the Subprime Mortgage Market," CEPR, February 2008.)

The increased popularity of subprime borrowing reflected the fact that house prices were going up much faster than earnings for the average American family. With real incomes squeezed, and the cost of health care and fuel rising rapidly, Americans had a choice: borrow more or give up hope of getting a foot on the housing ladder. Millions took the former option, even if it meant falsifying income records. In this, applicants were encouraged by the mortgage industry; more blind eyes were turned during this period in the U.S. than at a Horatio Nelson look-alike convention.

Some saw the growth in subprime lending as a positive breakthrough in extending credit to the less well-off. Yet, as the Center for Responsible Lending put it,

This increased access has come at great cost to many families, since the highest rate of home foreclosures occurs among subprime loans. In many communities, the pressing issue today is less the availability of home-secured credit than the terms on which credit is offered. For the average American, building wealth through homeownership is the most accessible path to economic progress, but progress is not achieved when a family buys or refinances a home only to lose the home or get caught in a cycle of escalating debt.

Subprime borrowers in 2005 and 2006 were vulnerable for three reasons. First, those who took out loans in 2005 and 2006 bought at the top of the market, when the big increases in house prices had already occurred. They either had no equity in their homes or—in many cases—had taken out loans that were bigger than the value of their property. Second, they had been seduced by loan conditions that looked attractive on the surface but were in fact inherently risky. These included low initial fixed—or teaser—rates that would rise, often sharply, after a two-year period. At that point, lenders would pay the full cost of their mortgage plus a premium to compensate for the interest deferred in the first twenty-four months. Finally, the Federal funds rate in 2006 was 5.25 percent. In 2002, it had been on its way down to 1 percent.

In the meantime, the subprime loans, riskier self-evidently than those granted to prime lenders who had well-paid employment or money in the bank, were then bundled up with better-quality loans and offered for sale in the financial markets. We looked at the process known as securitization in more depth in the previous chapter. Suffice it to say here that the complexity of modern financial markets meant that the initial bundle of mortgage-backed securities could be leveraged up many, many times, offering the prospect of easy money when real estate was booming but huge losses if and when the bubble burst, as it did from the summer of 2006 onward. At this point a slow-burning fuse was lit that a year later reached the barrels of gunpowder hidden deep in the foundations of Western financial markets.

From Miracle to Mirage: The U.S. Economy

Securitization in its modern form began in the early 1970s when the bright sparks in the financial markets realized that they could make use of assets that were illiquid (not easily traded). It was used back in the 1920s, during the bull market in shares that ended famously with the Wall Street crash of 1929. What they did was create asset-backed securities, financial instruments that used as collateral the cash flow from a specified pool of underlying assets, such as mortgages. Gradually the system became more sophisticated, with the original asset-backed securities (ABS) spawning a variety of financial derivatives, of which one was collateralized debt obligations (CDO).

As Diana Choyleva of Lombard Street Research puts it:

> Securitisation has allowed the banks to boost their income without increasing their risk. They offered the loans from their balance sheet, releasing capital for making new loans, but as well as fees from the origination of the loans they continue to earn the fees from their servicing, and then from the next round of the same process. The more banks securitise, the more profits they earn. Inevitably lending standards fall as banks no longer hold the risk. Revenue is solely governed by volume. ("US Liquidity Crunch: The Slow Motion Crisis," *LSR*, August 2007.)

The sense that these inherently risky trades were not risky at all fostered complacency in the markets. Investors normally expect to be offered far higher yields when they buy assets that are traditionally not rock-solid, but in the market frenzy of 2005 and 2006 they allowed good judgment to be subsumed by the classic trait of bubbles—greed.

The collapse of the U.S. real estate market had been predicted throughout 2006 and the first half of 2007 by a wide range of economists. Each half year, for example, the International Monetary Fund delivers its august view on the prospects for both developed and developing nations in its World Economic Outlook. While being a key part of the New Olympian movement, the WEO is a thoroughly researched and nonideological piece of work. IMF economists tend to be poor at forecasting precisely what is going to happen to the world economy, underestimating both the strength of booms and the savagery of downturns, but their assessment of longer-term trends tends to be accurate. In September 2006, when the IMF held its annual meeting in Singapore, the most likely source of a headwind for the U.S. economy was the housing market (IMF World Economic Outlook, September 2006). Rising home prices, it said, had provided a significant boost to consumption, residential investment, and employment in recent years, but the market now looked overvalued and activity had slowed as the Fed had belatedly tightened monetary policy, pushing up interest rates from 1 percent to 5.25 percent in quarter-point jumps at seventeen consecutive meetings of its open market committee. Rapidly declining mortgage applications, a rising supply of unsold homes, a decline in homebuilder confidence to a fifteen-year low, and a slowdown in the rate of home price inflation were all highlighted as possible signs of trouble ahead. The IMF stated that the world economy has been enjoying its longest spell of strong growth since the late 1960s and early 1970s, but noted "an abrupt slow down in the US housing market" as a source of uncertainty.

Six months later, the Fund returned to the same theme. In the next IMF World Economic Outlook, released in April 2007, the Fund said that a particular concern was the "potential for a sharper slowdown in the US if the housing sector continues to deteriorate." For good measure, the IMF was also the harbinger of the credit crisis that was to affect global markets some three months later, raising concerns about "the risk of a deeper and more sustained retrenchment from risky assets if financial markets remain volatile."

At a time when shares on Wall Street were rising and the talk was of which company was next to be targeted by a private equity firm, the Fund was rather more concerned about what was going on in subprime land. "The housing market downturn in the US has, if anything, been deeper than projected at the time of the September 2006 WEO," it said, adding perceptively that there was worse to come. "The housing correction still has a way to run. Housing starts and permits (to build) are still heading downward, while inventories of unsold homes are at their highest levels in 15 years."

As to the cause of the problem, the Fund noted—somewhat belatedly perhaps—that there had clearly been "an excessive relaxation of lending and underwriting standards." It was equally clear to other analysts and commentators that the U.S. housing market was an accident waiting to happen. The Cassandras included the analysts working for some of the big global investment houses that were heavily exposed to the vulnerable U.S. housing market.

This was what HSBC bank had to say in September 2006, almost a full year before the crisis broke. In a paper bluntly titled "US: Recession Warning Issued," the bank's analysts noted that the "miraculous" recovery in the world's biggest economy from the dot-com crash of 2000–2001 was ending.

> The US has become a "push-me, pull-you" economy: companies may be profitable but households, who have been the key drivers of growth, are in trouble. A cocktail of higher energy prices, tighter monetary policy, an end to tax cuts and, more recently, a housing market that appears to be in free-fall threatens to poison the upswing. Economic growth in the early years of this decade appears to have built on the most fragile of foundations.

At the time, this was a somewhat heretical view. And given the losses racked up by HSBC in U.S. mortgage, credit card, and other lending it seems to have been ignored by some inside the bank itself.

Legendary investor Warren Buffett put it this way:

> Nothing sedates rationality like large doses of effortless money. After a heady experience of that kind, normally sensible people drift into behavior akin to that of Cinderella at the ball. They know that overstaying the festivities—that is, continuing to speculate in companies that have gigantic valuations relative to the cash they are likely to generate in the future—will eventually bring on pumpkins and mice. But they nevertheless hate to miss a single minute of what is one helluva party. (Letter from the chairman, Berkshire Hathaway, 2000.)

The received wisdom about the U.S. economy was that it had experienced a renaissance since the deindustrialization of the rust belt during the deep recession of the 1980s. Rather like Britain, America was supposed to have emerged from a decade that included Watergate, the withdrawal from Vietnam, the Iranian hostage crisis, double-digit inflation, and the highest unemployment since the 1930s in a transformed state. When Bruce Springsteen was penning his songs of blue-collar melancholy, the U.S. was convinced that it was at risk of losing its economic hegemony to Germany and Japan. By the early part of the current decade, the tables had been turned. Japan was struggling to emerge from fifteen years of deflation; if Germany avoided being the exemplar of how not to run an economy, that was only because it was just one step up the ladder from the cheese-eating surrender monkeys west of the Rhine. The U.S., by contrast, was surfing the wave of the new technology. It had replaced the sunset industries of Ohio and Michigan with the sunrise industries of Texas and Arizona; it had boosted productivity and jobs; it had embraced the future at a time when Europe was stuck in the past.

In reality, the U.S. productivity miracle was something of a myth. As one study showed, the real difference between the efficiency of the American and the European economies could be explained by higher productivity in retailing. The U.S. retail sector used the interstate highway system to ferry goods between out-of-town distribution centers and hypermarkets using the latest IT equipment. Europe could only enjoy the same sort of productivity if it was prepared to abandon its stringent planning laws, allow 40-ton lorries to invade the centers of medieval cities, and perhaps knock down the odd Gothic cathedral or two. That, for some reason, the Europeans were reluctant to do (Adair Turner, "What's Wrong with Europe's Economy?" in *Challenges for Europe*, Palgrave, 2005).

By 2007, the data suggested that there had been no sustained improvement in U.S. productivity following the one-off boost provided by the widespread introduction of IT systems in the 1990s. One piece of research comparing the postwar golden age from 1947 to 1973 with the subsequent era concluded that there had been no evidence that trickle-down economics had increased the economy's long-term growth rate.

Adjusted productivity growth over the whole post-1973 period has badly trailed the pre-1973 rate. Even during the post-1995 speedup the adjusted annual rate of productivity growth was still more than a percentage point less than the 1947–73 average. In short, the economy has seen a sharp upward redistribution of income over the last three decades with little obvious growth dividend. Policies that redistribute income upward, yet fail to increase growth, are very costly to the vast majority of the US labour force. (Dean Baker, *The Productivity to Paycheck Gap: What the Data Show*, Center for Economic and Policy Research, 2007.)

In another piece of research from the same institution—one of the few left-of-center think tanks still swimming against the New Olympian tide in Washington—it was shown to be no longer true that the U.S. was leaving Europe for dead in terms of employment (John Schmitt, *Whatever Happened to the American Jobs Machine?* Center for Economic and Policy Research, October 2006). "In the 1990s, the United States developed an international reputation as a 'jobs machine' capable of creating jobs at a far faster rate than the European Union. Remarkably, however, in the current decade, the United States has been creating jobs at a slower pace than the European Union."

Schmitt said this characterization was true in the 1990s, particularly during the American boom of the second half of the decade. But in the first half of the current decade—between 2000 and 2005—employment growth in the U.S. was an annual 0.7 percent, compared to 0.9 percent a year for the European Union. True, the EU average was pulled up by the booming economies of Spain and Ireland, which had property bubbles to match those on the other side of the Atlantic Ocean, but American job growth was little better than that of allegedly "sclerotic" France, which increased employment by 0.5 percent a year.

Although exaggerated, the story of the U.S. economy reborn was partly true. America, unlike Britain, retained a strong manufacturing base, with technological innovation helped by lavish military spending, and world leadership in computer hardware, aerospace, and the audiovisual sector. It was this underlying strength that American policymakers took comfort in as the housing market weakened in late 2006 and early 2007. The fundamentals of the U.S. economy were strong, they said. The subprime problem would be contained, they insisted. There would be no contagion effects on the rest of the U.S. economy let alone the rest of the world, they reassured.

But on August 10, as the subprime tsunami crashed over Wall Street, the Bloomberg news agency reported that "Federal Reserve chairman Ben Bernanke was wrong. So were U.S. Treasury Secretary Henry Paulson and Merrill Lynch chief executive officer Stanley O'Neal. The subprime mortgage industry's problems were contained, they all said. It turns out that the turmoil was contagious."

With the benefit of perfect hindsight, many explanations were provided for the failure of the best brains in America—at the Fed, in the U.S. Treasury, and in the boardrooms of New York's investment banking community—to spot that something was seriously amiss. One was that sunny optimism is the natural disposition of Americans. Another, somewhat more politically pointed, was that those who extolled capitalism's ability to bounce back from any adversity had never themselves been at the sharp end of a factory closure or a wage cut.

A more convincing explanation, however, was that the U.S. had experienced a Minsky moment. In a paper for the Levy Institute based on the ideas of the late Hyman Minsky, Randall Wray, economics professor at the University of Missouri, said the long period of growth and low inflation had created an environment where markets were blind to the risks they were taking (L. Randall Wray, "Lessons from the Subprime Meltdown," 2007).

Minsky came up with a theory of financial instability based on two propositions. The first, not especially original, was that there are two types of regimes for financial markets—one that is consistent with stability and one not. The second proposition, however, was more striking because Minsky argued that stability was destabilizing and carried the seeds of its own destruction because those operating in a stable world would take actions that would push the system toward instability.

Making a case not just for the sort of curbs put on Wall Street after the excesses of the late 1920s but for a state of constant supervisory vigilance, Minsky noted, "Over a protracted period of good times, capitalist economies tend to move from a financial structure dominated by hedge finance units to a structure in which there is a large weight to units engaged in speculative and Ponzi finance" (*The Financial Instability Hypothesis*, Levy Institute, 1992).

Minsky argued that the strongest force in a capitalist economy operates toward an unfettered speculative boom, and in his paper Wray argued that the subprime crisis in the U.S. was a natural and inevitable outcome of those processes. "Minsky would not blame irrational exuberance or manias or bubbles. Those who had been caught up in the boom behaved rationally, at least according to the 'model or the models' they had developed to guide their behaviour."

"It is only in retrospect that we can see the boom for what it was—mass delusion propagated in part by policy makers and those with vested interests who should have known better."

America's vested interests, however, did not know better. Having created an economy in which real income for the bulk of the population (but not their own) as constrained, they needed a new mechanism for keeping the recovery of the early 2000s going. They were convinced that what they were doing was foolproof. They had forgotten the lessons of the Great Depression. They had stripped away, bit by bit, the New Deal reforms such as the Glass-Steagall Act, which had limited their freedom of action. Above all, they believed in their heart of hearts that if times turned really rough the government would step in, with cheap money, higher public spending, and an unlimited lender of last resort facility. In this last belief, Wall Street was right. The Great Depression had been the abiding American economic event of the twentieth century; it was part of what Jung called the collective unconscious in just the same way as the hyperinflation of 1923 haunted the Germans. Wall Street knew that the Fed tended to err on the side of caution when recession threatened, cutting interest rates to sustain growth.

So, as Minsky noted, a speculative boom became more difficult to control even as it became more likely. Responsibility for stripping away the constraints on finance was not Wall Street's alone. There was strong lobbying from Lower Manhattan for deregulation, but it found a willing ear at the U.S. Treasury and the Federal Reserve. Not only were so-called innovations tolerated, they were in many cases actively encouraged.

Wall Street had a touching faith in the ability of the Fed—and Greenspan in particular—to keep the good times rolling. Precious few analysts paid attention to America's burgeoning trade deficit, the clearest evidence that the country was living beyond its means. Nor did investment banks appear concerned about the buildup in personal debt that was necessary to purchase all the imported goods. There was, Wall Street insisted, no reason to be worried. The dollar was the world's reserve currency, so there would always be a demand for American financial assets. Foreign purchases of Treasury bills would finance the trade deficit and keep the dollar strong. A strong currency meant imports were cheap, and that in turn allowed Greenspan to keep interest rates low. In turn, low interest rates allowed people to borrow at cheap rates, fueling demand for real estate and so keeping property prices high. Rising property prices meant that there would be no problems with mortgage defaults and foreclosures, so all those securitized loans were surefire bets.

By the start of 2008, Wall Street's comfort blankets were looking somewhat threadbare. Greenspan had taken fright at the asset price bubble he had allowed to develop by cutting interest rates to 1 percent in June 2003 and leaving them there for a year. Even then it was probably not too late to control the wilder excesses of the real estate bubble. But instead of displaying to households and Wall Street that he was concerned that the boom might turn to bust, Greenspan proceeded to tighten monetary policy slowly and steadily. As *The Economist* said (October 2007), pushing up rates in predictable quarter-point steps intensified the housing boom and made the eventual bust more painful.

Eventually rising interest rates did have an effect and exposed how the precarious state of family finances in heartland America had been camouflaged by cheap money. Adjusted for inflation, median U.S. incomes have been falling for the past five years, yet consumption has been rising as a proportion of the economy. In the 1980s and 1990s, it hovered between 66 percent and 68 percent of GDP, but has since risen to almost 72 percent. This could be achieved only by borrowing more and saving less. Household debt is now three times as large as the annual output of the U.S. economy, higher than at any time since the Great Depression, while the savings ratio has been negative for more than two years, again without parallel since the slump of the 1930s.

As one commentator noted, Greenspan (aided and abetted by the U.S. Treasury) had solved the problem of high indebtedness in one sector of the U.S. economy—the heavily exposed business sector at the time the dot-com boom ended—by shifting the debt to two other sectors, households and the government (Brian Reading, "The Hangover," *Lombard Street Monthly Review*, October 2006). "After the Wall Street bubble burst the business sector retrenched savagely. Its financial balance went from a 2 percent deficit to near 4 percent surplus in the three years to mid-2003, a swing of 6 percent of GDP that would have knocked the economy for six had no other sectors given ground. Cheap and easy money boosted house prices, inflating a consumer borrowing bubble that together with tax cuts and the sharp deterioration into deficit in public finances, ensured a shallow recession (if technically there was one at all) followed by a recovery." The price of repairing corporate balance sheets was to impair those of households and the state.

The Dollar: A Slow-Motion Disintegration

The next part of the fantasy to be exposed was the notion that foreign investors would allow the U.S. to spend $107 for every $100 it produced—the difference being the country's trade deficit. Two Harvard economists, Ricardo Hausmann and Frederico Sturzenegger, found a novel way of getting round the problem by saying that the U.S. current account was not a question of imports far exceeding exports but of measurement problems that had persisted since 1980. The current account need not trouble economists and potential investors in the U.S. because it did not exist in the first place (Hausmann and Sturzenegger, *U.S. and Global Imbalances: Can Dark Matter Prevent a Big Bang?* CID Working Paper no. 124, January 2006).

There was no real evidence, however, that foreign exchange markets were convinced by this line of reasoning. On the contrary, the dollar fell by 30 percent against the euro between 2004 and 2007 as investors took the view that the U.S. current account deficit was fact not fiction, and that a drop in the value of the dollar to make exports cheaper and imports dearer was an inevitable part of any remedy. For a time, rising interest rates and strong U.S. growth meant foreign buying of American assets remained high enough to cover the current account deficit. But the warning signs were there of what might happen were overseas investors to decide that the prospect of a sharply falling dollar made the purchase of Treasury bills too risky, and that the euro looked a safer bet. One academic study showed that interest rates would have been a percentage point higher if foreigners were to cease buying U.S. Treasury bonds and two points higher were they to reverse the inflows off capital into the U.S. (Francis Warnock and Veronica Warnock, *International Capital Flows and U.S. Interest Rates*, National Bureau of Economic Research Paper no. 12560).

Former Fed chairman Paul Volcker, writing in the *Washington Post* (April 10, 2005), stated that he "didn't know of any country that has managed to consume and invest 6 percent more than it produces for long." The deficit worsened subsequently to 7 percent of GDP and despite improving in 2007 is still 6 percent of GDP.

The risks of the dollar losing its reserve currency status were highlighted long before the crisis broke in 2007. Avinash Persaud noted in an address to the annual Integrated Wealth Management Forum, Union League Club, in New York in 2006 that international currencies come and go and that by 2050 China and India were likely to have bigger economies—when judged by how much a dollar, a renminbi, or a rupee would buy—than the U.S., Western Europe, or Japan. Sterling had been a reserve currency in the first half of the twentieth century, but had lost that status as a result of the cost of fighting two world wars and the debt and inflation that followed.

In the case of the US today, the process is also being accelerated by wars where the end is as elusive as the enemy and by a consumerism built on a property bubble. Perhaps we will not have to wait until 2050. In my lifetime, the dollar will start to lose its reserve currency status, not to the euro, but to the renminbi or the rupee. The loss of reserve currency status for the US will bring economic and political crisis. If it was economically and politically painful for the UK, even though its international financial position did not begin from a position off heavy deficit, what will it be for the US which has become the world's largest debtor?

Persaud said the time it took for the dollar to lose its reserve status would depend on what the Fed did. It would take quite a long time were the U.S. central bank to tighten monetary policy in the face of inflation and currency weakness, but it would be accelerated should the Fed seek to boost short-term growth by cutting interest rates. "The Fed may have to take that decision sooner rather than later." That was September 2006. By the autumn of 2007, it was clear that the Fed had chosen the second option.

The climax of *Trading Places* is a scene on the dealing floor of the New York commodities exchange. Facing bankruptcy after being outsmarted by the hustler and the yuppie, the Duke brothers can see only one way out of their predicament. They demand that business be resumed on the deserted trading floor so that they can make good their losses. "Turn those machines back on," one of them screams.

Neither of us, sadly, knows Ben Bernanke, Henry Paulson, or George Bush well enough to know whether any or all of them are big fans of *Trading Places*. What we do know is that from the moment the full extent of the subprime crisis became apparent in the summer of 2007, it was a case of "turn those machines back on."

It was not hard to see why this was the response of American policymakers. Belatedly, they had woken up to the fact that the ebb tide in the housing market for the past year had left millions of borrowers stranded on the rocks of debt. In 2006, the U.S. mortgage market was worth $10 trillion, with 80 percent accounted for by prime loans, 15 percent by subprime mortgages, and 5 percent by Alt-A loans, believed the least risky of loans considered not to be of the highest quality. Those figures, however, said more about what had happened to the U.S. real estate market in previous years than it did about what was happening in 2006. Of the loans made in that year, 20 percent were subprime and 14 percent were Alt-A. A further 16 percent were known as jumbo loans, which meant they exceeded the maximum loan amount established by the Federal Home Loan Mortgage Corporation (Freddie Mac, as it is commonly known). Default rates by the summer of 2007 were already running at 14 percent, with the prospect of far worse to come in 2008 and 2009 as borrowers enticed by low-cost teaser loans had their monthly payments reset to much higher levels.

When Bear Stearns admitted that two of its hedge funds were no longer solvent as a result of the losses made on securities backed by subprime assets, there was the loud and unmistakable sound of stable doors being bolted. Wall Street realized that it did not know how big the losses were, nor who was sitting on them. It found that the highly complex models that its so-called rocket scientists had constructed to value CDOs and the other fruits of securitization were worthless, and it did what financial markets tend to do in those circumstances. It demanded help from the Big Government it normally affected to despise.

Help was not long in coming, with action proposed on several fronts simultaneously—a short-term injection of liquidity into the money markets to ensure that banks had enough cash to balance their books; cuts in short-term interest rates to boost confidence and help prevent the economy from slipping into recession; and a bailout plan for subprime borrowers to limit the number of defaults and foreclosures, and so put a floor under the housing market. Fears proved groundless that Bernanke was keen to expunge the belief on Wall Street that Greenspan's Fed had always been ready to protect reckless investors from the consequences of their own bad decisions by cutting interest rates. Instead, it was business as usual when the Fed told dealers in August that it would enter the money markets as often as necessary and would accept high-quality mortgage-backed securities as collateral for any financial assistance given. According to the *Financial Times* (August 11, 2007), it amounted to "the most extensive liquidity support operation undertaken by the US central bank since the 9/11 terrorist attacks and follows similar steps by the European Central Bank and the Japanese central bank in the past two days."

At the September meeting of its open market committee, the Fed cut interest rates by half a point and then announced quarter-point reductions in borrowing costs at its next two meetings in October and December. On January 22, 2008, it announced an emergency 0.75 percentage point cut, followed by a 0.5 point cut on January 30. Meanwhile, Treasury Secretary Henry Paulson was busy with a plan that involved some of Wall Street's biggest investment banks creating a $100 billion fund into which all the worthless subprime loans could be parked. The Bush administration announced in the autumn that interest rates would be frozen on some subprime mortgages.

This burst of frenetic action—in sharp contrast to the state of denial that had preceded it—was an attempt to replicate the operation in 1998 that had prevented the collapse of the hedge fund Long Term Capital Management from contaminating the financial markets and the wider economy. Some economists warned, however, that in 1998 the U.S. economy was booming and consumers were not nearly so deeply in debt. A quick and aggressive cut in interest rates coupled with a meeting in which the Fed told Wall Street that it had to bail out LTCM averted the crisis. But as Nouriel Roubini, economics professor at the Stern School of Business at New York University, wrote in his online blog on August 9, 2007, the difference between 1998 and 2007 was the difference between a cash flow problem and an insolvency problem.

> First, you have hundreds of thousands of US households who are insolvent on their mortgages. And this is not a subprime problem; the same reckless lending practices used in subprime—no down payment, no verification of income and assets, interest rate only loans, negative amortisation, teaser rates—were used for near prime Alt-A loans, hybrid prime ARMs, home equity loans, piggyback loans. More than 50 percent of all mortgage originations in 2005 and 2006 had this toxic waste characteristic. That is why you will have hundreds of thousands—perhaps over a

million—of subprime, near prime and prime borrowers who will end up in delinquency, default and foreclosure. Lots of insolvent borrowers.

But that was just the start, Professor Roubini noted. Insolvent borrowers meant insolvent lenders, insolvent builders, and insolvent hedge funds—not just in the United States but in Australia, Germany, and France. All the signs were of a credit and insolvency crisis that would affect the U.S. and the wider global economy.

We are indeed at a Minsky moment and this recent financial turmoil is the beginning of a much more serious and protracted US and global credit crunch. The risks of a systemic crisis are rising: liquidity injections and lender or last resort bail out of insolvent borrowers—however necessary and unavoidable during a liquidity panic—will not work; they will postpone and exacerbate the eventual and unavoidable insolvencies.

By the turn of the year, it was clear that Professor Roubini's assessment was right; the subprime crisis was proving far more intractable than the LTCM crisis of a decade earlier. The housing market remained in free fall, losses for the big financial institutions were still mounting, and economists were scrabbling to downgrade their forecasts for U.S. growth. Some remained confident that the Fed could keep the economy moving, while others predicted a short recession. One example of the downgrades came from the Economist Intelligence Unit, which in January 2008 said it expected U.S. growth of 1.5 percent in 2008 and 2 percent in 2009, but lowered them to 0.8 percent and 1.4 percent a month later (February 20, 2008).

There were signs, however, that it could be worse than that.

First, there was the prospect of mortgage rates on $1 trillion of teaser loans being reset in 2008 and 2009. Second, there was the fact that $6 trillion in mortgages had been securitized into mortgage-backed debt, and the rise in home loan delinquencies meant that the price of that debt had fallen sharply. Third, the sharp fall in the value of the dollar was leading to higher inflation, making it harder for the Fed to cut interest rates. Higher inflation was also eating into disposable incomes, making lower interest rates less effective as a stimulus

to higher borrowing and spending. Fourth, there were signs that foreign investors were becoming warier about increasing their exposure
to U.S. assets, particularly given the risk that the Fed would put a
higher priority on growth than on controlling inflation or safeguarding the value of the dollar. Finally, there was the less than reassuring
message from history that every previous crash in the U.S. housing
market had led to a full-blown recession and that by the end of 2007
the slump in real estate had only lasted about half as long as previous
downturns, none of which were nearly so serious. Bush's help for subprime borrowers was derided for being too little, too late since it
would only help borrowers who were not yet behind with their
monthly payments and had more than 3 percent equity in the property. The Bank of America calculated that this would leave around
$500 billion of subprime and Alt-A loans untouched.

With the crisis four months old, Persaud noted:

> Subprime was merely where the first Molotov cocktail was thrown not
> its source. The source of today's problem was a long period of predatory
> lending and there will be many more petrol bombs erupting wherever
> lending growth was excessively strong over the past few years. Secondly,
> the insidious problem for the financial sector is that the attempt to
> combine securitisation with financial statistics that blithely assumed
> away strategic behaviour by investors has so contaminated the asset
> pool that it has undermined confidence in collateral and those who own
> it more generally. ("We Are at a Riot Point in the Markets," November
> 27, 2007.)

By any measure, it was a serious situation, and one for which the
New Olympian class stood indicted. The Federal Reserve had mis-
managed the economy. Wall Street had ignored every warning sign as
it enriched itself at the expense of ordinary Americans. The Bush
administration had turned surplus into deficit, not just as a result of
expensive wars but also by pursuing tax policies that had favored corporations and wealthy individuals.

The charge sheet was a long one. Perhaps the most serious accusation for the New Olympians is that despite the job in security, despite

the pro-enterprise tax breaks, despite the IT revolution and two decades of growth, the United States is not nearly as mobile a society as Americans believe it is, and is becoming less so. To be sure, more people own stocks and shares than they used to, but only because they are being forced to plan for their own retirement now that companies have closed final salary pension schemes. Although 52 percent of households owned stock at the time of the dot-com meltdown in 2001, 70 percent of the stock was in mutual funds or 401(k) pension plans. As in the UK, risk in retirement has been shifted from employers to employees.

Jeff Faux says that in the three decades following the Second World War America did become a more mobile society and the distribution of income became more equal. "Labour unions gave greater bargaining power to workers, educational opportunities were expanded, and government-subsidised housing gave working-class Americans access to a wealth-building asset. Then, after the 1970s, both trends reversed." Back in the 1970s, 74 percent of people who were poor at the start of the decade were still poor at the end of the decade. In the 1990s, the comparable figure was 77 percent. It was the same story for those at the top; 73 percent of those who were rich in 1970 were still in the top 20 percent of earners in 1980; in the 1990s that figure had risen to 77 percent.

The political story of the U.S. over the same period is not, however, of a populist backlash but of a successful diversion of blue-collar anger and discontent into conservative culture wars, there being no outlet for the left-wing economic outlook of working-class Americans. There is more likely to be a furor about a pop star exposing a breast during the halftime entertainment at the Super Bowl than there is about the fact that it has been four decades since a president faced down the corporate lobby and forced business to do something it did not want to do. Even then, President Kennedy's insistence that the major steel companies rescind planned simultaneous price increases in October 1962 coincided with the Cuban missile crisis, a time when it would have been hard on patriotic grounds alone for corporate interests to push their luck.

J. K. Galbraith once paid backhanded tribute to the way in which America's elite had managed to fashion the new consensus in which "welfare queens" were demonized but the corporate dependency culture was not.

> It is the nature of privileged position that it develops its own political justification and often the economic and social doctrine that serves it best. No one likes to believe that his or her personal economic well-being is in conflict with the greater public need. To invent a plausible ideology in defence of self-interest is thus a natural course. A corps of willing and talented craftsmen is available for the task. (*The Good Society*, Houghton Mifflin, 1996.)

Professor Galbraith was also skeptical about independent central banks. He argued that the almost religious belief in a technocratic institution "removed from the pressures of democratic processes is a myth perpetuated by those" associated with large pools of money "to perpetuate their economic comfort at the expense of others" (*Good Society*).

America is central to this book. In part, that is because the financial crisis had its origins in the U.S. housing market. In part, that is because it has been apparent for the past fifteen years that the series of minitremors to the global economy were rippling back toward the epicenter of the global money system, Wall Street. In this respect, 2007 bore the hallmark of the period between 1890 and 1929, when problems first became apparent on the periphery of the global economy in countries like Argentina, then affected rich developed nations like Germany, and ultimately spread to the hub of the system itself, with far-reaching consequences. But there's a third and vital reason why the role of America is crucial. Any populist fight-back against the New Olympian hegemony is likely to begin in the United States, where—despite the conservative counterrevolution of the past thirty years—the deep-seated belief in local participatory democracy, states' rights, equal rights before the law, provide the raw ingredients for political change, however unlikely that seems at present.

Populism in the U.S. during the election year of 2008 was a much weaker beast than it had been in 1896, when William Jennings Bryan was the defeated Democratic candidate in the presidential race and fought the contest on the Jeffersonian principle that it was America's farmers, miners, and laborers who created the real wealth in the country, not "the few financial magnates who, in a back room, corner the money of the world." The explanation for this was that the Democratic Party had pretty much given up on populism. True, one of the candidates seeking to be nominated for the party's ticket in 2008, John Edwards, was a self-styled populist. But Edwards hardly looked capable of running a Harry Truman–style campaign. During his whistle-stop tour in 1948, Truman conjured up memories of the Wall Street crash and the Depression that followed, saying:

> You remember the big boom and the great crash of 1929. You remember that in 1932 the position of the farmer had become so desperate that there was actual violence in many farming communities. You remember that insurance companies and banks took over much of the land of small independent farmers—233,000 farmers lost their farms. . . . I wonder how many times you have to be hit on the head before you find out who's hitting you?
>
> The Democratic party represents the people. It is pledged to work for agriculture. . . . the Democratic party puts human rights and human welfare first. . . . These Republican gluttons of privilege are cold men. They are cunning men. . . . They want a return of the Wall Street economic dictatorship. (Quoted in David McCullough, *Truman*, Simon & Schuster, 1992, pp. 658–659.)

John Edwards, as one commentator put it, was made of less stern stuff. "Campaigning as a populist, Edwards comes across as a wealthy trial lawyer recycling his jury appeals to make corporations pay" (John O'Sullivan, *Spectator*, December 2007). By the standards of 1896 or 1948, Edwards would have been seen as a rather weak-kneed progressive; the state of the Democratic Party's mainstream in 2008 made him look a regular firebrand. Indeed, he proved far too radical for the Democrats and dropped out early in the race. By contrast, the personable but, in policy terms, elusive Barack Obama stormed past him.

Wall Street had every reason to feel comfortable about the idea of Hillary Clinton becoming the first woman president. After all, when Clinton's husband, Bill, had been in the White House, the U.S. Treasury had bailed America's big banks out of every scrape they got into. And during Clinton's eight-year presidency, there were plenty of those—from Mexico to Thailand, from South Korea to Russia. Clinton had the choice when he arrived in office to spend his political capital either on pushing through health care reform in the teeth of opposition from the big pharmaceutical companies and the medical insurers or pushing through the NAFTA (North American Free Trade Agreement) free trade deal with Mexico and Canada in the teeth of opposition from the labor unions, who argued (correctly as it turned out) that the point of the treaty was not to make the individual countries more competitive but to make corporations more competitive and profitable. The Democrats' loss of Congress in 1994 was in part attributable to Clinton's decision to turn his back on his own natural supporters. It was a decision, however, entirely in keeping with the party's gradual shift over the past forty years, away from politics of class to politics of identity. In the new politics, the big economic issues were settled. Open markets, free trade, capital liberalization, labor market flexibility, welfare reform, tax breaks to encourage innovation, higher investment on human capital, technological advance: these were the building blocks of the new economic orthodoxy and there was little difference between the two main parties. What separated them was culture: abortion, religion, gay marriage, race. As Faux rightly noted, the big shift came in 1968 and the years immediately following.

The civil rights and Vietnam conflicts of the 1960s splintered the Democratic Party's broad-based New Deal coalition that had been united around issues of economic class. Since then, liberal identity has been defined by issues of gender, race, sexual preference, disability, and other subclass categories that emphasize differences among their own core constituencies. The institutions that unite the traditional Democratic constituencies but make business uncomfortable, such as the labor unions and the local political clubs, were gradually marginalized by the party, a process that accelerated in the 1980s with the expanded influence of corporate money. The result was that liberalism's accomplishments have been aimed at niche political constituencies. Thus, notes Elaine Bernard, executive director of the Trade Union Program at Harvard University, "The boss cannot fire you because of your race. He cannot fire you because of your gender. He cannot fire you because of your sexual preference or your disability. He can just fire you for no reason at all."

The crisis of 2007 and 2008 provided the perfect conditions for a new populism. Americans had grudgingly accepted that the labor market dice were loaded in favor of the employers. They had responded to the top 1 percent of earners grabbing 90 percent of any increase in income not by taking to the streets but by taking another job. The threat of 2 million foreclosures was of a different order or magnitude, however. It conjured up memories of the dust bowl years of the 1930s and the last time Wall Street had been allowed to mess things up. It created the impression that America was facing an economic crisis unprecedented since the Great Depression. Which indeed it was.

CHAPTER 9

Thunder in the West

Scanning the Horizon for the Perfect Storm

There is no cause for worry. The high tide of prosperity will continue.

—U.S. TREASURY SECRETARY ANDREW MELLON

I expect to see the stock market a good deal higher than it is today within a few months.

—PROFESSOR IRVING FISHER

The global credit problem that started in America is now the most immediate challenge for every economy, and addressing it the most immediate priority. But just as we withstood the Asia crisis, the American recession, the end of the IT bubble and the trebling of oil prices and continued to grow, Britain will meet and master this new challenge by our determination to maintain stability and low inflation.

—GORDON BROWN

Each year Lake Superior State University in Sault Ste. Marie, Michigan, offers a prize to the most overused word or phrase that has affronted the English language over the past twelve months. There were no surprises when on January 1, 2008, it was announced that the award for 2007 had been given to "the perfect storm."

Originally "perfect storm" had a precise meteorological meaning: a mixture of tropical moisture with warm air from a low pressure weather system and cool air from a high pressure system converging on a single point. By the start of 2008, it had become a theory of everything. The *Financial Times* said Guy Hands, the private equity entrepreneur trying to revive the fortunes of EMI in the face of opposition not just from staff but the record label's roster of stars, was facing a perfect storm (January 13, 2008). After being caught flat-footed by Hillary Clinton's unexpected victory in the New Hampshire primaries, the media needed to find a way of explaining a forecasting faux pas on a par with the *Chicago Times* front-page headline in 1948: "Dewey Defeats Truman." Rather than admit they simply got it wrong, the humbled psephologists said a combination of baby boomer feminism and the alleged superficiality of Barack Obama had resulted in Hillary Clinton's victory. "Barackwave Crashed in Hillary's Perfect Storm," said one headline (*Boston Globe*, January 10, 2008). Perhaps best of all, however, was a report in the *Los Angeles Times* the previous summer in which the mayor of the city described the drought conditions as—you guessed it—a perfect storm. The students of Lake Superior State University were right; the phrase was threatening to make the leap from meaning a confluence of warm air and cold air to signifying instead billowing gusts of hot air. The word "crisis" was no longer good enough.

The state of the global economy in the first half of 2008 made it a prime candidate for the perfect storm thesis. Nor was it merely a craze among the end-of-the-world brigade. The chief economist of the International Monetary Fund, Simon Johnson, is hardly one for apocalyptic visions of the future, but in November 2007 he popped up to warn of a perfect storm caused by the interaction of turmoil on the financial markets and the spiraling cost of energy. "The combination of the credit crunch and high oil prices could bring a big reduction in international trade from which no one would be immune," he said. It says something about the febrile mood in that autumn that only a month previously, Johnson had unveiled half yearly forecasts for the global economy in which the Fund said it barely expected growth to miss a beat in 2008, edging down from 5.2 percent to 4.8 percent.

Robert Kuttner, editor of the *American Prospect*, was convinced that 2008 would see a witch's brew of bad news. Writing in the *Boston*

Globe (December 21, 2007), he said, "America now faces an economic perfect storm: a weakened financial system, diminished consumer purchasing power, a swooning dollar, and rising inflation. Ours is a resilient nation. The eventual recovery will require a repudiation of free-market economics, as bold as the New Deal. But like so much else about the Bush legacy, recovery will be far more agonizing than it had to be."

While avoiding use of the phrase, Joseph Stiglitz, the Nobel Prize winner and former chairman of the council of economic advisers under Bill Clinton mentioned earlier in this book, had a message similar to Kuttner's. A tax code weighted in favor of the rich, a 70 percent rise in the budget deficit, a nearly $850 billion trade deficit, record oil prices, a depreciating dollar, a dearth of investment in education, science, and research: all this, according to Stiglitz, made George Bush a candidate to seize the unenvied mantle of America's worst president from Herbert Hoover, someone with hands-on experience of a perfect economic storm.

> Whoever moves into the White House in January 2009 will face an unenviable set of economic circumstances. Extricating the country from Iraq will be the bloodier task, but putting America's economic house in order will be wrenching and take years.

> What is required is in some ways simple to describe: it amounts to ceasing our current behavior and doing exactly the opposite. It means not spending money that we don't have, increasing taxes on the rich, reducing corporate welfare, strengthening the safety net for the less well off, and making greater investment in education, technology, and infrastructure.

Inevitably newspapers embraced the new sound bite. "The storm clouds are gathering over the jobs market; the climate on the high street is growing distinctly chilly; a typhoon of bad debt is buffeting the banks," the *Independent* noted on December 5, 2007. "Could a 'perfect storm' be about to hit the British economy?" A month later the *Guardian* asked, "Is This the Big One?" It added, "It is 15 years since Britain last suffered a recession. But now the housing market is slumping, oil prices are soaring, and a credit crisis is paralysing the banking world. Are the conditions right for a 'perfect economic storm'?" (January 3, 2008). It should be admitted at this point that the author of that piece was also the coauthor of this book.

In many cases, the use of the phrase "perfect storm" was inappropriate; a reduction in America's growth rate to around 2 percent in the light of the subprime crisis did not merit the description. Nor did forecasts from City of London economists that Britain was about to have its toughest year since the early 1990s but still avoid suffering a single quarter of falling output. In previous eras, such outcomes would have been described as the stop phase of a stop-go cycle or a soft landing. It appeared, however, that a long period of rapid growth (the five-year period from 2003 to 2007 marked the strongest performance by the global economy since the climax of the post-war boom in the late 1960s and 1970s) had made commentators forget what tough times were really like, and they lurched into hyperbole at the first hint of trouble.

So let us be clear. We do not consider it to be a "perfect storm" should British house prices fall by 5 percent while simultaneously a weaker pound makes it less appealing for British consumers to increase their carbon footprint with a weekend shopping trip to Manhattan. Nor do we consider it to be a perfect storm should higher oil prices occasion two or three years of belt tightening in the U.S. that result in weaker corporate profits and smaller bonuses for Wall Street traders. If it is to justify the nomenclature, a perfect storm has to meet a far tougher test: a concatenation of events, serious enough in themselves, that taken together ensure an outcome that is bad, perhaps worse, than any informed commentator could envisage. Our view is that some of the headwinds facing the global economy—the financial losses sustained as a result of the U.S. subprime crisis, for example—are serious enough to cause quite significant damage to growth and living standards over the coming years, but that the outcome would be far more serious were the problems of injudicious lending to be amplified by energy shortages, environmental disaster, policy error, rising inflation, terrorism, and tension between the

United States and China. The arrival of all of these horrors at once would be akin to Odysseus being left at the mercy of the elements after the crew on his ship opened the bag of winds presented to him by King Aeolus.

Before describing what a genuine perfect storm might look like, it is worth noting that the next few years may see the status quo restored: Odysseus may be able to get all the winds back into the bag bar the West Wind drifting him gently home to Ithaca. More often than not, the worst does not happen. Despite the scare stories, the world's computers did not all malfunction as a result of a Millennium Bug when the clock struck midnight on December 31, 1999; the West's population had, at the time of writing, remained unaffected by SARS or Asian bird flu; the record of the past quarter of a century has been that every setback to the global economy—from the Latin American debt crisis to the terrorist attacks on New York and Washington in September 2001—had been shrugged off.

The philosopher Karl Popper always insisted on making the best possible case for his opponents before seeking to refute it; doing so, he said, made his argument all the stronger. Popper would have little trouble constructing a case for business as usual over the coming years; a market-based system has withstood anything and everything that has been thrown at it over the past 250 years, and a graph of global output since the middle of the eighteenth century shows a steady upward trend, with even the Great Depression registering as an almost imperceptible downward blip. Capitalism has proved itself to be malleable and adaptable; the profit motive has emerged, albeit sometimes battered, from world wars, hyperinflation, speculative manias, crashes, and depressions. It has found a home in states run by economic liberals, social democrats, and communists. The system has learned how to bend with the wind (the current vogue for environmentally friendly forms of production being a prime example of firms knowing when and how to give ground to the prevailing political orthodoxy), how to coopt its critics, how to keep a low profile when necessary, and, most important of all, how to learn from its mistakes.

Policymakers learn from past experience. Nobody would seriously suggest today, for example, that finance ministries should seek to balance budgets during economic downturns, as was the accepted wisdom at the time of the Wall Street crash of 1929. Ben Bernanke, the current chairman of the Federal Reserve Board, was an academic before he was a central banker, and made his reputation for his work on the causes of the Great Depression. More than anyone in early 2008, Bernanke was alive to the risk of repeating the policy errors that turned a stock market crash into a slump—leaving interest rates too high for too long and raising taxes or cutting spending in a misguided belief that the budget needs to be balanced even when the economy is in free fall.

As a governor of the Fed under Alan Greenspan, Bernanke outlined his thinking in a speech in 2002 ("Deflation: Making Sure It Doesn't Happen Here," National Economists Club, Washington, November 21, 2002). The Fed, he said, would "take whatever means necessary" to prevent the U.S. from repeating the deflationary experience of Japan in the 1990s. Coping with the threat of a period of falling prices was straightforward; the Fed and the U.S. Treasury had the means to do the job, and although the best cure for deflation was to make sure it did not appear in the first place, Bernanke was prepared to crank up the printing presses. "By increasing the number of U.S. dollars in circulation, or even by credibly threatening to do so, the U.S. government can also reduce the value of a dollar in terms of goods and services, which is equivalent to raising the prices in dollars of those goods and services. We conclude that, under a paper-money system, a determined government can always generate higher spending and hence positive inflation." This speech won Bernanke the nickname Helicopter Ben, since it assumed that in a deflationary crisis the Fed would, figuratively speaking, take to the skies and dump wads of dollar bills on the economy, a policy response first raised by Milton Friedman. By 2008, Helicopter Ben's theories had ceased to be academic. While he was cutting interest rates, the White House was suggesting a tax cut worth 1 percent of American GDP—$140 billion—to encourage spending.

Again, this owed much to the postmortem examination of the Great Depression. In the jargon of the profession, politicians now allow the economic stabilizers to work in recessions; they accept lower tax revenues and higher public spending even as budget deficits increase. The government thereby leans against the wind, supporting economic activity until, as Lord Keynes said, the animal spirits of the private sector revive.

And revive they do, eventually. Britain could be said to have suffered two perfect storms under the long period of Conservative control from 1979 to 1997: the recession that wiped out a quarter of the country's manufacturing capacity in the early 1980s and a downturn of almost equal severity that laid low the property market a decade later. In the early 1980s, industry was faced with inflation at 20 percent, a doubling of oil prices, interest rates of 17 percent, and a pound artificially boosted in value by the arrival in the late 1970s of North Sea oil. At a time when global demand was weak, UK companies were internationally uncompetitive and they went out of business in droves, pushing unemployment to levels not seen since the 1930s. Within five years of the economic trough in 1981, however, the economy was growing strongly again. Oil prices were below $10 a barrel, the pound had collapsed, interest rates had been cut, and inflation was just above 2 percent.

Five years later, Britain was back in recession. The recovery of the mid-1980s turned into a wild speculative boom in 1988 that necessitated interest rates of 15 percent to bring it under control. Inflation picked up once more, hitting almost 11 percent and—despairing of finding a domestic solution to rising prices—the Conservative government pegged the pound to the Deutschmark in the hope that it could import some anti-inflationary rigor from Germany. Two extra ingredients made up the perfect storm: rising oil prices as a result of the first Gulf War and German reunification. The latter triggered a surge in inflation, prompting the German central bank—the Bundesbank—to keep interest rates high. That had knock-on effects for other European countries, including Britain, because they too were required to keep interest rates high in order to maintain the value of their currencies against the mark. In Britain, high interest rates led to a rapid cooling of the economy and a doubling of unemployment, which returned to almost 3 million. People who had bought their homes at the top of the market in 1988 found that they could no longer keep up the mortgage payments. Home repossessions and bankruptcies rose to record levels; house prices entered a six-year decline.

Again, however, recovery was relatively swift. Britain ceased to peg its currency against the mark and the pound dropped in value by 30 percent, making exports cheaper on world markets. Without the need to defend the pound, interest rates were cut from 10 percent to 6 percent in four months. Oil prices again tumbled once the short war against Saddam Hussein was over. The years immediately after Black Wednesday were not easy for consumers, since taxes were raised aggressively as the government sought to repair the damage to the public finances caused by the recession, and even with interest rates at 6 percent rather than 15 percent house prices did not start to rise again until 1995. Even so, by the time Tony Blair took office in May 1997, the economy was growing strongly, consumer spending was buoyant, and exports from a more competitive manufacturing sector meant Britain's trade gap with the rest of the world had been closed.

Periods such as the early 1980s and the early 1990s are the exception rather than the rule. In only five years since the Second World War has Britain experienced years when gross domestic product (GDP)—the yardstick for measuring growth—has declined. That is, perhaps, not entirely surprising since technological advance and improvements in working practices mean that historically the economy has grown by 2.5 percent on average for the past six decades. Years when output is actually falling indicate that the economy is performing a long way below its potential.

It is for that reason—and not just innate optimism—that economic forecasters rarely see recessions coming. J. K. Galbraith had enormous fun at the expense of American economic pundits in *The Great Crash* (1954; Penguin, 1992), a book peppered with bittersweet examples of how the great and the good failed to see the stock-market crash coming, predicted that the fall in share prices would be a short-lived affair and completely failed to realize that America was facing the biggest depression in its history, even when factories were closing and the bread lines were lengthening.

Most of the time, those who take a cautious approach to forecasting are proved right. Economies tend to operate at around their potential growth rate—in Britain's case GDP tends to expand in the range of 2–3 percent each year. Those who habitually say that the economy is about to plunge into recession are sometimes right, but so are stopped clocks.

At the start of 2008, the prevailing view was that both the U.S. and the UK were going to have a year of subtrend growth, and that while there was a risk that America would have a brief recession, Britain would grow at between 1.5 and 2 percent. Even the most bullish forecasters did not expect developed economies to escape unscathed from the financial crisis prompted by the souring of subprime loans, but it remained a possibility—albeit a slim one—that aggressive cuts in interest rates coupled with coordinated central bank action to unfreeze financial markets might allow the global economy to continue serenely on its way.

Anatole Kaletsky, the distinguished commentator at *The Times* newspaper, was confident that things would turn out better than the Cassandras were predicting. In his article "Goodbye to All That: The Worst Is Over for the Global Credit Crunch" (*The Times*, January 14, 2008), Kaletsky said there would be no recession in the U.S. and stock markets would rise in 2008. "I believe that the global credit crisis, far from taking a turn for the worse, is now almost over," he added. This was a minority view, even in the City and on Wall Street, two geographical locations not normally known for their rampant pessimism. Goldman Sachs, Merrill Lynch, Citigroup, Morgan Stanley, just about every big beast of the U.S. investment banking world had, by the end of 2007 or the start of 2008, penciled in a recession for America in 2008 and a pronounced slowdown for Britain and the rest of Europe. This was not desperately surprising, given that most of these banks were reporting record quarterly losses as a result of their exposure to subprime securities; the gloom spread downward from the boardroom to the analysts.

That said, there was still a chance that Kaletsky would be proved right. Although there was more and more news coming in to refute the Fed's confident assertion in early 2007 that subprime would be contained and cause problems only to the real estate market, not all the news was gloomy. Consumers still appeared to be spending; unemployment had picked up, but at 5 percent the jobless rate was much lower than it had been in previous downturns, and lower than in continental Europe. It was the same story in the UK. The last set of figures from the labor market in 2007 showed a quarterly rise in employment of 175,000 and the fifteenth successive monthly fall in the number of people out of work and claiming benefit. So, as we seek to assess the impact of the financial turmoil, the starting point is that there may not be even a shower or squall let alone a storm, but merely a gust of wind.

In the past, this has certainly been the case. Warwick University economist Andrew Oswald has noted that every sharp increase in the oil price in the past thirty-five years (1973–1974, 1979–1980, and 1990–1991) has prompted a global recession. "The single best cyclical indicator for the world economy is the price of oil," he told the *New York Times* as the American-led coalition prepared to invade Iraq in early 2003 ("Jump in Price of Oil Puts New Strains on the Economy," March 2, 2003). Far from flooding the global energy market with cheap crude, the defeat of Saddam Hussein was the catalyst for a long and pronounced increase in the cost of oil, and every time it hit a new benchmark—first $40, then $50, then $60, and finally $100 a barrel—there were predictions of impending recession. But as noted earlier in this chapter, the fivefold increase in the cost of crude failed to prevent the global economy from having its best period of growth since the days of Edward Heath and Richard Nixon. Indeed, one explanation for the rising cost of energy was that the rapid expansion of the global economy had led to the voracious demand of newly industrializing countries such as China and India outstripping supply.

Even so, there were few takers for the Kaletsky view of the world in the first few months of 2008, not least because those running developed economies—and the Federal Reserve in particular—had ceased to be confident that the problems from the subprime crisis would be contained. Instead, there was a recognition that there were already contagion effects. In late 2007, Bill Gross, the managing director of the fund manager Pimco, predicted a further 10 percent fall in U.S. house prices and said the only real question was how bad 2008 would be. "The 2008 outlook for housing prices will be a function of whether the Fed can cut off a worst-case scenario, but we think continued weakness in housing and slower economic growth are already baked into the cake for next year" (Pimco Spotlight, December 2007). U.S. growth, Gross added, would slow to 1 percent—a view shared by the leading Wall Street investment banks, where the consensus view was that the U.S. would suffer two quarters of negative growth—the technical definition of recession.

In the UK, the Royal Institution of Chartered Surveyors, the body that represents estate agents, produced its gloomiest survey in sixteen years in January 2008 against a backdrop of credit becoming more expensive and less easily available. The number of mortgage products on the market was sharply down, and one-eighth of first-time buyers had to pay 7 percent or more to obtain a mortgage. In May 2007, less than 1 percent had been forced to pay such expensive rates. House prices in Greater London, the center of the boom in the property market over the previous ten years, were down more than 6 percent in the final three months of 2007 (Halifax Regional House Price Index, January 19, 2008).

One piece of good news was that actions by the Bank of England, the Fed, and the European Central Bank to pump funds into the financial markets had helped to make it cheaper and easier for banks to borrow from each other. The bad news, however, was that a belated mood of caution and the need to repair balance sheets damaged by losses on "toxic waste" securities meant that these benefits were not being passed on to the banks' customers. Michael Saunders, UK economist at Citibank, summed up the mood when he said it would be wrong to assume that easing strains in money markets meant the crisis was over. "The economic slowdown has barely begun. Most of the bad news—in terms of soft consumer spending, job losses, cuts to profit forecasts and falling property values—still lies ahead" ("Still Getting Worse," *Citigroup Sterling Weekly*, January 18, 2008). Admittedly the Saunders missive did appear in the week that Citigroup was left contemplating a nearly $20 billion write-off on subprime debt, a 42 percent cut in its dividend, and a record quarterly loss. But Saunders was by no means alone. Nor was his the most gloomy prognostication for the UK economy.

Mainstream City thinking went like this. With the U.S. housing market still declining, banks would likely have to own up to much bigger losses on their speculative activities. In addition, tighter credit conditions would expose some other examples of excess that the markets had conveniently ignored during the good years. Britain's commercial property sector, for example, received far less attention than its residential counterpart, but had experienced a boom of equivalent size. Billions of pounds had been invested in property funds; as with real estate, securitized derivatives, and the global economy, the feeling was that the only way was up. By the early months of 2008, property prices were plunging, prompting hefty selling by small investors. Aware that their cash balances were inadequate in the event of a Northern Rock–style run, the property funds responded by putting a freeze on withdrawals.

Nervous attention was also being paid to the companies that guaranteed bonds—the so-called monoline insurers. As with almost everything else in the world of modern financial markets, the mundane name disguised what these companies were up to, and how their possible collapse could add a fresh leg to the subprime crisis. When banks in the U.S. and Europe bought CDOs they protected themselves with monoline insurers, highly leveraged by AAA-rated firms that ostensibly specialize in taking the risk out of risky investments. Like any insurance operation, this was a good business to be in when the number of claims was small. But as it became evident that most of the bonds guaranteed by the monoline insurers were worthless, their losses mounted and their credit ratings were cut. This raised the possibility that they would have to sell assets to meet their commitments or, even worse, collapse. Merrill Lynch, nursing its own $16.7 billion of losses on virtually worthless subprime debt, announced in January 2008 that it was putting aside $3.1 billion connected to mortgage-backed securities that it had thought were off its books.

Indeed, the monolines were in a highly exposed position. They had guaranteed $150 billion of derivatives backed by subprime mortgages and as much as $1.5 trillion in municipal bonds. They had very little actual capital and were leveraged 100 to 1, similar to the hedge fund Long Term Capital Management in 1998. By early 2008, some monoline insurers were on the brink of insolvency and the U.S. government was trying to piece together a rescue package. Investment sage Warren Buffett said he was interested in taking over the parts of the business that dealt with municipal bonds but did not want the subprime arm, hardly surprising since Buffet once famously called derivatives "financial instruments of mass destruction" (Letter from the chairman, Berkshire Hathaway, 2002).

What the banks feared was that the monolines would lose their Triple-A rating, which would mean that they could not meet their commitments to insure the big banks for subprime exposure and would prompt an estimated further $150 billion in write-downs. That, in turn, would lead to a further tightening of credit conditions and lead to both a deeper recession and further downward pressure on share prices.

While Gordon Brown was seeking at every opportunity to stress Britain's ability to shrug off a crisis that had started in the U.S., City analysts were far less sanguine. "To a very large extent, the risks to the UK are the same as those in the US, though they are arguably even more severe," said Rob Camell of ING in London ("2008: Where Could It All Go Wrong," *ING*, January 11, 2008). "The UK housing market has risen faster and further than that in the US, though without the same supply imbalance, and perhaps with greater fundamental support. Nevertheless, household balance sheets in the UK are more stretched relative to the US in terms of household debt to disposable income. And government finances are in much poorer shape to help the economy, should that be needed."

Britain, it was argued, could have a mini–perfect storm all of its own. First, there was no guarantee that the collapse of Northern Rock would be the last should the UK suffer the sort of residential property crash that had been seen in the U.S. As the City firm Kleinwort Dresdner noted (conversation with the authors, December 2007), there had been three previous booms in British house prices in the post–Second World War era; after each there had been a subsequent 30 percent fall in prices when adjusted for inflation. Second, there were warnings that years of consumer profligacy followed by a period of negative equity and tougher criteria for borrowers could lead to a rising number of bankruptcies and mortgage delinquencies, thereby putting even more stress on the UK banking system. Third, the Bank of England's ability to respond to a slowing economy was constrained by rising inflation, which meant the chances of deep cuts in interest rates was less likely in the UK than in the U.S. Finally, the government was in no position to take up the slack through tax cuts or spending increases, as had happened in the first few years of the decade when Britain avoided the recession that affected the U.S., Germany, France, and Japan by spending its way out of trouble. Budget deficits usually come down when economies are growing fast, and by the start of 2008 the UK had been growing at an annual rate of 3 percent or more for almost two years. Yet far from getting better, the budget deficit continued to rise, forcing the government to cut back the rate of spending growth and to impose below inflation pay rises on the public sector. The title of a report on the global economy from HSBC summed up the mood: *Goodbye to All That* (December 2007).

We have much sympathy with this analysis. In our previous book (*Fantasy Island*, Constable, 2007) we argued that Britain's economy had been overreliant on debt and that the chronic tendency to spend more than we earn and consume more than we produce would, sooner or later, come back to haunt policymakers. Labour's decade in power had been marked by a continuation of the decline in manufacturing, leaving the economy flying on three engines: the City of London, the housing market, and the public sector. In 2008, all three were in danger of stalling.

It is our contention, nevertheless, that this would still not constitute a perfect storm, or anything like it. The most pessimistic City analysts were still predicting a moderation in UK growth rather than a recession; their counterparts on Wall Street believed that by the end of 2008 cheaper money and tax cuts from the U.S. Treasury would ensure that the American economy was expanding once more.

Our view is that the phrase "perfect storm" is rendered meaningless without a more stringent test and that this will require more than a slowdown in the UK turning into a recession and a short recession in the U.S. becoming a more prolonged hard landing. As has no doubt become clear in the earlier chapters of this book, we have some sympathy with those like Albert Edwards at Société Générale who wonder whether there is not going to be a much higher price to be paid for the years of living dangerously. "The debate is shifting from whether the US economy will go into recession, to how long and how deep it will be. Strangely, no one seems to be contemplating a deep recession. I'm not sure why, given the unprecedented consumer debt excess that could easily unwind. As profits slump, investors are relying on equity cheapness to limit any bear market. They should not" ("Is the Penny Finally Dropping?" Société Générale, January 8, 2008).

The debt-soaked economies of the U.S. and the UK may indeed be the Ponzi schemes that Edwards considers them to be. He may also be right in doubting whether the great moderation attributed to central banks is no such thing if the periods of strong, stable growth with shallow recessions have been deliberately "bought" at the cost of successive credit and asset bubbles. But even if all that is true, it would merely be one of the ingredients—albeit a vital one—for a perfect storm. Worryingly, the other ingredients appear to be readily available.

High Anxiety: Oil, Hurricanes, Rumors of Wars

Excessive levels of debt and financial stress provide necessary but not sufficient conditions for a perfect storm. It would, for example, have been unimaginable for policymakers in the 1950s and 1960s to contemplate a period of loose credit leading to a freezing up of global credit markets. For one thing, credit markets were domestic, not global; but more importantly, the activities of the financial sector were carefully monitored following the debacle of the late 1920s and any suggestion that borrowing conditions were becoming too loose was met with the imposition of credit controls. The globalization of finance, the abandonment of the policy instruments used to control speculation, the increasing importance of finance in domestic economies, and the complacency engendered by a long period of low-inflationary growth have all made the economies of the UK and the U.S. more vulnerable to a crisis. But not every slowdown turns into a recession and not every recession turns into a slump.

One current danger is the reemergence of inflationary pressure. Even as economies were slowing in the winter of 2008, there was unmistakable evidence of rising fuel and food prices. Some of these increases were beyond the control of policymakers in London or Washington; one reason, for example, that butter prices in UK supermarkets were up by 50 percent in a year was that the growing prosperity of Chinese consumers meant that for the first time they could afford to buy refrigerators and store dairy products.

The effects of rising prices were starting to be felt beyond the West. The UN Food Program said in February 2008 that the rising cost of food meant it no longer had the money to keep malnutrition at bay in the world's poorest countries. Josette Sheeran, head of the program, called it "the new face of hunger."

Central banks responded to this pressure in different ways. The European Central Bank, still dominated by memories of marks being carried around in wheelbarrows in the Germany of 1923, discussed whether it should raise interest rates to combat inflationary pressure. The Bank of England adopted a middle-way approach. Having expressed concern in the first half of 2007 about the cost of living in the UK, it first shelved plans for dearer borrowing and then cut rates modestly. It stressed, however, that it was still concerned that the higher cost of energy and food might be the start of a wage-price spiral. The Federal Reserve, despite presiding over the economy with the highest inflation, had no such reservations; the Fed had no wish to be blamed for a second Great Depression (or even, in an presidential election year, a common or garden recession) and it cut rates quickly and deeply.

Unless the conditions facing the three central banks were wildly different, at least two of them were making a policy error. Either they were worried about an inflation problem that didn't exist, leaving themselves open to the charge of failing to spot the risk of a downturn until it was too late. If so, they were guilty of the mistake made by the Fed after the 1929 crash. Alternatively, they were playing with inflationary fire and by pumping cheap money into the economy would simply put off the reckoning to another day. Graham Turner, an expert on the Japanese economy, said from the early days of the crisis that the Fed needed to act quickly and decisively. "Until the Fed recognises the seriousness of the US housing market crisis and starts cutting, equity markets will continue to correct lower, increasing the risks of recession in 2008" ("Leverage, Contagion, and Stocks," *GFC Economics*, August 15, 2007).

Stephen Lewis was in the opposite camp. He compared Ben Bernanke with Bill Miller, the chairman of the Federal Reserve who in the late 1970s ignored inflationary warning signs in an attempt to reflate the economy. Lewis said that while Bernanke may not be the growth "nutter" that Miller had been, he had precious little to say about the risks of rising prices.

> Bernanke gave the impression he had been unnerved by the scale of the problem facing U.S. financial institutions. In assessing the prospects for the economy, he hardly got beyond the subprime market and the financial turmoil. If, in the past, market participants have complained that the Fed has not heard what they are saying about their distress, they could hardly maintain that charge after yesterday's speech (in which Bernanke said he stood ready to continue cutting interest rates). The Fed chairman at least is 100 percent focused on the financial sector's woes. ("Economic Insights," Insinger de Beaufort, January 11, 2008.)

Lewis made the point that Miller had allowed inflation to spiral to 13.5 percent in 1980, and it took draconian action from his successor, Paul Volcker, to bring it back under control. It involved pushing the Fed funds rate back up to 21 percent. The underlying inflationary backdrop was less threatening than in the late 1970s and early 1980s, but U.S. households were far better able to withstand tough anti-inflation medicine from the Fed under Bernanke than they had been under Volcker or than they would be today, because mortgages were almost exclusively fixed rate in the late 1970s and early 1980s. "A similar loss of confidence in today's circumstances would bring on the kind of crisis in household finances that Bernanke is trying to avoid."

Wall Street and the City retained a tender, almost touching faith in policymakers even as it became clearer and clearer that they were no longer fully in control of events. Every utterance was greeted with reverence, although the impact on the markets seemed to grow weaker and weaker as the months went by. The belief that the Fed, the Bank of England, and the ECB knew what they were doing and could steer a path between the Scylla of recession and the Charybdis of inflation was strong. A soft landing was, however, one of only three possibilities; the others were that cutting interest rates (and it was assumed that eventually the Bank of England and the ECB would follow the Fed's lead) would be the equivalent of a fix for the world's debt junkies, the effects of which would wear off even more quickly than they had in the past. Alternatively, there was the risk that cutting interest rates would have no effect on borrowers long overdue for a period of cold turkey.

The oil market provided an added complication. Historically, periods of slow economic growth have led to a drop in the price of crude, with falling demand for energy leading to lower prices. In 2008, there was no guarantee that this pattern would be repeated, in part because the bigger developing economies—China and India— were still growing fast. Even with demand in the West threatening to slow, there were doubts about whether there was enough supply capacity to cope—the legacy of a long period of scant investment in new refining capacity. More importantly, there was the question of whether the days of cheap oil were over.

There have been no major new discoveries of crude since 2002 and—as with food—rising demand has been pushing up prices. In the mid-1950s, M. King Hubbert accurately predicted that oil production in the U.S. would peak at the start of the 1970s and then start declining. Many oil experts believe that peak oil for the world is now rapidly approaching, if it has not already arrived, for cheap crude that is easy to extract. Colin Campbell, former chief geologist at a number of major oil companies, put it this way: "It's quite a simple theory and one any beer drinker understands. The glass starts full and ends empty and the faster you drink it the quicker it's gone" (*Independent on Sunday*, June 14, 2007). The green movement has latched on to peak oil, since it believes the projected doubling of demand for oil from 80 million barrels per day to 160 million barrels would be disastrous for the environment, pushing the world over the edge of runaway climate change. It is not only environmentalists who believe peak oil is a reality, however. Matthew Simmons, who worked as an energy adviser to George W. Bush, believes that $100 oil prices are the inevitable consequence of demand outstripping supply.

"The world expects several decades of growing supplies of generally affordable oil," said the energy economist Jeremy Leggett in a published note ("The Trouble with Oil," December 2007). "Every corporate and ministerial plan is geared to this assumption. Beyond the peak of global oil production the world will face shrinking supplies of increasingly expensive oil. That is a manageable proposition if the peak is several decades away. It is a major problem if the peak is imminent. Growing numbers of people well qualified to offer an opinion fear that it is indeed imminent."

Global oil production currently stands at around 85 million barrels per day. By 2030, projected demand is expected to be 116 million barrels per day, a figure the oil cartel OPEC, the International Energy Agency, and the leading oil companies believe will be almost impossible to meet on current trends. If the world is really close to, or at, the moment of peak oil, prices will not just remain at $100 a barrel but could easily rise further. In April 2005, Jim Rogers, who founded the Quantum hedge fund with George Soros, predicted that crude could cost $150 a barrel within ten years (Hedge Funds Global Opportunities Conference in New York), a forecast that looked far less fanciful three years later.

> The question on oil will be how high the price goes and stays, because there may be vast amounts of oil in the world but no one has discovered a great oilfield in over 35 years.
>
> The Alaskan and Mexican fields are in decline, and while the North Sea has made the UK one of the great oil exporters in the last 20 years, within the decade the UK will be a net importer.

Optimists argue that the date for peak oil has constantly been pushed back and that with global prices high there will be an incentive to find and develop fields in the more inhospitable parts of the world. Leggett says the optimists are in denial; fewer and fewer giant oil fields are being discovered, large portions of supposedly proved reserves might not exist, while it is an illusion that large amounts of crude can be extracted from Canadian tar sands. The cold wastes of Alberta are unlikely to rival the deserts of the Middle East; the oil from the tar sands is hard to get at, expensive to extract, and will provide little more than 2.5 million barrels per day by 2015 (Leggett, "The Trouble with Oil").

The very real prospect is that oil prices continue to be high. And while it is certainly true that the shift in production in developed economies from manufacturing to services means that each unit of output is now less energy intensive, oil is still vital for the West. Higher crude prices mean higher costs for business and lower disposable income for consumers. In the short run, the impact is inflationary but in the longer run the squeeze on corporate profits and consumer spending is deflationary. The fact that the world economy continued to grow strongly in the five years during which oil prices rose from $20 a barrel in early 2003 to $100 a barrel in early 2008 does not mean that the impact of dearer energy can be permanently shrugged off.

Painful though this would be for Western economies, the impact would be far more grievous if oil supplies were cut off. One possible cause of shortages would be environmental disaster of the sort that was wrought to U.S. production in the Gulf of Mexico by Hurricane Katrina in August 2005. The other threat stems from geopolitical risk.

Climate change experts say that the risk of environmental disaster as a result of climate change is growing, noting that there has been a correlation since 1970 between sea temperature and the increased frequency of cyclones. The year 2005 saw the most destructive hurricane season on record, culminating in the loss of more than 2,000 lives and an estimated $125 billion worth of damage in the violent storm that flooded large parts on New Orleans. Even more violent hurricanes, with larger peak wind speeds and heavier rainfall, are predicted for the future (*Hurricanes: A Compendium of Hurricane Information*, U.S. Global Change Research Program, June 2007). The global insurance industry, facing the prospect of ever larger claims, has, unsurprisingly perhaps, been in the vanguard of attempts to persuade policymakers to take climate change more seriously.

Global political developments provide the final piece of the jigsaw. At one level, the threat is obvious: the attacks on New York and Washington on September 11, 2001, had an immediate impact on Western economies. Wall Street was shut for several days and when it reopened share prices fell abruptly, consumer confidence collapsed, and certain sectors of the economy—airlines especially—suffered considerable commercial damage. Any repetition of 9/11 at a time when financial markets are feeling the effects of the credit crunch, falling home prices, and dearer energy would amplify the impact of a downturn.

But there are two more geopolitical threats. The first arises from the fact that large quantities of the global reserves of oil and natural gas are in countries that are either politically unstable (the Middle East) or controlled by regimes prepared to use energy as a strategic weapon in international relations (Russia). With Western governments acutely aware of how vulnerable they are to regime change in Saudi Arabia, terrorist attacks on oil installations in Iraq, religious fundamentalism in Iran, and sabre-rattling in Moscow, energy security has moved up the policy agenda and is one reason why the British government has, in the face of considerable domestic opposition, supported the building of a new generation of nuclear reactors.

All this is happening against the background of profound changes to the international balance of power, mirroring changes seen a century ago that made the world a far more dangerous place in the years 1890 to 1945 than it had been in the previous three-quarters of a century.

There were no major wars involving all the great powers between Waterloo and 1914. Historians attribute this period of peace to the fact that Britain, the global hegemon, was committed to the peaceful exploitation of its largely maritime interests and to the balance of power between the other great powers. From the late nineteenth century, this balance of power was affected by the rise of some powers—the United States, Germany, Japan, Russia—and the decline of others, Austria-Hungary, the Ottoman Empire. Britain became involved in two costly world wars for the reasons it had always reluctantly involved itself in Continental adventures—to prevent one continental power achieving dominance. The Cambridge historian Harry Hinsley wrote in the early 1960s (*Power and the Pursuit of Peace*, Cambridge University Press, 1963) that the balance of power was restored in 1945 when neither the United States nor the Soviet Union could normally consider invading each other or letting loose their nuclear weapons, the 1962 Cuban missile crisis and the 1983 "hot autumn" being exceptional and highly dangerous moments in history. This did not prevent the two great powers from fighting proxy wars in other parts of the world—Asia, Africa, and Latin America—but it did mean that there was no chance of a third world war. Hinsley dates the challenge to the nineteenth-century balance of power as 1890, and future historians may date 1990 as the moment when the post–Second World War balance of power started to come apart. This was the year when the reunification of Germany heralded the end of Moscow's dominance in Eastern Europe and the breakup of the Soviet Union. In Asia, there were signs that the pro-market reforms introduced by Beijing in the late 1970s were turning China into an industrial power of real clout; India was a year away from introducing its own attempt at moving away from a command economy.

And just as the tensions from the breakup of the nineteenth-century balance of power quickly became evident, so the period of tranquillity that followed America's elevation to unrivaled global superpower was also brief. The emergence of the new Asian powers—not just China but also a Russia reinvigorated by the economic strength it attained by virtue of its considerable reserves of ever more valuable oil and gas—posed a discernible threat to American hegemony. As Paul Kennedy stressed in his seminal work on the link between economic and political power, the U.S. should not assume that it will remain unchallenged for ever.

> Although the United States is at present still in a class of its own economically and perhaps even militarily, it cannot avoid confronting the two great tests which challenge the longevity of every major power that occupies the "number one" position in world affairs: whether, in the military/strategic realm, it can preserve a reasonable balance between the nation's perceived defence requirements and the means it possesses

to maintain those commitments; and whether, as an intimately related point, it can preserve the technological and economics bases of its power from relative erosion in the face of the ever-shifting patterns of global production. (*The Rise and Fall of the Great Powers*, Fontana, 1988.)

What Professor Kennedy did not realize, perhaps, was just how quickly these political changes could occur. Writing in 1988, he failed to spot that the Soviet Union was atrophying economically and on the point of collapse.

So how could this threat to the U.S. materialize? One theory is that America's international creditors—China and the Gulf States—will put the sort of pressure on Washington that Washington put on Britain and France at the time of the Suez crisis in 1956. Flynt Leverett, writing in the *National Interest* magazine (January–February 2008), said the U.S. is now facing an "axis of oil," a loose and shifting coalition of energy-exporting and importing states, anchored by Russia and China. "The ability of such a coalition to resist American hegemony is now compounded by the vulnerability of the United States to financial and monetary pressure by its major international creditors—most of which are at least putative members of the axis of oil." Should China and Russia choose to do so, they have the power to put coordinated financial and monetary pressure on the U.S. for strategic ends.

Most importantly, there is the question of how the U.S. would cope should the dollar cease to be the "world's money." At the time of the Asian crisis in 1997 and 1998 such a suggestion would have been unthinkable; since then U.S. trade deficits have grown bigger, China has grown rapidly, the euro has appeared as a rival reserve currency, and the U.S.-led invasion of Iraq has led to increased tension in the Middle East. The Chinese have financed the American trade deficit by buying vast quantities of U.S. Treasury bonds and have quietly made it plain that they would be prepared to make life difficult for Washington by selling assets should the White House continue to threaten the imposition of trade sanctions. In the Middle East, the Iranian government has openly suggested pricing oil in euros rather than dollars, while even the traditionally pro-Washington Saudi government has cultivated a strategic partnership with Beijing.

A true perfect storm, therefore, might look like this. In October 2008, on the thirty-fifth anniversary of the start of the Yom Kippur War, George Bush finally loses patience with Tehran and, in the last big decision of his presidency, launches air strikes against Iran's nuclear capability. The Iranians retaliate by shutting off supplies to the West and, in a further blow to crude supplies, militants in Saudi Arabia launch a coup attempt against the royal family. On the same day, just as the citizens of Louisiana, Mississippi, and Texas think they have seen the last of the stormiest summers on record, a category five hurricane sweeps across the Gulf of Mexico and shuts down half of America's oil refining capacity.

The military action in the Middle East and natural disaster combine to send the price of oil—already close to record levels—shooting up to $150 a barrel, pushing up inflation in all Western economies. Central banks, fearful of another 1970s-style surge in the cost of living, raise interest rates, intensifying the effects of the worst economic downturn seen since the 1980s. Financial markets suffer a spasm of selling. Banks stop lending and as businesses fail in their droves, lengthening dole queues prompt a meltdown in the housing market. No part of the world is left untouched by the turmoil, although the impact is severest on the country that was the root of the problem—the United States. China does not fall into recession but is hit by the curse that often afflicts countries that host the Olympics. With the games over, Beijing cuts back on investment and takes action to curb inflation just at the time that exports to the U.S. are being choked off. China's growth rate halves to 5 percent and there is a domino effect through the rest of Asia. A bill imposing trade sanctions on Beijing for its refusal to revalue its currency is passed by Congress; China responds by dumping a quarter of its dollar assets, sending the U.S. currency and global markets into free fall.

In the recent past, predicting doom and gloom has been a game for losers, the financial markets equivalent of the boy who cried wolf. There is good reason for this: policymakers act to stop recessions from developing. When times are tough businesses cut prices in order to keep consumers spending; at a global level there is no obvious reason why the Chinese or the Saudis would want to cripple the American economy since to do so would cost them hundreds of billions of dollars in lost exports. The perfect storm may never happen.

Yet ultimately, the message of the tale of the boy who cried wolf was that there was indeed a wolf. Consider the following facts: debt in America stands at 300 percent of GDP and the last time it was at this level hundreds of banks were going bust in the Great Depression; credit has been expanding in the U.S. at more than double the rate it was in the 1920s; banks in the U.S., Britain, and Europe are nursing as yet unknown losses as a result of subprime mortgages; Britain has seen the first run on a high street bank in almost a century and a half; real wages in Britain and the U.S. have been squeezed; oil prices have quintupled in the past five years; the Middle East from Gaza in the west to Afghanistan in the east is in political and economic turmoil; China is becoming relatively stronger and is seeking to expand its influence in the Pacific; the U.S. is becoming relatively weaker; a series of environmental disasters has highlighted the risk of climate change to the global economy.

None of which means there is going to be a perfect storm, let alone that there is the economic equivalent of Britain's Meteorological Office that can precisely time its arrival. Yet the sky is growing darker not just with storm clouds but with chickens coming home to roost. There is a very real risk that economies already enfeebled by a borrowing binge and untrammelled speculation will be further weakened by policy error, higher oil prices, environmental collapse, and rising geopolitical tension. Should that occur—as it might within the next five years—three things will happen. There will be an economic crisis the like of which has not been seen since the 1930s. The gods that have failed will be pilloried in a new era of populism. And there will be a hunger for new and better ways of doing things. It is to the policies for a saner world that we turn in the last chapter of this book.

CHAPTER 10

After the Gold Rush

How the New Populism
Makes the Financial System Safer,
Gives Ordinary People a Bigger
Slice of the Cake, and Puts the New
Olympians Back in Their Cage

Faced by failure of credit they have proposed only the lending of more money. Stripped of the lure of profit by which to induce our people to follow their false leadership, they have resorted to exhortations, pleading tearfully for restored confidence. They know only the rules of a generation of self-seekers.

— FRANKLIN ROOSEVELT,
inaugural address, March 1933

Ultimately what one loves about life are the things that last, because those who care, see to it that they do.

— STEVEN BACH, *Final Cut*

If the creation of wealth itself destroys and wastes humanity, that wealth, however vast, will never suffice to repair the ravages it has wrought.

— JEREMY SEABROOK, *The Race for Riches*

243

With the world reeling from a global financial crisis, Gordon Brown flew to Japan to spell out a few home truths to both his hosts and other leaders of the main economic powers. Brown stressed the need for the Group of Seven club of rich nations to work together to restore international stability and renewed growth. "But this is only possible if the industrialised world provides the engine for growth by sustaining demand in the world economy," Brown wisely added. "All industrialised countries—in Europe and Japan as well as North America—must bear their share of that adjustment. No one country can either escape its responsibility to play its part in sustaining global demand or be required to bear the whole burden and thereby encourage protectionist sentiment."

In an impressive *tour d'horizon*, Brown added that fears of the dumping of cheap Asian products must not lead to the West closing its markets, and reaffirmed there could be no relaxation of the British government's tough anti-inflationary policy.

Finally, and unsurprisingly, he rejected claims from Britain's Tory opposition that the government was responsible.

A freehand summary of Brown's remarks to the international summit held in Japan in early February 2008? It could be read in that way. But it is actually a résumé of a more youthful Gordon Brown's opinions as expressed on September 16, 1998, during a trip to Tokyo in the wake of turmoil caused by the currency crises in the Far East and the Russian decision the previous month to default on some of its external debt. In 1998 and 1999, Gordon Brown urged the G7, the International Monetary Fund, and pretty much any gathering of finance ministers or central bankers, or both, to bolster the international financial system against future crises by improving surveillance of cross-border money flows, by establishing early warning systems that would whistle like a boiling kettle when ill-conceived economic policy in one country threatened to spill over and create problems for other countries, by improving the transparency of financial markets to ensure nobody would have the chance to make a killing out of general market ignorance and generally to establish a new "world financial architecture" that would allow everybody to enjoy the full benefits of financial globalization while ensuring that all the risks were safely encased in an intergovernmental version of the sort of concrete tomb used to store radioactive nuclear waste.

Does any of this ring a bell? In light of the earlier discussion in this book, does the notion that all rewards can be preserved while all risks can be parked somewhere out of sight and out of mind sound eerily familiar? It is, we would argue, merely the political version of the financial market fantasy that suggests ever more complex instruments can be used to disperse risk while allowing banks, hedge funds, and others to hang on to the rewards.

As the current storm broke upon the leading economies, there was every sign that Brown, now British prime minister, remained committed to the notion that large-scale problems in large-scale financial markets among large-scale participants requires a large-scale political response from the G7, the IMF, and any other worthy international forum that wishes to get involved. Key to this is the notion that markets will become less volatile if they can be made more transparent. Brown has been pushing this notion with regard to the oil market since at least the autumn of 2004, and has set up an information gathering initiative to that end with the Saudi Arabian authorities. Since the autumn of 2004, the price per barrel for North Sea Brent crude has soared from about $46 to smash through the $100 a barrel level, suggesting that Brown's "transparency" may not be all it is cracked up to be.

As 2008 dawned, however, the old songbook was dusted down as Brown and his colleagues tried to find a way out of the encircling gloom. As ten years earlier, the first reaction was to huddle with other G7 ministers and officials and work on a communiqué. Perhaps the subconscious hope is that even if the assembled big-wigs produce wrong-headed answers, this will matter less if blame for these "solutions" can be spread over different countries. Again, there is an echo of the financial engineers' belief that risk, if smashed into sufficiently tiny pieces and dispersed among a great range of institutions and other investors, effectively ceases to be risky. That this notion is wrong by about 180 degrees was amply demonstrated in the global market crisis that first struck in the summer of 2007. Far from making markets less risky, by spreading risk the wizards in the banks had managed to globalize the consequences of reckless lending in specific markets.

Thus on January 17, 2008, Alistair Darling flew to Paris for talks with the finance ministers of the three other G7 members of the European Union: France, Germany, and Italy. The chancellor was keen to get agreement on the need for better market surveillance from the IMF and the G7's Financial Stability Forum ahead of the meeting of the Group of Eight in Tokyo early the following month (the G8 is the political version of the G7, at which Britain is represented by the prime minister rather than the chancellor and which comprises all the G7 members plus Russia). The UK's faith in the efficacy of better market surveillance was especially touching in light of the fact that the FSF was set up in April 1999 in the wake of the Asian and Russian financial crises precisely to ensure such shocks could not recur. That they did so, with much greater force, from mid-2007 onward suggests the FSF has not fulfilled its promise.

Watching Brown and Darling fly to international meetings, call for greater surveillance and transparency, and suggest new ways of "tackling imbalances" and "reducing volatility," the private citizen may well conclude, with the former baseball player and manager Yogi Berra, that "this is like déjà vu all over again." Or perhaps Darling's performance is reminiscent of a former Archbishop of Canterbury, Robert Runcie, whose globe-trotting method of operation was described thus by the writer A. N. Wilson: "He has said bland things to the Pope. He said bland things to the Lutherans. He is saying bland things now he is home again" (quoted in *The Young Fogey Handbook*, Javelin, 1985).

Another figure with good reason to feel much the same way would be the New Olympian hedge fund manager, speculator, or investment banker. At gatherings of the G7, the IMF, or EU finance ministers, and so forth, they would quickly have established that, despite the chaos they had unleashed on the world economy, nobody was really gunning for them. At the first sight of the popping flashbulbs at ministerial press conferences, of delegates reaching for the translation headsets, of the trolleys of coffee and pastries wheeled by waiters or waitresses dressed in dark trousers or skirts and trim green waistcoats, of the bar-coded conference security passes whose efficacy seems predicated on the idea that any terrorist will have the decency to give his real name, of the police helicopter overhead, of the ranks of official Lincoln Town Cars clogging up central Washington, they will assume that, whatever their current business problems, they have nothing to worry about from politicians and regulators. And on present showing they will be right.

We do not need any more New Olympian institutions to "monitor" world markets and to give "early warning" of the next crisis. Those that we already have did little good in heading off the present debacle. Nor do we need endless meetings of the type described in the last paragraph, bulging with the terracotta army of look-alike and think-alike ministers, central bankers, and bureaucrats. But we had better resign ourselves to the prospect of international conferences galore. None is likely to get to the root of the problem. They will resemble gatherings of liberal schoolmasters who, bewildered by the destructive consequences of having allowed the kids to express themselves, wring their hands as they survey the devastation, unwilling to contemplate the admission that they were horribly, utterly wrong and fearful, anyway, that it may be too late to take any meaningful action.

Such toothless gatherings, we shall be told, will produce codes of conduct for hedge funds, and tough new standards for accounting and for prudential banking standards. Their existence will be predicated on the concept that finance is now an affair of huge, multinational entities, thus only huge global governmental get-togethers have the slightest chance of bringing even a semblance of order to the activities of these entities. This idea reaches back at least until the 1970s, and was adumbrated in a hugely enjoyable, very well-written, and (in our view) quite mistaken book by journalist and writer Axel Madsen (*Private Power*, Abacus, 1981).

Madsen declared that multinationals enjoy "power beyond flag and country," adding, "Of the 100 wealthiest entities on the international scene, well over half are corporations." The argument that for a private entity to be wealthier than a political entity somehow damages the legitimacy or potency of the latter is reminiscent of the fuss in Britain in the early 1960s after it emerged that the pop singer Adam Faith earned more than the prime minister. That Faith's earnings and the prime minister's authority had no connection whatever with each other was, it seems, in sore need of being forcefully pointed out.

Indeed, elsewhere in Madsen's book, the cat is very nearly let out of the bag by none other than Sir David Orr, then chairman of consumer goods multinational Unilever. Here was someone who clearly did not believe that huge multinationals somehow had the nation state at their mercy:

> If anyone asks him if it isn't true that that polyglot companies are largely beyond the control of any single government, Orr smiles and says that's, of course, true, "but only because we come under the control of all the governments of the countries in which we operate for everything over which those governments exercise jurisdiction. Our problem is to ensure any given action is only controlled by one government; and, quite often, especially in tax matters, we fail."

It is worth noting, in passing, that Sir David's comments cast a new light on the creation of entities such as the European Union. Far from such large entities being essential in order to exercise some sort of control over large companies, they look rather more like being essential to the simplification of large companies' dealings with political authorities.

One final excerpt from *Private Power* discloses a rather more sinister side to the much touted New Olympian myth that the nation-state has a strictly truncated future in the brave new world of global finance. Madsen quotes journalist Norman Macrae on the question of worker participation in industry. We are not expressing a view one way or another on this issue, but are deeply concerned by the rationale behind Macrae's objection to it:

> To the proponents of worker participation who say that the arguments for it are the same as those for universal suffrage in the 19th Century,

Macrae says: "Exactly, the arguments for it belong entirely to this land of look-behind. Voter control of anything in the 20th Century, like monarchy in the 19th Century, is where the world is coming from, but not where it is going to."

Macrae's words are taken from a piece in *The Economist* entitled "The Coming Entrepreneurial Revolution: A Survey." It was published in the early days of the New Olympian revolution on December 25, 1976. But then the idea of the mobile and ungovernable corporation appeals to politicians who prefer the patronage of the superrich to the tedious work of public administration. Increasingly, they see their job as providing public relations expertise to "the big end of town": they sell the "inevitable" erosion of pension rights, the "inevitable" decline of public services, and the "necessity" of yet more privatization through the full range of market research and "perception management" techniques.

In exchange for their services they are flattered by the plutocratically inclined media, and they get to experience the jet-set lifestyle of the superrich. Key to the New Olympian project has been the notion that mere mortals and their governments need the Olympians a lot more than the Olympians need them. This piece of propaganda has enjoyed extraordinary success across the decades, across the continents, and across political party lines. Even after the current crisis saw Big Finance whining like drug addicts facing cold turkey for public bailouts and state-supplied cheap credit, the illusion persists, a feat of mass hallucination worthy of the classical gods of antiquity.

We believe that only when this illusion is dispelled can work really begin on creating a robust postcrisis financial structure.

A Demeaning Dependency Culture: Big Finance and Big Business Today

With all due respect to Norman Macrae, our inspiration for understanding the respective roles of government on the one hand and large-scale business, finance, and industry on the other is Theodore Roosevelt, U.S. president from 1901 to 1909 and cousin of Franklin

Roosevelt, whom we quote at the head of this chapter. Teddy Roosevelt—a Republican and an imperialist—was about as far from being a dangerous leftist as it is possible to be, but he had this to say:

> The vast individual and corporate fortunes, the vast combinations of capital which have marked the development of our industrial system, create new conditions and necessitate a change from the old attitude of the state and the nation toward property. . . . More and more it is evident that the state, and if necessary the nation, has got to possess the right of supervision and control as regards the great corporations which are its creatures. (Quoted by Edmund Morris, *Theodore Rex*, Random House, 2001.)

> In his presidential message to Congress on December 3, 1901, Roosevelt declared, "It is no limitation upon property rights or freedom of contract to require that when they receive from the government the privilege of doing business under corporate form . . . they shall do so upon absolutely truthful representations. . . . Great corporations exist only because they are created and safeguarded by our institutions and it is therefore our right and duty to see that they work in harmony with those institutions." (Morris, *Theodore Rex*.)

In other words, we made you and we can break you. In that spirit we offer our suggestions, not in the spirit of establishing yet another international quango sitting in agreeable premises in New York, or Geneva or Paris, monitoring, consulting, surveilling, and early-warning, headed by the very able chap who used to be deputy to another very able chap who has been tipped as the next head of the Bank for International Settlements, or the IMF, or similar. Britain's New Olympians are never happier than when comparing themselves to the salty merchant adventures of the nation's past, and no after-dinner speech in the City or glossy magazine article about London's dominance as a financial center is complete without some reference to the swashbuckling traders whose galleons plied the seven seas and whose DNA has somehow been passed down to the bankers, dealers, and asset-strippers of the modern Square Mile. The reality is that the investment banks, hedge funds, and others are creatures of our law, incapable of existence without life support from our legal system, entirely dependent on the juridical and political systems they effect to despise, just as the moon astronauts were utterly dependent for life itself on the items they had brought with them from earth, to which they were effectively attached by a sort of invisible umbilical cord.

It is we, through our elected representatives, who have created the limited liability company (which allows corporations to enjoy all the rewards of their successful activities while passing on much of the losses of their failed ones to society at large), the fractional reserve bank (which allows banks to create new money out of thin air), and the trust (which conveniently allows assets to own themselves).

The limited company is not only an extraordinary mechanism for privatizing profit and socializing losses, but allows shareholders and executives to escape much of any bad consequences of their behavior:

> In Britain, corporate signatures end in 'ltd', that means 'limited liability'. The Latins are more poetic and descriptive: they use 'SA'—Sociedad Anonima, or Society of the Nameless. It all adds up to the same thing: when the cops come, there's nobody home. . . . This legal anomaly has led to all sorts of aberrant corporate behaviour. (Robert Townsend, *Up the Organisation*, Coronet, 1971.)

Fractional reserve banking, as already noted, allows banks to behave in a way that would be considered fraudulent in any other walk of life—to lend out money that does not exist and, by doing so, to bring into existence the great majority of money in use in the economy. Those with loans or overdrafts may imagine their borrowings are made up of money belonging to depositors. Almost all of it is not; it is bank-created imaginary money, legally spun out of thin air by the bank in the form of loans. When banks create too much of it, generating inflation, they put up interest rates, which increases their return on their loans. Furthermore, central banks will usually step in to rescue any bank that has recklessly abused its credit creation ability.

Trusts, the slightly mysterious third sibling in this trio, perform one very simple task: they allow assets to be parked, away from any named owner. One iron law of finance is that every asset is ultimately owned by individuals. Companies, banks, partnerships, and investment funds are merely intermediate, artificial entities. Trusts are the one exception to this rule; they can be owners in their own right, without any immediate human beneficiary. The potential advantages of keeping assets for a time off any person's books in terms of tax planning and many other maneuvers are obvious.

This trio—limited companies, fractional reserve banks, and trusts—are all creatures of law, creations of the political system. Their existence renders unintentionally amusing the following entry in a dictionary of economics:

> Law and economics: . . . The economics of law and economics is firmly in the liberal economics camp, favouring free markets and arguing that regulation often does more harm than good. (Matthew Bishop, *Pocket Economist*, Economist Books, 2000.)

Show us a real-life merchant adventurer who abjures these three vital legal props and instead hazards his own fortune, day in and day out, in the pursuit of business and we will be lusty in our demands that the state get off his back. We may even help him aboard his galleon and wave him off from the quayside. But we will offer long odds on his ever reappearing.

This, then, must be the starting point of reform—nothing more nor less than saying boo to the New Olympians, to breaking their spell and telling them that we are well within our rights to bring their activities back under democratic control.

We do not mean them to be brought under the oversight of the New Olympians' technocratic opposite numbers in unelected national and transnational bodies, whether Britain's Financial Services Authority or the International Monetary Fund. These Olympian officials exist precisely to promote the financial Olympians' agendas; their answer to every systemic problem is more "competition," freer trade, a smoother functioning of the very machine that caused the trouble in the first place. On the contrary, we would argue that the New Olympians have hollowed out the democratic process precisely by removing more and more powers from political control and handing them over to this cadre of technocrats. The result in the first decade of the twenty-first century was, at best, the view among voters that it was not worth voting because their views were never listened to and, at worst, the rise of extreme parties eager to exploit grievances about job insecurity and stagnant real incomes. Action to redress the democratic deficit would have been necessary even were it the case that rule by the New Olympians had ensured a permanent economic nirvana. As it is, we are all in the happy position that the entirely benign project of bringing the Olympians to account for their economic misdemeanors will have the wholly desirable effect of reviving democracy.

But having asserted our right to control the private sector New Olympians and to give instructions to the public sector Olympians, rather than take instructions from them, what sort of control ought to be asserted and what sort of instructions ought to be issued?

Not the sort that have proved so ineffectual in the past. As we said above, the last thing we need is another monitoring forum, another code of conduct, another "information exchange and transparency initiative" or another "benchmark of best practice." These and similar proposals are rooted in the assumption that there is nothing much wrong with the New Olympian system that cannot be put right by mild admonition and oversight or by removing obstacles to the better functioning of the Olympian system itself. This is the worldview of the Institute of Economic Affairs, of the Adam Smith Institute, of the business schools, and of the financial section of many newspapers. The asset—be it a landholding, a shareholding, or a business enterprise—exists in some state of nature. Then politicians or state employees come along with their laws and their taxes and "distort" it.

All true enough, in the sense of personal private property: a car, a home, a piece of jewelry. Property brought into being and guaranteed by the state and by law, however, cannot, as Theodore Roosevelt explained, be seen in the same light or treated in the same way. It is partly because we have allowed ourselves to be persuaded that the two types of property are identical that we are in the current position. It will be objected that we, society, already ask a great deal from the financial and big business interest in return for privileges such as limited liability and credit creation. Do we not insist that they treat their employees fairly, that they comply with reams of business principles, and that that they disburse assorted state benefits through pay packets? True enough. Moneybags Bank is regulated as an employer, as a potential polluter, as a potential discriminator, as a subject of anti–money laundering regulations and as a possessor of large amounts of personal data. It is regulated as almost everything, but it is not regulated as a bank. Its actual business is entirely deregulated. Irresponsible lending, dangerous speculation, investment in toxic securities—there is practically no limit to the use the bank is allowed to make of the government-guaranteed product in which it is allowed to traffic: money. Much the same goes for the large limited liability public company, required to show what passes for virtue in the modern world in every aspect of its activities—except its business. Takeovers, layoffs, outsourcing . . . the pursuit of "shareholder value" is overriding.

As with the hollowing-out of democracy, these abuses of legal privileges would be obnoxious in principle even had they produced permanent stability and prosperity. That they have not should make it easier to get to grips with them.

Love of the Common People: Roosevelt, Attlee, and Continental Social Democracy

So we propose, first and foremost, root and branch reform of the financial system. We eschew the word "radical," which has become too all-encompassing in its application to have real meaning. Nigel Lawson was a self-styled "Tory radical."

What happened the last time a new generation of leaders came to grips with the wreckage of a speculative financial system run riot? The most notable example, and the most lustrous, after all these years, was the accession to power of the man whose quotation heads this chapter—President Franklin Roosevelt.

As he took office in March 1933, amid a chronic slump that closed almost all of the nation's banks and brought its economic life to a halt, the new president's mixture of dynamism and self-confidence excited even those not his natural admirers, such as Churchill:

> A single man, whom accident, destiny or Providence, has placed at the head of one hundred and twenty millions of active, educated, excitable and harassed people, has set out upon this momentous expedition. Many doubt if he will succeed. Some hope he will fail. Although the policies of President Roosevelt are conceived in many respects from a narrow view of American self-interest, the courage, the power and the scale of his effort must enlist the ardent sympathy of every country, and his success could not fail to lift the whole world forward into the sunlight of an easier and more genial age. (*Great Contemporaries*, 1937.)

At a distance, Roosevelt's New Deal seems a many-tentacled beast, whose aspects range from arts funding and job creation schemes to the foundations of a rudimentary welfare state. But for simplicity's sake, we can discern five main pillars: reflation of the economy, public works programs (such as the electrification of the Tennessee Valley), strict control of banking and finance, improved welfare for the very poor, and pro-trade unionism (this latter aspect receiving comparatively little attention these days). There is certainly a left-wing case against President Roosevelt as someone who patched up American capitalism after its reckless driving had resulted in a spectacular crash, but who had achieved little else. Anthony J. Badger of Newcastle University states that case:

> The deficiencies of the New Deal were glaring. As the nine million unemployed in 1939 testified, the policies for industrial recovery did not work. . . . The commitment to deficit spending was belated and half-hearted. Neither through taxation nor through anti-trust prosecution was the Roosevelt administration able to break up the economic power of large corporations or to redistribute wealth. . . . The ambitious plans to resolve the problems of rural poverty were largely

stillborn. Spending on direct relief was always inadequate. . . . Too often relief perpetuated traditional and degrading attitudes towards welfare recipients. Work relief never reached more than 40 percent of the unemployed.

But Badger continues:

It is equally easy to replace this bleak catalogue of New Deal failure with a positive achievement of its success—the more so when New Deal activism is contrasted to the inaction of the federal government under [Herbert] Hoover [the previous president].

In contrast to Hoover's vain exhortations to keep wages up . . . [Roosevelt] put a statutory floor under wages, checked the downwards deflationary spiral, and halted the relentless erosion of labour standards. Together with direct federal public works expenditure, the NRA [National Recovery Administration, a government body] seemed to prevent matters from getting worse and, through 1936, government intervention in the economy paralleled, if it did not cause, modest but definite recovery. A stabilised banking and securities system, eventual deficit spending, and protected labour standards gave hope for ultimately orderly recovery. (*The New Deal*, Macmillan, 1989.)

The programs of the Labour administrations of 1945–1951 differed from the New Deal as in as many ways as it resembled it, the most obvious difference being that it occurred after the Second World War rather than before. Indeed, it may be argued (although this is not the place to do so) that the war was to Britain what the Great Depression had been to the United States—a defining national moment after which the ordinary people, having suffered so much, would be invited to society's high table, never to be turned away again.

Public works were a far smaller feature of Clement Attlee's "New Jerusalem," as it has become known, than of President Roosevelt's New Deal, for the simple reason that large-scale job creation was a less pressing need in a postwar command economy. Similarly, publicly financed farm support was less totemic in postwar Britain that in prewar America; *The Grapes of Wrath* was set in California, not Shrop-shire. And one of the great reforms of the Attlee years—the granting of independence to India and Pakistan—had no echo of any kind in the U.S. Neither did another, the large-scale nationalization of min-ing, transport, health care, and other activities.

That said, the similarities are striking, in particular the intertwin-ing of more generous welfare benefits with an interventionist and reflationary economic policy. On both sides of the Atlantic, the em-phasis was on greater personal and social security, to be sustained by a mightily productive economic base, working at full stretch at all times, from which depression and recession would be banished.

As with President Roosevelt, Attlee's legacy has been criticized from the liberal left:

> The Labour Government of 1945–51, whatever its reformist aspira-tions, was never really a group of social radicals. They adhered to the em-pire; many of them believed in white supremacy; they, or most of them, upheld the extreme penalty of the rope; they refused to upset the min-ers by abolishing fox hunting (popular in some mining areas at this time) or other traditional rural pursuits such as hare coursing. (Kenneth O. Morgan, *The People's Peace*, Oxford University Press, 1992.)

One may argue that treating economic security as a higher prior-ity than stopping people from hunting foxes was one of the great strengths of the Attlee governments. Certainly, the way its accession to office was greeted suggests many people would have agreed. This is former *Picture Post* editor Tom Hopkinson:

> In 1943 . . . [our proprietor Edward Hulton] published a book—*The New Age*—which Tom Clarke, former editor of the News Chronicle, described in a review as ". . . a brave and eager book, a refreshing adventure among ideas." It called for "a change of heart and a new spiritual and social urge," and the reviewer described the Utopia it envisaged: "There will be no Stock Exchange . . . no speculations in shares, no genuflexions before an obsolete gold standard. No money 'talking' as if it were a commodity. Business will be more controlled, internationally and internally, in an

economic system combining nationalization and private enterprise." The mood continued into August 1945, when Hulton wrote a resounding welcome to Mr Attlee's new Labour Government.

> The great victory of the Labour Party at the General Election was a surprise to everybody, to Labour people almost as much as to anyone else. We now have, for the first time in British history, a Labour Government in power with a large majority. Wise men have long realised that Labour must some day come to power; and it is well that it should do so unfettered. More will be relieved that the form of Conservatism represented by Lord Beaverbrook, and aided and abetted by Mr Churchill in his latest phase, has been flung indignantly overboard. . . .
>
> I am not personally a Socialist . . . still less am I a materialist. Yet I rejoice that latter-day Conservatism has been overthrown. (*Picture Post 1938–50*, Penguin, 1970.)

Images of the 1945 Labour government's economic reforms are dominated, for some, by the plaques placed at the entrance of every British coal mine on January 1, 1947, declaring: "This colliery is now managed by the National Coal Board on behalf of the People," for others by hazier images of idealistic young doctors welcoming their first National Health Service patients. Yet the Attlee government's policies toward finance and the City were every bit as far-reaching as those pursued in the United States under the New Deal. While nationalization of the Bank of England in 1946 made little practical difference, it was hugely symbolic, parking an enormous tank on the front lawn of the City. Henceforth, banking, insurance, and finance would be subordinated to national economic policy. Unlike in post-Depression America, there was no immediate need to separate stock broking, market making, and commercial banking from one another—the City's own closed-shop rules did that already. All that was needed was to ensure the rules were properly enforced, that brokers and market makers would remain as separate, relatively small partnerships, that merchant banks would be grouped under the Accepting Houses Committee, where an eye could be kept on them, that the discounted bill market would transmit the Treasury's interest rate decisions to the wider world, and that the Bank governor would, as the cliché has it, raise an eyebrow at any untoward speculative activity. The Bank would police exchange controls, and the Stock Exchange would decline in relevance as key industries were taken into public ownership.

Across the Channel, postwar social democracy took different forms in different countries. France had a large public sector; West Germany's was relatively smaller. Italy maintained some of the large state holding companies inherited from the fascist era. Swedish social democracy relied on the need to compete in export markets to discipline large companies and keep the economy in trim. France preferred to devalue the franc early and often, confident that French people would buy French cars, eat and drink French produce, and take their holidays in France, thus shielding themselves from the inflationary effects of a weaker currency while gaining competitive advantage overseas.

All that said, there are a number of common themes in continental postwar social democracy running through most of the economies of what was then Western Europe. "[In] the late 1950s and 1960s another Europe appeared. This was a Europe which put emphasis on unity, on creating a great centre of production, on being modern and progressive, on establishing uniform systems of justice and welfare, on giving an example of international co-operation" (Richard Hoggart and Douglas Johnson, *An Idea of Europe*, Chatto & Windus, 1987).

The first theme was a stress on peaceful labor relations and partnership between capital and labor. This was obviously more successful in some countries (Germany, for example) than others (France). But everywhere it was a theme.

The second was a stress on creating national and, later, European "champion" companies in different industries, under the guidance of national governments.

The third relates to social cohesion and the compression of income differences. Ostentation was frowned on, glaring inequality was thought impermissible, and progressive taxation bit significantly into the top slice of higher earners' incomes. West Germany, for all its powerhouse status, never produced a breed of superrich tycoons. Leading industrialists were expected to live comfortably, not luxuriously.

A fourth theme was the relative insignificance of banking and finance, even in countries such as the Netherlands in which the financial sector had traditionally been strong. In some countries, parts of the banking system were in public ownership. Germany's lavishly praised central bank, the Bundesbank, pursued hard money policies for political and social reasons, not to foster a large financial sector with an international reach. On the Continent, only Switzerland provided an echo to the pre-1945 and post-1976 British obsession with a strong currency linked to a powerful banking sector, and Switzerland was rather more successful in this endeavor, at least in terms of keeping the Swiss franc as a hard currency.

And the fifth theme of European social democracy was a stress on competitive markets to deliver higher living standards. This may seem to jar with the first four themes, but it does not. After all, the Common Market was the postwar European institution. Competition between European businesses would, it was believed, raise productivity; indeed, productivity may almost be seen as a separate theme in its own right. The quid pro quo for the higher pay and shorter hours enjoyed by Continental European workers was a constant rise in output per person. In tripartite Europe, the company supplied the best machinery, the workers operated it to the limit of its potential, and the government redistributed some of the company's profits back to the workers in social benefits.

It was a far cry from much of British industry, bedeviled by restrictive practices, go slow–type industrial action, and "who does what" demarcation disputes. Indeed, the notion of Continental Europe as an intrinsically more social democratic, welfarist, left-of-center sort of place in contrast to the savage Anglo-Saxon capitalism of modern Britain did not take root in the UK until the late 1980s. For most of the postwar period, the Continent's more vocal British admirers were on the right and in business circles, where the "responsible" trade unions of West Germany, in particular, were highly regarded.

He [Edward Heath] had been deeply impressed by the German success in co-operation between government, employers and trade unions which enabled their workers to produce more and to live so much more prosperously than British workers. On one occasion, as Heath was taking his leave after a visit to Bonn, Chancellor Willy Brandt mentioned the people waiting for his next appointment: "There are 16 union leaders out there. They are the men I run Germany with." (Richard Clutterbuck, *Britain in Agony*, Penguin, 1980.)

But as right-of-center British admirers of the Continental approach were to find out from the late 1980s onward, the European notion of an open market was not the free-fire zone of the Anglo-Saxon model, but a social construct to be carefully supervised by institutions such as the European Commission, in the years before it became so enthusiastic about untrammeled trade and capital movements and the European Court of Justice.

Back to the Future: Some Pointers for the Present

What can be drawn from this brief historical exploration of economic and social policy in the mid-twentieth century? In place of the New Olympianism we propose a New Populism, a creed that puts ravenous finance back into its cage and concentrates on a real-world agenda of jobs, living standards, and secure retirement instead of the Olympian agenda of free trade, free capital movement, and the primacy of finance. The New Populism we envisage would rest on the following principles.

First and foremost, we would argue, however separated in time and place, these mid-twentieth-century policies all stressed the subordination of finance. From Washington in the 1930s to London in the 1940s to Paris and Bonn in the 1950s and 1960s, financial sector activities were kept on a tight rein, their destructive potential fully realized and their proper, auxiliary role in relation to the real economy kept firmly in focus. Banks and other large corporations are creatures of law, and it is the public's right and duty to supervise them. Furthermore, they, the financial New Olympians, have had their chance.

The result of letting them off the leash has been a disaster. This, then, is our first and possibly most important principle.

The second is personal and social security, the principle that society should insure its members against misfortune, protect their savings, and make proper provision for their old age. This is what we tried to do in the past, and, in Britain, are trying again to do, with very mixed results, using a range of entitlements of frequently baffling complexity. The loss of a person's job ought to be a problem, not a cosmic disaster. Savings in approved schemes ought to be guaranteed. Why are the type of high-quality pensions on offer in the postwar period now unaffordable, and why did that unaffordability mysteriously emerge after the Soviet Union and its allies had disappeared? It would rightly be thought extraordinary were policymakers to agonize today over the difficulty of ensuring that the average family can buy an Austin Cambridge car and a black and white television. Our society is greatly wealthier than it was forty years ago, and improved cars and consumer goods are relatively less expensive. Why retirement schemes should be any different is not clear.

A third principle is accountability or democracy, to put it slightly differently. The leeching away of powers from national parliaments to the New Olympians' mandarin allies in bodies such as the IMF, the World Trade Organization, independent central banks, and the European Commission (these days a far more pro-finance and pro-free trade organization than in the early decades of the European Economic Community), is, we stated earlier, the Olympians' antidemocratic project. It would be obnoxious even without the economic and financial turmoil that it has created. So great is the democratic deficit that people increasingly either do not bother to vote or vote for nonmainstream parties. The answer from left-of-center parties, terrified of crossing the Olympian orthodoxy, has been more of the same. Thus the UK's Labour Party is losing votes to the British National Party, and the Irish Labour Party is losing votes to Sinn Fein. The response of both parties has been to cede more powers to Brussels and to insist on the need for another world trade agreement that will transfer more authority to the WTO.

There have been suggestions in the UK that Gordon Brown is planning a bill reasserting the primacy of British over EU law. That would be a most welcome blow against the Olympian system, but we fear it is unlikely to be proposed by Brown, a fundamentally conformist person with an apparent yearning for respectability.

A fourth principle is the undesirability of a semidetached superrich class. Not only does such a class pull money values completely out of shape, in the housing market for example, but it tends to be the *fons et origo* of the horrendous errors from which the world economy is now reeling. It was superrich investment bankers and derivatives traders who dreamed up collateralized debt obligations and exotic derivative products. It was the superrich who have demanded cheap money for most of the last decade and cheered on the inflating of the credit bubble.

This leads to our fifth principle, the protection and strengthening of an independent middle class. The superrich and their political allies are destroying the middle class. Lawyers and doctors are to be faced with a stark choice between corporate employment and unemployment, while deskilling and outsourcing are eating into occupations such as accountancy, journalism, and technical design. Much of this is attributed to "market forces" when in fact it stems from legislative changes designed to tear down time-honored protection for professionals. But even were the market to be driving all these changes, we believe the value of a professional middle class, independent of both the state and of corporate power, greatly outweighs any efficiency losses and that the market ought to be curbed. Besides, professions exist to offset market failures caused by inequalities of information—a deregulated market for health care would be a free-for-all for entrepreneurs offering a glittering array of "choices" to "consumers," many of whom would of course end up dead. Professions must be subject to public scrutiny, and they should be subject to sensible independent regulation too. But they cannot be adequately replaced by corporate forms of employment.

Which leads neatly to our sixth principle: social stability and tranquillity are more important than market efficiency or shareholder value. In other words, to the specific protections from the market for the professions ought to be added a general protection for everybody. If market forces dictate paving over the south of England, or the obliteration of British manufacturing, or the closure of the rural Post Office network, then they should be resisted. This is, of course, an impeccably conservative as well as a center-left position. This is T. E. Utley, writing in the *Daily Telegraph* on January 10, 1977:

> I simply do not believe that if society decides that some evil produced by the spontaneous forces of competition (i.e. mass unemployment in an area like Ulster, afflicted by civil disturbance, or the destruction of the farming industry) calls stridently for governmental action to temper it, that action is bound to prove disastrous, however prudently and deliberately it is conceived and carried out.

Our seventh and final principle may surprise some readers: liberty of the person. Hang on, you may say. You propose all sorts of controls on financial and business activity. It is a bit late in the day for you to start banging on about individual freedom.

Not at all. The New Olympians have been keen to assert that their right to move colossal sums around the world, speculate, and generate credit is indivisible from the right of humbler folk to live their lives as they choose, but we argue otherwise. The Olympians are in receipt of huge legal and other support from the state; ordinary people, including the self-employed and those running small businesses, are not. Limited liability and fractional reserve banking mean nothing to them. And yet as the financial interest has been progressively freed over recent decades, the liberty of the person has been increasingly restricted. Spot-tested at work for drugs, monitored by closed-circuit television, subject to rules prohibiting "inappropriate" language, soon, if a government program proceeds to its original conclusion, to be burdened with a national identity card, the individual is having a thin time of it. It is time to restore privacy and autonomy to the private citizen.

Much is made of the need to make trade-offs between liberty and security in the age of terrorism. We are told that we must face restrictions on our liberty to prevent terrorist attacks, and few object to sensible restrictions in this respect. But the New Olympians must concede the same point. They have been merrily transporting the financial equivalent of fissile material around the world for several years now, and the result is widespread contamination of the financial system. Irresponsible lending has caused genuine suffering.

So yes, our principles would give rise to much greater control of finance and big business. The "liberty" of the Olympians' institutions would be severely restricted. And this in turn gives rise to the suggestion that such controls would be ineffective, because, "in a globalized world," nothing much can be done to control the investment banks, hedge funds, and others. This deprecation of old-fashioned controls has been the orthodoxy for at least twenty years. It depicts interventionist governments as hopelessly flailing about, trying to get a grip on capital movements, an exercise as futile as trying to control the wind. This notion is not new. Addressing the Massachusetts legislature in 1867, writer and lawyer Richard Henry Dana spoke of the undesirability of passing laws against usury: "The market of the world moves with the irresistible power of ocean tides" (quoted in Lewis Hyde, *The Gift*, Random House, 1979).

This notion is quite misleading, for two reasons. First, the technology that makes possible almost instantaneous money transfers round the world and split-second dealings in cash and securities makes possible also the tracking of such funds by national authorities. Indeed, large financial movements are tracked already, in the name of anti–money laundering measures. No one suggests this is a pointless activity. Should some form of capital controls be thought desirable, the surveillance and enforcement machinery should not be impossibly difficult to bring into existence. As we noted, the technology is already there.

Second, there is a low-tech reinforcement for this high-tech equipment. Contracts or deals entered into in offshore jurisdictions, or anywhere else, in defiance of financial controls could be declared void in British law. This "negative enforcement" is highly attractive. It requires no police and relies simply on British courts not doing something—recognizing and enforcing financial arrangements made without authorization.

Both these methods of enforcement also give the lie to the objection that financial controls can work only with international agreement. In some cases, the objector is genuine and really hopes for every country in the world to sign up to a grand treaty on controlling speculative activity. In others, the objection is a ploy from those with no desire to see finance put back in its cage, rather like the child who declares he is only too happy to tidy up his bedroom but only when his left thumb stops hurting.

Not that international agreements are to be despised, provided two things are kept in mind. First, that, as things stand, such agreements are likely to be drawn up and enforced by the New Olympians' political and bureaucratic allies. Second, even when drawn up in good faith, such agreements tend to represent the minimum that all countries can sign up to. Individual nations serious about dismantling the New Olympian system will find they need to go it alone, at least to begin with.

So given the above-mentioned principles, and given that, contrary to myth, measures can be enforced, what ought those measures to be, in practical detail? In our limited experience, it is when critical commentators put forward their own ten-point plan that they get shot down. To vary the metaphor, we ended our last book in true professional boxer fashion, presenting the smallest possible target to our opponents. A two-point plan confined itself to suggesting the UK ought to curb its enormous borrowings and stop destroying the natural environment. We are prepared to be a little more expansive this time.

First, we suggest tighter controls on lending and on the generation of credit. Second and linked to this is the forced demerger of large banking and finance groups, splitting retail banking from both corporate finance (merchant banking) and securities dealing. This would echo the Glass-Steagall legislation of interwar America, which separated retail and investment banking but was repealed in the 1990s.

Third, even the remaining demerged units are likely, in many cases, to be large entities. We suggest breaking them into smaller banks, on the principle that megabanks make megamistakes that affect us all. Instead of institutions that are "too big to fail," we should aim for institutions that are small enough to fail without creating problems for depositors and the wider public.

Fourth, we suggest subjecting all derivative products and other exotic instruments to official inspection. Only those approved would be permitted to be traded. Anyone trying to circumvent the rules by going offshore or onto the Internet would face the negative enforcement mentioned above—their contracts would be unenforceable in law.

Fifth, we would seek to offer the same protection for our remaining top-class industrial companies as is routine in France or the United States—and perhaps go further. Ultimately, the aim must be an orderly downsizing of the financial sector, much as postwar France and Italy sought an orderly move of employment from agriculture to industry. More of the engineers and technical experts from our best universities would end up making things. Some of the famed "rocket scientists" who spend their days in the City cooking up ever more abstract financial entities may even end up making . . . rockets.

Certainly, at a moment when the survival of human life of the planet may depend on our finding new technologies to generate energy and reduce our disruptive impact on natural systems, it seems perverse to the point of madness to corral our brightest and best technicians on to open-plan trading floors in air-conditioned skyscrapers.

Sixth, we suggest sharply increasing taxes on the hedge fund operators and private equity partners, to ensure at the very least that they pay the same rate of tax as their cleaners. The loophole whereby income can be disguised as a capital gain and thus taxed at a lower rate was closed by a previous Labour government in the mid-1960s, only, bizarrely, to be reopened by Labour more than three decades later. It is time to close it again.

Seventh, we suggest deregulating genuinely private businesses and the self-employed (frequently the two are synonymous). One byproduct of the Olympian myth that vast financial institutions are part of the "enterprise culture" has been the imposition on genuine enterprises of the sort of employment and other legislation used to extract at least some payback from the New Olympians for the benefits of limited liability and other privileges. The self-employed and small firms ought to be regulated only with regard to their activities (e.g., a jam maker would have to obey the food and hygiene laws) and not as businesses. Indeed, by greatly enhancing the attractiveness of the partnership or the small firm, such deregulation may divert many talented people from the pursuit of Olympian status to gentler, more rewarding, and more socially useful business careers.

None of this will be easy. Some of it may involve abrogating Britain's signature to various international treaties, those enshrining New Olympian objectives, not least the various European treaties. Nor does much of this New Populism appear to be immediately in prospect, despite the darkening clouds over the world economy. And whereas it could move rapidly onto the agenda should the crisis worsen markedly and suddenly, it is possible also that it will take time to piece together a populist coalition.

We have touched already on some of the elements that may join such an alliance: small business people and farmers (if there are any left); independent middle-class professionals and shopkeepers. Then there are those filling the basic supervisory roles that ought to be the backbone of society: railway station managers and their equivalents in bus depots and motorway service stations, police sergeants, prison officers, main street store managers, noncommissioned officers in the forces and similar. We would seek to add two significant blocks of members: manufacturing and export businesses and trade union members. Industry and those working in it have been the biggest losers from the Olympian experiment as productive capacity has been destroyed and millions of manufacturing jobs wiped out. Those owning, running, and working in industry know better than anyone the virulence with which New Olympianism has blighted the economy. Both union members and managers have much to gain from a more sensible attitude to industry.

And those within such a coalition will always have the inestimable advantage of the fact that, beneath the shiny packaging, the Olympians' creed is and always has been the reverse of their own. It is "Unpopulism," the belief system that sacrifices jobs and productive assets on the altar of deal making, that demands schools and post offices be "rationalized" (i.e., closed), that insists on lower tax rates for the rich than for their domestic servants, that has created a vast debt bubble and chronic global instability and which, even at this late hour, has the effrontery to suggest that the answer to the crisis lies in the even more enthusiastic application of New Olympian ideas in terms of untrammeled free market activity.

Unpopulism ought to make the selling of the New Populism a lot easier. But there is likely to be plenty of work to do in terms of spreading the word. The independent professionals need to grasp the dangers of being assimilated by commercial entities and to cease to regard corporate Britain as an essentially friendly place, respectful of the status of lawyers, accountants, and the rest. Similarly, liberal writers, artists, senior left-leaning white-collar personnel—those who tend, lazily, although not entirely inaccurately, to be labeled with the names of their presumed favorite newspapers or with the London boroughs where they like to live—need to be made aware of the urgent need to build alliances with the remnants of organized labor. Export-oriented business needs to agitate for a state system that supports them rationally and effectively, in terms of financial support, trade policy, and exchange rate. State employees need to recognize that the notion of a "public sector" as traditionally understood is under attack, from New Labour as much as from the right. Rather than support either "market reforms" (which often mean worse services provided by lavishly rewarded private contractors) or the bloated social-engineering sector (which seems designed, in part at least, to soak up many of the additional graduates generated by the breakneck expansion of higher education), public sector workers should call for more democratic accountability and the reestablishment of honest, cost-effective, and competent public services, provided on clear and, as far as possible, nondiscretionary premises on the straightforward basis of entitlement.

This may sound like hard, dusty work. Certainly it does not offer the excitement of revolutionary agitation. But it is a political response to the current situation that offers some chance of success. And if those who met on Mont Pelerin all those years ago were not daunted, neither should we be.

Beyond all this we would hope for a cultural shift toward decency, fairness, and social stability, away from the demented pursuit of "shareholder value" and "yield." There are signs of a reaction to the excesses of the past two decades and the chaos they have wrought. In Britain, there has been a greater emphasis on thrift, on not throwing perfectly good food away, and on cutting out conspicuous waste.

Symptoms of a new mood of disgust at the excesses have appeared in various places and for various reasons. There was the groundswell of discontent at plans for further expansion of Heathrow Airport. On January 29, 2008, Chris Blackhurst, city editor of the *Evening Standard*, summed up the mood of many: "BAA [the airport's operator] wants to build a third runway and a sixth terminal. . . . Why not put a plea in now for a fifth runway and an eighth terminal? In fact why not do away with planning restraints completely and bulldoze chunks of west London to give BAA the model it seeks?"

There was an article entitled "Confessions of a Graduating MBA Student" in the *Financial Times* on December 24, 2008, from recent INSEAD graduate Neil Courtis: "Overconfident, overpaid and everywhere—the 2007 vintage of MBAs [Master of Business Administration, a mis-named bachelor degree in business]. Last year Ben Bernanke, the chairman of the US Federal Reserve, earned $183,500. With bonuses included, this is almost exactly what a graduate MBA now expects to be paid to create PowerPoint slides for a bank or consulting firm. . . . No wonder recruiters think we are arrogant."

He added, "Perhaps this is simply evidence of the euphoria of the last few inches of the upswing."

Yes, quite.

There was a seasonal article by business journalist and former banker Martin Vander Weyer in the *Daily Telegraph* on December 28, 2007, "Philanthropy Is Good: Remorse Is Better," comparing the hedge fund and private equity millionaires of today unfavorably with Charles Dickens's Scrooge. The latter, he pointed out, did not merely give to charity; he repented of his ways. "When the hedge fund boys get together for a black-tie charity auction and raise casual millions, there is something distasteful about it all . . . we should ask whether the trend towards business philanthropy is disguising another trend, towards social damage caused by market excess."

It has been a long time since anyone suggested the New Olympians may have anything about which to feel remorseful. Meanwhile, for ordinary mortals, the financial crisis and the credit crunch give an added urgency to a revival of prudence and saving. But these pressures aside, there seems to be a yearning for a less frantic and greedy way of life, one less geared to the needs of a plutocracy and less in awe of it.

As we now draw close to the end of our narrative, it is appropriate to turn to one of Graham Greene's more uplifting tales.

In his 1955 novel *Loser Takes All*, Graham Greene's narrator, Bertram, is a recently married lowly white-collar employee who finds himself with his wife in Monte Carlo. Stony broke after a few days, Bertram devises an apparently successful system for winning at roulette. He is, briefly, fabulously rich. He jousts among the three Olympians—Dreuther, Blixon, and Bowles—who own the firm for which he works. For a brief moment, he controls the firm, having lent one of the Olympians money against a crucial packet of shares. His marriage falls apart, as his wife tells him, "I didn't marry a well-off man. I married a man I met in the bar of the Volunteer—someone who liked cold sausages and travelled by bus because taxis were too expensive."

The novel closes with the couple reunited in a cabin onboard ship, leaving the Olympian playground of Monaco behind them. "'We shan't be rich,' I added quickly. . . . I got up and took the great system out of my jacket pocket and tore it in little pieces and threw them through the porthole—the white scraps blew back in our wake."

The gods promised us paradise if only we would obey and pamper their hero-servants and allow their strange titans and monsters to flourish. We did as they asked, and have placidly swallowed the prescriptions of the lavishly rewarded bankers, central bankers, hedge fund managers, and private equity tycoons, while turning a blind eye to the rampaging of the exotic derivatives, the offshore trusts, and the toxic financial instruments. Had they delivered, there would, at least, be a debate to be held as to whether the price was too high, in terms of the loss of democratic control and widening social inequality. But they have not. Chronic financial instability and the prospect of, at the best, years of sluggish economic activity as we pay off borrowings of a debt-burdened society are the fruits of their guidance.

These gods have failed. It is time to live without them.

AFTERWORD

July 12, 2007, was not an easy day to persuade a publisher to put time and money into a book predicting imminent disaster in the world financial system. In Britain, a fifteen-year boom was apparently roaring on and its architect, Gordon Brown, had just moved up from chancellor to prime minister. In particular, 2006 had been a golden year and all indications were that 2007 would bring more of the same.

Nevertheless, it was on that day that we visited the British head office of Random House in central London to make our case for what became *The Gods That Failed*. It was our contention that free market ideology had allowed a cadre of financiers to indulge in such reckless behavior that there was a clear and imminent risk to the global economy. At that stage, our publishers could see the merit of our analysis but thought we might be going somewhat over the top.

There was a comic moment when we threw into the discussion the suggestion, nothing more, that some financial instruments lodged with banks as "securities" were so complex that no one knew whose liability they would prove to be were anything to go wrong. Asked to elucidate, we fell back on good old-fashioned waffle. We cannot claim that in July 2007 we had heard of the collateralized debt obligations that were shortly to become known as "toxic waste."

Our publishers asked, "Do you really think it is going to be that bad?" Although we answered in the affirmative, even we have been taken aback by the speed and savagery of the collapse, and by the need for such widespread intervention to prevent in October 2008 what Dominique Strauss-Kahn, the managing director of the International

273

Monetary Fund, called the risk of system-wide global financial meltdown.

Back in the summer of 2007, Gordon Brown made his last speech as chancellor of the exchequer to the City's great and good at the Mansion House. He boasted of London's "risk-based regulatory approach." In October 2008, Brown's government took a controlling stake in the Royal Bank of Scotland and a more than 40 percent share of both Lloyds TSB and Halifax Bank of Scotland, or HBoS. The prime minister no longer bragged about the City's light-touch regime. Instead, he compared the need to rescue the world's banks from collapse to the wartime exploits of Roosevelt and Churchill, by implication giving himself, somewhat improbably, a role comparable to that of the two great men.

Our opening chapter covers the extraordinary month from September 7, 2008, to October 7, 2008, thirty-one days that changed the world. On October 8, 2008, began the coda to that mad month of bank failures and government panic as delegates arrived in Washington for meetings of the Group of Seven rich nations, the International Monetary Fund, and the World Bank. Against a background of plunging share prices on both sides of the Atlantic, finance ministers and central bankers set aside decades of economic orthodoxy and agreed to the partial nationalization of their banks, initially a British scheme that was adopted by the G7 on the evening of October 10 and by the wider IMF membership the following day.

On Monday, October 13, the British government announced £37 billion in help to the banks that would leave it holding 57 percent of Royal Bank of Scotland, 43.5 percent of HBoS, and 43.5 percent of Lloyds TSB. The U.S. government announced a similar scheme the following day. In 1929, the Wall Street crash and subsequent Great Depression left the City and Wall Street utterly discredited. In 1973, the energy crisis and the great inflation gave advocates of the unfettered free market an economic shock that could be blamed on ministers and civil servants. Intellectually, this was the free marketeers' 1929.

Now turbocharged capitalism has crashed spectacularly, and the once despised politicians and bureaucrats are having to supply hugely expensive emergency surgery. True entrepreneurs, with whom we have no quarrel, do not demand billions of dollars of taxpayer support once things go wrong. The big institutions of the City and Wall Street were never really entrepreneurs at all, but state-licensed traffickers in a state-manufactured and state-guaranteed product—money. The events of 2008 have shone a glaring light on this truth, which must not be forgotten in years to come when these events start to recede in the rearview mirror of history.

Some have compared the Anglo-Saxon economies to a casino. In fact, most casinos in Britain and America are well run and properly regulated. It is time for our economies to be more like them, not less.

The world has changed utterly during the past fifteen months. For the disciples of anything-goes finance, the events of 2007 and 2008 have been as traumatic as the demolition of the Berlin Wall in 1989 to communist apparatchiks and their Western apologists. The collapse of communism marked the dawn of market fundamentalism; the necessity for the U.S. government to take a stake in Goldman Sachs and Morgan Stanley saw the sun going down on that era.

For us, the widespread acceptance that we were right is, of course, immensely gratifying. Friends, colleagues, and family have grown weary of us saying "we told you so." It gives us no satisfaction, however, to contemplate the human cost of the folly of finance. The prospect of a 1930s-style depression seemed to have been averted by the unprecedented action by governments in October 2008, but clearly there would still be long and painful recessions across the developed world. Rather than end on a downbeat note, however, we argue that the collapse of the free market model and the validation of state intervention has opened up the possibility of real and radical reform of the global financial system. Governments have been forced to work together to bail out the banks; they could clearly do the same to put the squeeze on tax havens and introduce currency transaction taxes. The emergency forced policymakers to act quickly and decisively to meet the global threat of economic and financial chaos. They could and should do the same to meet two other looming challenges: climate change and inevitable energy shortages in the decade ahead.

In doing so, they need to bear in mind a truth that was forgotten during the years of free market excess: economies and markets exist not for their own sake but in order to promote the fullest possible development of the human person.

Larry Elliott and Dan Atkinson, October 2008

INDEX